FROM ONE TO MANY

FROM ONE TO MANY

Best Practices for Team and Group Coaching

Jennifer J. Britton

JB JOSSEY-BASS™
A Wiley Brand

National Library of Canada Cataloguing in Publication Data
Britton, Jennifer J., author
   From one to many : best practices for team and group coaching / Jennifer J. Britton.

Includes bibliographical references and index.
Issued in print and electronic formats.
ISBN 978-1-118-54927-8 (bound).—ISBN 978-1-118-54928-5 (pdf).—ISBN 978-1-118-54930-8 (epub)

   1. Teams in the workplace. 2. Employees—Coaching of. 3. Organizational effectiveness. I. Title.

HD66.B74 2013   658.4'022   C2013-902762-9
                                             C2013-902763-7

Production Credits
Cover design: Adrian So
Typesetting: Thomson Digital
Cover image: iStockphoto
Printer: Courier Westford

Editorial Credits
Executive editor: Don Loney
Managing editor: Alison Maclean
Production editor: Pamela Vokey

John Wiley & Sons Canada, Ltd.
6045 Freemont Blvd.
Mississauga, Ontario
L5R 4J3

Printed in Canada

1 2 3 4 5 CW 17 16 15 14 13

This book is dedicated to coaches, leaders and other professionals looking to enhance their own coaching conversations with groups and teams.

We are strengthened by those around us, particularly our loved ones and family. Thank you to Andray, Matthew, Mom and Dad.

Contents

List of Figures and Tables

Acknowledgments

From One to Many has grown out of the many questions I have been asked and the conversations I have had with coaches since the publication of *Effective Group Coaching* in 2010. Whether it has been in the coaching training programs I run through Potentials Realized, or during presentations I have made at ICF conferences and chapter meetings, one of the most common questions I have been asked is, "What's the difference between team and group coaching?" Increasingly coaches, leaders and other professionals are straddling the realms of coaching teams and groups, and are eager for more resources to undertake their work. I am pleased to take a deeper look at the related realms of team and group coaching— the processes and practices behind our work.

This book has been infused by the experiences of the groups and teams I have worked with over the last two-plus decades. My work has now taken me to work with teams and groups in five continents, and in recent years has connected me virtually with more countries than I will physically ever visit.

Incorporating the voices of many is critical in our work with groups and teams. I would like to thank the following coaches who generously shared their examples and insights around group and team coaching for this book: Renee Brotman, Catherine Carr, Michael Cullen, Ursula Lesic, Sharon Miller, Lynda Monk, Shana Montesol, Jacqueline Peters, Ray Rigoglioso, Phil Sandahl and Kevin Stebbings. It should be noted that all quotations from these coaches are taken from my interviews with them, unless otherwise documented.

It has been a pleasure to work with the team at John Wiley and Sons Canada again. I have enjoyed the many conversations with my executive editor, Don Loney, and also want to thank Nicole Langlois for her editing work. Thanks as well to Leslie Bendaly, who reviewed the manuscript.

A big thank you to my family—Matthew and Andray, and of course my mom and dad. Without your support I would not be able to do the work that I do.

Jennifer J. Britton
East Gwillimbury, February 2013

Introduction

From One to Many: Best Practices for Team and Group Coaching explores the continued evolution of two sub-disciplines of the coaching profession: team coaching and group coaching. Whether you are an internal or external coach working with teams, corporate groups or public groups, or you are a leader working with your own team, this book is geared to provide you with practical tools, insights and best practices around team and group coaching. *From One to Many* is geared to professionals who want to explore the skills and best practices behind exceptional team and group coaching. It is also for professionals who are looking for practical tools and approaches they can adapt and implement in their own programs right away, without having to reinvent the wheel. *From One to Many* has been shaped by my own work with teams and groups over more than two decades. The book has also been shaped by the questions and learning of hundreds of practitioner coaches from around the world with whom I have had the opportunity to work in the Group Coaching Essentials program, the Advanced Group Coaching Practicum and the Group Coaching Intensive programs since 2006.

Just as current business challenges require new ways of thinking and working across boundaries, the work of a coach is also spanning these boundaries and silos. In fact, group coaching is playing an important role in facilitating communication across the silos. Likewise, team coaching has the potential to break down the silos that exist within a team, as well as the silos that exist within a wider organizational context. At the same time, coaches are increasingly collaborating with more partners in organizations, often working with them to develop a cadre of peer coaches and to train leaders as coaches.

Since the publication of my first book, *Effective Group Coaching*, in January 2010, the global reach of coaches who are active in group and team coaching has continued to grow. Economic realities have continued to turn individuals and organizations onto these as modalities of choice. The collaborative nature of the coaching conversation and the connectivity it creates have been underpinnings of group and team coaching approaches. In contrast to 2009, when I wrote the last book, I regularly hear of organizations incorporating group coaching into their work, as a standalone program or as a follow-on to training. Team coaching is increasingly becoming a popular choice as more organizations turn to the team as the engine of business and also as the luster of one-off team-building initiatives continues to wane quickly after the offsite or retreat.

Based on the requests of practitioner coaches, leaders and HR professionals, this book expands the focus of coaching to groups and teams—that is, into the realm of "coaching many." The shift from one-on-one coaching to working with many, whether in a team or group, is often perceived as a large step. As we will explore, there are many foundational similarities in team and group coaching, and several chapters will look at these commonalities. Several other chapters will address the differences between these two related "sibling" modalities.

As with coaching itself, my hope is that *From One to Many* will stimulate dialogue and debate among coaches, leaders and other professionals undertaking this work, as well as add to the growing foundation of literature on the topics of team and group coaching. Thankfully, there is a growing number of books that provide more of a theoretical and conceptual look at team and group coaching. Just as *Effective Group Coaching* has been embraced by practitioner coaches and as the learning text by many coach training schools, my hope is that this book will also become a trusted go-to resource for new and experienced coaches, HR professionals, leaders and others undertaking work with teams and groups. My aim for the book was to make it practical, impactful and relevant.

As a graduate student 20 years ago, I was motivated by the concept of "praxis"—or the interplay of theory and action. Praxis continues to shape my work. Throughout this book I open a window to my own work with teams and groups and include Field Journal notes. My approaches and insights have been shaped by real-time experience with groups and teams over the last 25 years—virtual teams, intact teams, global teams, public groups and corporate groups—designing and delivering programs in person as well as through virtual programs.

This book takes a multidisciplinary approach, cutting across boundaries. It reflects practically how coaches are coming to this work and shaping it in partnership with their clients. Several undertaking this work today bring a background in learning and development, some as former leaders and managers, while others have entered the coaching domain through intensive coaching skills training. Readers are encouraged to explore areas that may be new terrain—for example, capacity development and leadership. Others may be revisiting topics they are very familiar with, such as group process and coaching skills. *From One to Many* also reflects this expansion of seeing how coaching fits into the broader business context today.

Part III of the book—Expanding Our View of Coaching Many—particularly addresses this. While there are still many "pure" coaching rollouts, as more professionals are trained in coaching skills, it is likely that the boundaries between related disciplines will continue to be spanned. Likewise, leaders and other internal resources are entering into the domains of team and group coaching. It is not uncommon for me to see experienced group facilitators embrace this work in team and group coaching very quickly. A key focus of this book is on the subtle but important different focus and orientation a group and team coach brings, with a strong emphasis on goal setting, accountability and focus on supporting action and awareness.

As with *Effective Group Coaching*, I found that it was important to also have other voices represented in the book. Throughout the book you will meet 10 coaches who undertake work in the realm of team and group coaching around the world. Each has each offered his or her own case study, as well as thoughts on team and group coaching processes: best practices, key skills, recommendations and thoughts on trends. Their voices provide a sampling of the variety of experiences that are common with the groups and teams we work with. At the same time, as you read through their varied voices, note the synergies that exist among them.

It has been truly an honor to have the active participation of senior coaches such as *Co-Active Coaching* co-author Phil Sandahl, MCC, chief coaching officer of Team Coaching International. You will also meet coach Kim Ades, founder of JournalEngine, an innovative online journaling platform with great potential for team and group coaching. We also reconnect with two coaches who were first spotlighted in *Effective Group Coaching*: Lynda Monk, CPCC, who talks about using a coaching approach in workshops as well as her virtual retreat group coaching; and Sharon Miller, CPCC, PCC, who shares her insights around team coaching. You can also find a case study from the financial services industry that illustrates how Sharon Miller's coaching engagements over time integrate for significant impact and culture change in the digital chapter Team Coaching in Action, located at www.groupcoaching essentials.com. Dr. Jacqueline Peters, PCC, and Dr. Catherine Carr, PCC, share their insights around team coaching and team effectiveness. Jacqueline offers a case study from the oil and gas industry entitled "Coaching as a Lever for Cultural Change."

Many coaches are engaged with team and group coaching in the context of leadership development. In Chapter 10, Ursula Lesic, ACC, offers a group coaching case study based on her work. Renee Brotman, PCC, shares insights around using tools with leadership groups. Coach Michael Cullen, PPCC, shares his insights based on working with public groups, and Ray Rigoglioso, ACC, offers insights based on his work with nonprofit professionals and public programs for gay men. A case study has also been provided by performance coaches with the British Columbia Public Service Agency, which provides a detailed look at an actual team coaching engagement.

THE 30,000-FOOT VIEW: A SNAPSHOT OF THE TERRAIN WE WILL COVER IN *FROM ONE TO MANY*

The book has three parts. Part I explores the foundation of coaching many, and provides a framework for expanding individual coaching work into coaching many. Chapter 1 looks at team and group coaching as "related sisters." The first chapter looks at some of the differences and similarities between team and group coaching. Chapter 2 explores the program continuum and how coaches may find themselves using a "pure" coaching approach or may incorporate more training and/or facilitation. In today's era of complex challenges and rapid change, hybridization is a welcomed approach. Chapter 3 takes a deep dive, looking at the core coaching competencies of the International Coach Federation (ICF) and how these play out in the group and team coaching contexts.

Part II of the book takes a look at group and team coaching: common process pieces, different approaches for working with groups and teams, and what this work looks like, along with case studies or "Voices from the Field." Four examples are presented from practitioner coaches in the area of group coaching, and four in the area of team coaching. You are encouraged to consider how the spotlighted coaches' experience and learning can infuse your own work with clients. Chapter 4 looks at design practices and principles for creating team and group coaching programs. Chapter 5 looks at group coaching processes. A digital accompaniment at www.groupcoachingessentials.com includes team coaching approaches. It also looks at different approaches for working with groups and a selection of case studies of group coaching in action. Chapter 6 explores team coaching processes. A digital accompaniment at www.group coachingessentials.com includes team coaching activities and case studies. Discussion about team and group coaching would not be complete without a focus on virtual programming options (Chapter 7), and also on techniques for engaging your groups (Chapter 8). A digital chapter on marketing also accompanies the book.

In Part III, the book widens the scope and connects us with the larger context of coaching many in organizations today, namely the topics of capacity development and developing a new cohort of leaders. In shifting your coaching from *one to many* it is also likely that you will be involved at some level with discussions around systems and performance at a larger level. Chapter 9 addresses the topic of capacity building, that is, developing internal skills and capacity through peer coaching, supervisor as coach, and linking support with mentoring. Chapter 10 addresses the topic of developing a new cohort of leaders, as many coaches today are involved in supporting and feeding into related talent management initiatives such as leadership development training.

Co-facilitation is increasingly called upon and is an art form for coaches working in the team and group coaching domain. This topic, along with collaboration, is covered in Chapter 11. Trends and where our work is evolving are the subjects of Chapter 12.

Finally, questions, exercises and resources continue to be the backbone of our work as coaches. Everyone is eager for more tools and ideas in their toolbox. The appendix focuses on activities and resources you may wish to incorporate into your own work.

It is my intent that this book will stimulate conversation and action in the coaching community and with leaders. It is focused on providing practical insights. It is also geared to providing a look at the skills below the surface of our work. *How is our work different with team and group coaching? What are the things we want to ensure we are always doing? What best practices can we incorporate into our work with teams and groups?* The final section of the book explores trends, collaboration, leadership and capacity development, which I believe point to future arcs of where our work is headed, if it's not there already.

I hope that you will engage with this book and in the conversation. I look forward to connecting with you to continue the conversation in person, virtually (through Facebook, Pinterest, Twitter, email) or by good old fashioned telephone.

THE CONTEXT OF COACHING TODAY

"Individually, we are one drop. Together, we are an ocean."
—Ryunosuke Satoro[1]

Teams, collaboration, globalization, working across differences, and doing more with less are all key themes in today's business world. Coaching as a modality of support to personal and professional development has also grown and changed in response to this evolving context in which we operate. Team and group coaching are now well rooted as possible approaches for coaches, and leaders, to draw on, in support of better business results, better relationships and enhanced personal and collective goals.

Coaching continues to expand in size and reach. The 2012 Global Coaching Survey from the International Coach Federation estimates 47,500 professional

---

[1] http://www.brainyquote.com/quotes/quotes/r/ryunosukes167565.html.

coaches worldwide, of which 41,300 are active coaches. Coaches participating in this global survey came from 131 countries around the world.[2]

Coaching as a profession continues to become more rooted, and the survey notes that "the coaching profession appears to be showing more rapid growth in emerging regions outside the established high-income regions" of North America, Western Europe, Australia and New Zealand. In the past few years I have seen team and group coaching continuing to expand around the world, as I have seen coaches from countries such as Bolivia, Peru and the Czech Republic explore how it can be added to their coaching mix.

The coaching profession has grown out of diverse fields such as social psychology, quantum physics, the humanities and group dynamics. As Vikki Brock writes about the emergence of coaching in her dissertation, "Grounded Theory of the Roots and Emergence of Coaching":[3]

> Five points summarize my observations about the emergence of coaching:
>
> 1. coaching sprang from several independent sources at the same time and spread through relationships;
> 2. coaching has a broad intellectual framework that draws on the synergy, cross-fertilization, and practices of many disciplines;
> 3. modern patterns and practices of coaching are dynamic and contextual;
> 4. coaching came into existence to fill an unmet need in an interactive, fluid world of rapid change and complexity; and
> 5. coaching came into being in an open integral social network from a perspective of diversity and inclusion.

The first global coaching survey undertaken by the International Coach Federation asked coaching clients how they perceived coaching to be different from other interventions. A focus on goal setting, awareness building and accountability all were identified as distinguishers for coaching versus other modalities.

Research from the ICF has identified increased productivity, increased positivity and return on investment (ROI) from coaching.[4]

---

[2] International Coach Federation, 2012 Global Coaching Survey, Executive Summary, 16.

[3] Vikki Brock, "Grounded Theory of the Roots and Emergence of Coaching," Dissertation for Doctor of Philosophy in Human Development and Coaching, International University of Professional Studies, Maui, 2008, vii.

[4] International Coach Federation, 2009 Global Coaching Client Survey.

Increased productivity measures include:

- Improved work performance (70 percent)
- Improved business management (61 percent)
- Improved time management (57 percent)
- Improved team effectiveness (51 percent)

Improved positivity measures include:

- Increased self-confidence (80 percent)
- Increased relationships (73 percent)
- Improved communication skills (72 percent)
- Improved work/life balance (67 percent)

It is with these roots that coaching continues to expand in form and reach.

THE SHIFT FROM ONE TO MANY

Against the backdrop of global and economic events, opportunities and pressures, team and group coaching have evolved into their own over the last decade.

This shift in the coaching conversation from a one-on-one conversation between coach and client (also known as the "coachee" in some models), to conversations between coach or coaches and team and group clients is what I call "the many."

As more and more coaches add group and team coaching to their mixes, it is important for us to have a series of best practices and approaches grounding our work. What you will find as you move through this book is a variety of examples, and practical suggestions of how team and group coaching is playing out around the world. The intention of the book is to be a practitioner's resource guide, while providing a light touch on the theory underpinning the work.

So, what are the key themes we encounter as we expand our work to teams and groups (the many)? What areas should those looking to create exceptional experiences with our clients consider? Figure I.1 looks at the foundations of coaching, as well as five areas of consideration as we expand our work.

Figure I.1: From One to Many

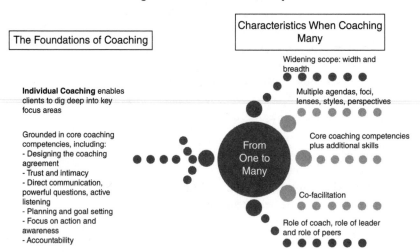

THE FOUNDATIONS OF COACHING

Coaching is all about a conversation. It's not just any conversation. It's a focused conversation, one that is geared to expedite the insights and actions around issues of importance for the people we are working with. As one of my favorite subject matter expert (SME) partners, Doug McLaren, says, "Coaching is a conversation with intent." In any type of coaching work—with individuals, teams and groups—we want to remember that coaching is not just any conversation. Coaching is all about a conversation with purpose, to expedite the results for the person or persons being coached.

In moving from coaching one to many, our core coaching competencies and skills continue to provide the foundation for exceptional and impactful coaching conversations. Whether we are external or internal coaches[5] or leaders integrating these skills into portfolios—and working with teams, groups or individuals—we will want to "lean into" foundational coaching skills. Most, if not all, coaching models will be founded on, or connected to, the 11 core coaching competencies of the International Coach Federation.

Foundational to any coaching conversation are these skills:

---

[5] An internal coach is an employee of an organization, coaching others within the organization; this may be a full-time role, or one part of their portfolio. An external coach is one brought in by an organization for a specific coaching initiative.

Designing the Coaching Agreement

Every coaching relationship should be grounded in a shared agreement between coach and client(s). This includes partnering with the client to design what the coaching will look like, including agreeing on what the coaching focus will be, and will not be. It will include the "ways of working" or "agreements for the work" we do together. Part of designing the coaching agreement identifies what measures of success and focus areas will ground the work we do. An evolving best practice of the profession of coaching is having formalized written coaching agreements in place.

Trust and Intimacy

Coaching is a relationship that is based in trust and "knowing the client." Without trust, coaching cannot occur. In the team and group coaching context, the trust and knowing is not only with the coach, but also between and among group and team members. The coaching process often explores the different needs, preferences, and what is important with the group members individually, and in the case of teams, individually and collectively.

Communicating Effectively

Communication is the foundation for any coaching conversation. The "triad of communication" includes what the International Coach Federation (ICF) calls "direct communication, powerful questions and active listening." Practically this involves coaching using language that is appropriate for the client, asking powerful questions, and listening at multiple levels inviting exploration, new awareness and action on the part of those being coached.

A Focus on Goals

A key component of the coaching process is working with the person being coached to set and work on goals that are important to them, personally or professionally. These goals become the foundation and focus for our work as coaches with our clients, whether they are individuals, teams or groups. Throughout the conversation it is important to explore with the client(s) the 30,000-foot metaview or "big picture" level of their goals and priorities, as well as the "micro" view, which is more tangible or immediate.

Awareness and Action

Throughout the coaching process we want to maintain a focus on deepening awareness around those key areas of interest to the individuals we are working with, as well as supporting them in taking action.

Coaching involves a regular series of coaching touch points, creating an accountability framework. The coaching process takes place over time, and is generally not a "one-off" conversation, but rather a series of touch points. It is this enhanced "sticky factor" that has led to coaching being seen as an excellent add-on to training, boosting the transfer of learning and integration of new insights and behaviors.

Accountability

The hard focus on accountability distinguishes coaching from other related modalities. In the context of coaching, accountability involves clients making commitments (individually or collectively) around key action steps that will move them toward the goals that are important. A critical part of the coaching conversation involves checking in around these actions and insights at each touch point or meeting.

These skill areas continue to serve as the foundation for all team and group coaching work. Chapter 3 takes a deep dive into looking at what the core coaching competencies look like in both the team and group coaching domain. It starts the conversation around specific techniques and approaches coaches and leaders can integrate into their coaching of teams and groups.

EXPANDING INTO THE REALM OF MANY

In "working with many," in either a team or group context, our focus expands.

While we continue to lead from our core coaching skills, coaches working in this domain will notice:

A Widening Scope

Group and team coaching conversations often feel like they are going broad and wide, and not always deep. In an individual coaching conversation our focus is to have deep conversation with each client around the one or two key areas they are interested in. In coaching many, the scope widens with more voices, with peers playing a key role in the coaching process. We often talk about the "collective wisdom" of a group. It is the breadth and width that have many learning as much from their peers as from themselves and the questions coaches ask.

Multiple Agendas, Foci, Lenses, Styles and Perspectives

Coaches who work in the realm of coaching many will need to be comfortable and confident in working with multiple focus areas or "agendas" at play. In working with more than one person there will be different styles at play, including different learning styles and generational styles, in addition to varying perspectives that show up in any given conversation. This multiplicity creates both enormous opportunity and challenge for coaches in working with tremendous amounts of diversity. It often calls for a stretch on the part of team and group coaches. The book explores varying approaches in structuring coaching processes to maximize impact at both individual and collective levels.

This work is grounded in relationships. Team and group coaching conversations are rich due to the peer learning and sharing that take place. Conversation is the medium in which coaching takes place.

Core Competencies Plus Additional Skills

In addition to leveraging the core coaching competencies explored in Chapter 3, in coaching many, team and group coaches need to develop skills in the following areas:

- Adult education
- Group process
- Group facilitation skills and experience
- Experiential education
- Instructional design
- Relationship systems awareness

Chapters 2 and 8 explore related topic areas, including the introduction of the Group Program Continuum, a way to look at related skills that may be useful in supporting your groups or teams.

Co-facilitation

Given the variety of personalities, focus areas and numbers of coachees/clients involved in the coaching of many process, it is common for coaching work with teams, and in some instances, larger groups, to be undertaken by co-facilitators. Virtual coaching programs may also benefit from a co-facilitation approach. Chapter 11 looks at the rich topic of co-facilitation and partnering with others to support the team and group coaching processes. Bringing in a co-facilitator to coach with provides yet another voice, set of eyes and modeling of co-leadership for the clients we work with. At the same time, group and team coaching are two modalities that are critical in building a collaborative workplace. The second part of Chapter 11 looks at what collaboration is and building collaborative cultures.

The Role of Coach, Leader and Peers

In an individual coaching conversation the coach is in the spotlight with the client, creating a tight partnership with the client. The role of the coach shifts in team and group coaching contexts. She or he is no longer the center of attention. Masterful group and team coaches understand the importance of being able to "fade in and out"; they are able to step back and let the group do the work, stepping back in at times with new questions or insights. Masterful team and group coaches place a lot of emphasis on process. Creating a strong process for the group or team to step into and interact with creates the context for exceptional team and group coaching.

Peers or other team members play a key part in the impact and learning of coaching many. In fact, the peer conversation is just as important, if not more so, than the dialogue with the coach. Coaches play a key role in creating the structure and process of the experience, using powerful questions and various approaches to help teams and groups deepen their awareness and undertake action.

Leaders of teams are enablers of this work. This book explores key conversations that are important to have with the leader before the coaching work starts. It is also likely that leaders may look to integrate many of these approaches with their own, and other, teams. Chapters 9 and 10 look at coaching skills for leaders and developing a new cohort of leaders.

Other Considerations for Coaching Many

Coaches working in the realm of many will want to transport several foundational principles from our individual coaching work, including curiosity, "unattachment" and flexibility. Masterful team and group coaches come from a place of curiosity rather than judgment. Exceptional coaches are flexible in their approaches, able to respond and work with the client in a way that meets their goals in the moment. This requires a level of "unattachment" to how the work may play out. Masterful team and group coaches should feel confident in throwing out ideas and questions (based on intuition, listening and observations) and seeing how they land in the moment. This is often called the "spaghetti factor," since the ideas might stick like wet spaghetti or just slide down the wall. Being able to adjust "on the fly" is critical. Group and team coaching is often light on content, and heavier on process. The emphasis in a coaching conversation is the conversation, and the ensuing insights and actions as a result of the conversation.

A key anchor point to making this work successful is keeping the client—in this case the group or team entity—front and center. Our clients need to be the driving force of the focus and direction of the coaching, and will influence decisions around structure, approaches and pacing. Flexibility sometimes requires merging, morphing and hybridizing skills and approaches from different domains. Master coaches such as Phil Sandahl have commented that some of the most successful team coaches are those who bring additional skills to the table for teams. At the same time a dynamic tension exists for team and group coaching—preparing and thinking through the various possibilities that can transpire, and being ready to "dance" and move with the client in the moment.

This introduction has provided an overview of the terrain of the book, as well as providing a high-level view of some of the foundational skills and considerations as we expand our focus from coaching one to many.

Before we move on, I want to invite you to reflect on the end-of-chapter questions. Each chapter will include several questions for you to reflect on, and many times, self-assessments to undertake. As a team and group coach I often speak about the importance of writing things down, not only as a reminder tool, or as a tool in setting intention, but also as a support in developing new neural pathways in our brains. I encourage you to write at will—mark up the book, or even better yet, start a new notebook, journal or file on your computer or tablet.

End-of-Chapter Questions

What opportunities currently exist for you in expanding your coaching work to many?
What differences do you see with this work?
What strengths do you already bring as a team or group coach?
What additional skills will you need to, or do you want to, develop?

Reflection

In your work, what do you see as the importance of these areas?

- Widening scope
- Multiple agendas, focuses, lenses, styles and perspectives
- Core coaching competencies, plus additional skills
- Co-facilitation
- Role of coach, leader and peers

PART I

TEAM AND GROUP COACHING DEFINED

As we will explore throughout the book, at first glance, team and group coaching may appear very similar as approaches. As we will discover in the following chapters, there are subtle and significant differences between team and group coaching. Chapter 1 explores the distinctions between team and group coaching, and Chapter 2 looks at the fusion of approaches needed for success in coaching many. Chapter 3 explores core skills for exceptional team and group coaching.

CHAPTER 1

TEAM AND GROUP COACHING: RELATED SISTERS

If you want to go fast, go alone; if you want to go far, go with others.
—African proverb

This chapter explores the following topics:

- Group and team coaching defined
- The context of team and group coaching
- The differences and similarities between team and group coaching
- Focus areas in team and group coaching
- Best practices when working with many (team and group coaching)
- Design principles for coaching many

What is group and team coaching? Consider these examples:

Example 1: An intact team in health care with a new leader engages two coaches to work with them, over a six-month period, to help them improve communication, strengthen relationships and results and become more effective working as a diverse team.

Example 2: A virtual team spread across three continents has been brought together after a merger and acquisition (M&A). The leader engages a team coach to help them "hit the ground running."

Example 3: An international organization wants to equip its senior leaders and key personnel with enhanced coaching skills so they can start developing capacity at country levels. The organization engages two coaches to provide coaching skills training, followed by six months of group coaching calls to support the transfer of learning.

Example 4: A group of female leaders engages a coach to work with them over the span of several months to explore "doing more with less," and the implications for their work and their lives.

Example 5: A group of parents work with a coach through the local PTA to explore what it means to be a better parent.

Example 6: A government-funded program for women in business engages a coach to work with two cohorts at the start of a nine-month business development program. The program coordinator is confident that the business leaders will be getting enough technical skills through their curriculum. A group coach is engaged to work with each cohort for the first two weeks of the program (half-day sessions) to explore the "softer" foundational side of creating a business vision, exploring values and strengths.

TEAM COACHING DEFINED

As examples one and two illustrate, team coaching can take many forms. There are several widely accepted definitions of team coaching, including:

- "Helping the team improve performance, and the processes by which performance is achieved, through reflection and dialogue."[1]
- "Coaching a team to achieve a common goal, paying attention to both individual performance and group collaboration and performance."[2]

Key to these definitions is a focus on goals and performance, and the processes behind them. Throughout my work as a coach practitioner I define team coaching as "a sustained series of conversations, supported by core coaching skills. The focus is on goal setting, deepening awareness, supporting action and creating accountability. The focus of the coaching may be on the team as a system and/or strengthening individuals within the team. Team coaching links back to business goals, focusing on results and relationships."

Team coaching is a sustained process of dialogue, reflection, learning and action, occurring over time. Chapter 5 addresses team coaching processes. A digital chapter illustrates Team Coaching in Action and provides several activities coaches may want to incorporate.

---

[1] David Clutterbuck, *Coaching the Team at Work* (Boston: Nicholas Brealey Publishing, 2007), 77.
[2] Christine Thornton, *Group and Team Coaching: The Essential Guide* (New York and London: Routledge, 2010), 122.

GROUP COACHING DEFINED

In my last book, *Effective Group Coaching*, I explored the width and depth of the group coaching field. Examples three through six (above) are snapshots of how group coaching work is occurring.

Group coaching is "the application of coaching principles to a small group for the purposes of personal or professional development, the achievement of goals, or greater self-awareness, along thematic or non-thematic lines."[3]

Group coaching continues to expand in reach, with group coaching initiatives becoming more commonplace in organizations, as well as with individuals joining public groups. In her book *Group Coaching: A Comprehensive Blueprint*, Ginger Cockerham offers this definition of group coaching: "a facilitated group process led by a skilled professional coach and created with the intention of maximizing the combined energy, experience, and wisdom of individuals who choose to join in order to achieve organizational objectives or individual goals."[4]

Many coaches are often surprised at how small group coaching work really is. The ICF placed a threshold of 15 persons as the maximum group size several years ago. Many coach practitioners may find that to really reap the benefits of coaching, group size needs to be much smaller, often in the four to eight range. This smaller grouping allows for more opportunities for individual group members to engage at a deeper level with the coaching process. Larger groups often become more training focused.

"Group coaching is an intimate conversation space, focused on goal setting, awareness building and accountability."
—Jennifer J. Britton in *Choice Magazine*, March 2011

Chapter 5 explores the realm of group coaching, discussing the group coaching process. A digital chapter on Group Coaching in Action illustrates different ways that group coaching work is rolling out into the world through several case studies.

THE CONTEXT OF TEAM AND GROUP COACHING

Team and group coaching are related sisters. They are separate sub-disciplines of the coaching profession. They share a common foundational skill set, and in

---

[3] Jennifer Britton, *Effective Group Coaching* (Toronto: John Wiley & Sons, 2010).
[4] Ginger Cockherham, *Group Coaching: A Comprehensive Blueprint* (iUniverse.com, 2011), 1.

many instances will utilize the same approaches in terms of design, marketing and implementation. What makes the two very different is the *role of relationships,* the *role of leadership,* the *lifecycle of the grouping* (team versus group), the *stance* (or position/philosophy) *of the coach* and also *what may be at stake.*

A key distinction between team and group coaching is the context in which the coaching takes place. Team coaching engagements take place in the context of an organization or collective body, which operates with a purpose and reason for being. Goals, vision and values will exist, and will be shared by all team members to differing degrees. In the team coaching context, coaches will be connecting the conversation and focus to three levels of impact: self/individual, team and organization. Team coaches need to be able to support teams as a whole system as well as a team of individual group members.

In group coaching, the focus is often more on the development of the individual within the group context, especially in the case of public groups where coaches may be bringing together groups of individuals. There may be no common goals, vision or values linking the group members. The context within which individual group members operate may be radically different, or it may be similar, such as in the case of the women leaders. A challenge for group coaches is to ensure that there are opportunities for individual group members to explore the synergies that do exist and to find points of commonality or similarity.

In a group coaching process, it is likely that the layers of context and impact are different for each group member. As we will see throughout the book, this leads to a different stance in our work. Whereas team coaches may be working with the team as a system, or supporting individual member development toward the team goals, in group coaching, by its nature, coaches are often putting the focus on individual development in the group context. One instance where this may not be the case is in the organizational context, where you may be working with groups of new managers who do not report to each other. In this context of offering group coaching within an organization, it is important for the group coach to support individual group members to reflect on the learning and insights as it relates to themselves, as well as the teams they are part of, and the overall organization they belong to.

The Role of Relationships

Teams usually have relationships that exist before, and will exist after, the coaching relationship. As we often say, teams exist to produce results, so the web of team relationships is a key focus in team coaching. This may not always be the case with group coaching. Members of groups that are to be coached may know one another, but hold disparate positions and levels of relationship. For example, if I am working with a group of new business owners, chances are that they may be meeting each other for the first time. Each owner's focus will likely be on strengthening their own businesses first, and getting to know each other second. It is still important to be aware of the team and group dynamics issues in both.

It is important to note that not every group coaching process takes place in an organizational context or even a shared one. Some coaches may find themselves working with groups of business owners or working with groups of parents, where relationships may not exist before or after the coaching process. Relationships in many group coaching processes start and end with the engagement. Likewise, the context of the different group coaching members may be different. Coaches can bring together business owners from across industries, or new managers in a global organization who work in different divisions or countries. In this last instance, there may be some shared experiences, but very different contexts and priorities.

The Role of Leadership

A key issue in the team coaching process that does not exist within the group coaching process is the formal and informal leadership roles that exist within teams. Where formal leadership exists there are key considerations in the design and pre-work with the leader.

Engagement and Role of the Leader

A key success factor in any team coaching process is the engagement and role of the leader. It is critical to have a conversation with the leader before the start of the engagement around:

- What their role will be throughout the coaching process
- From their perspective, what they see as important areas of focus
- Connection between the work of the team coaching and the organizational and team goals and priorities
- The culture of the organization
- The openness of the leader and the organization to change (how will the leader react to criticism?)

Teams will have some form of leadership that needs to be taken into consideration in designing the type of coaching that will happen. In all the team coaching and team systems coaching work I do, team leaders play a key role. In fact, the team coaching process may be started because of a new team leader coming on board.

Typically a group coaching process in organizations is not as directly impacted by leadership. For example, if I am working with a group of new managers in an organization, they are likely to have different leaders that they report to. Part of our coaching may involve having them share their learning with their leaders, without the leaders being directly involved in the coaching.

The Lifecycle of the Grouping

The lifecycle of the grouping is another key difference between group and team coaching. Some groups undertaking a group coaching process may come together for a short period of time, disbanding at the end of the coaching engagement. In contrast, team coaching builds capacity within the team. The team exists before and after the coaching engagement.

Key to masterful team coaching is supporting the team in creating agreements that will last beyond the coaching work. Agreements usually spell out the accepted behaviors of a team. Likewise, in masterful team coaching, coaches will be asking the team to sustain the focus. This may involve bringing the tools and models that participants are learning back to their work, as well as integrating structures and ideas into their work and processes. For example, a coach may work with a team on having more difficult conversations, and may introduce the team to a common model or framework they can use to surface difficult issues. It is important for the coach to encourage the team to think about how their learning throughout the coaching process, and the models and tools, can be brought back to the office in everyday activities such as team meetings.

What Is At Stake?

The context of team coaching can be perceived as having more at stake or higher risk than some group coaching contexts. In the team environment, the ability for a team member to become vulnerable with their peers, as well as their leader, requires a certain level of trust in the process. Individuals' livelihoods are at stake within the team coaching process. As such, team members may take time becoming open in the coaching conversation if they do not feel that the coaching space is nonjudgmental and safe, not only with the coach, but also with all team members. This trust is essential for the coaching conversation to ensue.

DIFFERENCES BETWEEN TEAM AND GROUP COACHING

Many coaches may find themselves working across both domains—team and group. Table 1.1 outlines some of the key distinctions, as well as the common foundation for "coaching many"—that is, team and group coaching.

Table 1.1: Group versus Team Coaching

Group Coaching	Team Coaching
Group agreements	Team agreements
Individual development in group context	Team and/or individual development in team context
Relationships typically last only during the coaching relationship *(exceptions: boards, committees)*	Relationships exist beyond the coaching relationship
Often no shared leadership *(exceptions: boards, committees)*	Formal and informal leadership
Peer conversation	Team conversation—may have internal and external focus
Vision, values and purpose may be different	Shared vision and purpose; common team and organizational values
"I" focus	"We" focus
Closure critical at end: may not be together again	Closure at the end of each session should challenge the team to consider how they will take learning back to the workplace
Development of the individual: focus on how individuals can build skills and integrate the tools and processes into their work	Capacity development: focus on integration of tools and processes to their business/world

Common Foundations:

- Designed agreements
- Multiple agendas
- Goal setting and SMART-E goals
- Action and awareness
- Accountability
- Trust and intimacy
- Confidentiality
- Powerful questions and active listening
- Process focus

As we explored in the introduction and will see in Chapter 2, our core coaching skills remain a foundation, but may need adaptation with groups or teams.

D. J. Mitsch and Ginger Cockerham make the following distinctions between group and team coaching:

- Choice versus enrollment (selection)
- Co-creation (with group) versus collaboration (team leader)
- Environment of confidentiality versus transparency
- Varying levels of personal commitment

Levels of personal commitment can vary between group and team coaching, depending on whether group coaching is mandated, as in the case of programming for new managers. Another distinction to be aware of is the importance of confidentiality in both processes, but also the transparency that is required in team coaching. Team coaching is "risky" work, and transparency allows for deeper levels of coaching conversations to happen.

FOCUS AREAS FOR TEAM AND GROUP COACHES

As much as there are differences, there are also a number of similarities between team and group coaching, including common focus areas such as difficult conversations, identifying and leveraging strengths, goal setting, vision and values. What is different in many of these cases is the focus of our work. For group coaches, the unit will usually be the individual; for team coaches, the focus may be on the team as a system, the individuals within the team, and the context in which the team operates.

Table 1.2 includes possible focus areas for team and group coaching.

Table 1.2: Focus Areas for Group and Team Coaching

Group Coaches	Team Coaches
Becoming a better parent, teacher or business owner	Enhanced collaboration
Enhanced individual productivity	Better team productivity
Clearer goal setting	Clearer goal setting or achievement as individuals and a collective
Accountability	Mutual accountability

Leadership	Shared leadership
Difficult conversations	Difficult conversations
Strengths	Strengths: individual/team/organizational
Vision	Vision: individual/team/organizational
Values	Values: individual/team/organizational
Group member roles	Team member roles
Emotional intelligence	Emotional intelligence: individual/team/context
Styles	Styles: individual and team
	Feedback

Group coaching can occur in the context of coaching the individual members of the group (for example, individual business owners to become better owners of their own businesses) or it can occur in the context of strengthening a group, which may not necessarily be a team (for example, a parenting group).

FOUNDATIONAL ISSUE: ADULT LEARNING PRINCIPLES

Foundational to any group coaching or team coaching process with adults is that we incorporate adult learning principles. As it relates to our work as coaches we want to ensure that we:[5]

- Leverage the life experience and expertise of the group
- Create a safe and confidential learning environment
- Create opportunities for client ownership and co-create the agenda and exercise
- Make sure the approach and focus of the program are clear
- Create opportunities for clients to discover knowledge
- Establish coach and participant/client expectations at the start of the program
- Make it stick (link the learning to real life)

---

[5] Britton, *Effective Group Coaching*, 52.

Many of these topics are addressed in other chapters, namely Chapter 3 on core skills, as well as Chapter 8 on connection and engagement. The appendix includes a range of activities. Consider which ones can be used to support these different areas.

BEST PRACTICES WHEN COACHING MANY (TEAM AND GROUP COACHING)

Regardless of whether we are working with teams or groups, there are similar strategies, techniques and approaches in our work. Coaches will want to review the core coaching competencies covered in Chapter 3.

Dictionary.com defines *best practice* as "the recognized methods of correctly running businesses or providing services."[6] In my mind, best practices are an evolving signpost for practitioners, and practice to build onto for our own context, as well as an opportunity to not have to reinvent the wheel.

Wikipedia[7] defines *best practice* as "a method or technique that has consistently shown results superior to those achieved with other means, and that is used as a benchmark. In addition, a 'best' practice can evolve to become better as improvements are discovered."

Foundational best practices for **coaching many** include:

1. Less is more.
2. Know your client.
3. Remember that all participants learn in different ways.
4. Meet with each participant before the start of the program.
5. The impact of coaching happens between sessions.
6. Building trust and intimacy is key.
7. Keep it simple, not simplistic.
8. Remain flexible.
9. Have a strong focus on process and a light touch on direction.
10. Let the group/team do the work—it's not all about you.
11. Ensure you evaluate.
12. Follow up as a "value add."

Let us take a look at each one of these.

---

[6] Dictionary.com. *Collins English Dictionary, Complete & Unabridged 10th Edition*, HarperCollins Publishers, accessed April 03, 2013, http://dictionary.reference.com/browse/best%20practice.

[7] Wikipedia. "Best Practice," accessed April 29, 2013, http://en.wikipedia.org/wiki/Best_practice.

Less Is More

The power of the group or team coaching process is in the conversation. Conversation with intent takes time. As such, in designing group or team coaching programs, coaches will want to incorporate the "less is more" principle. Practicing the principle of less is more requires that coaches consider what will add value for the group—whether adding an exercise, question or even content. In initial design it may be useful to put aside 20 percent or more of your initial program ideas. It may be useful to consider these elements: What is the focus of each of your sessions? What do you want to incorporate around this theme?

> **The key to coaching many is to avoid overdesign. You want to ensure that there is sufficient space and time for exploration.**

Know Your Client

Foundational to any team or group coaching process is knowing your clients. Your clients will shape everything from the coaching approaches you use to the balance of coaching, and in some instances content or skill development (e.g., difficult conversations). In the one-to-one coaching conversation, everything is created with the client and at first there may be a very loose structure or focus. Many times we start our coaching conversation with the question: "What do you want to focus on today?" Our individual client will provide direction. In coaching many, there are multiple agendas at play, and providing structure and a process to identify and work around these multiple issues and perspectives is important.

The Knowing Your Client profile included in Chapter 4 can support us in thinking through what will be useful for the groups we work with. For those working in a team context, it may be used on a much higher level to think through some of the items of concern facing the team's industry.

Remember that Participants Learn in Different Ways

Coaches need to consider the different learning needs in each group and team they work with. You may be working with a combination of visual, auditory and

kinesthetic learners. Note the balance that works for each group you are supporting. Depending on the composition and preferences of the group you will want
to look to incorporate a number of different approaches to working with groups,
highlighted in Group Coaching in Action, a digital accompaniment to the book.

Knowing your client, coupled with what you learn in any pre-calls, via assessments or in sessions, will enable you to adapt the program for the different needs
that show up. There can be tremendous diversity among the group, including:

- Generational differences
- Learning styles: visual/auditory/kinesthetic
- Cultural differences, particularly if you are working with virtual teams
- Differences in processing times and preferences: slow/fast, written/verbal
- Personality styles: introverted/extraverted

Chapter 8 explores how to work with different styles and preferences.

Meet with Clients Prior to the Start of a Team and Group Coaching Process

So much can be learned in the pre-program one-on-ones before the program even
starts. A key message throughout the book is that successful coaching engagements
happen when expectations are shared. Chapter 8 provides more information on
specific questions you may wish to incorporate into pre-program calls for team or
group coaching. The pre-program one-on-ones will give you insight as to themes
and areas of interest, specific goals participants are bringing, learning styles and
pacing. They also provide an important opportunity to ensure a good fit between
the program and the participant, and answer any questions the participants have.
One instance where a meeting with individual clients may be problematic is if you
are working with the team as a system and ensuring complete transparency in all
conversations. If this is the case, you will want to leave ample time in the first conversation with the team to create shared expectations, identify themes or priority
areas of focus, review process and answer any questions team members have.

The Impact of Coaching Happens between Sessions

Coaching is a sustained process of change. In fact, some of the greatest impacts of
coaching happen in between our sessions or touch points, when action is taken
around important goals by the client. Leaving space for goal setting, action planning

and checking in and sharing successes as well as weak points is key to the coaching process in the team and group domains.

Just because there are multiple group members, do not shy away from creating field work (or, in the language of the International Coach Federation, "designing actions") with your group members. Coaching requests, challenges and inquiries may be some of the coaching tools you incorporate. The focus in a group context may be individual, or group focused, as we will see below, and the focus in the team coaching context can be individual or team.

Depending on your group/team size and/or delivery mechanism, pre-work and post-work may be important considerations in leveraging the time you have together to devote to the coaching conversation. Pre-work and post-work can be important to expedite engagement and "deepen the dive" around key coaching issues. This is especially true in the virtual environment, even where capping of group size at four to eight individuals may enable only a few rounds during the sessions. Virtual programs can benefit from an increased focus on pre-work and field work.

Field Work

Field work and homework are important parts of the coaching process in both the team and group coaching contexts. In the group coaching context, where individuals may be working on their own individual goals, you will want to co-create field work, homework and commitments with them. This may be a combination of individually identified items, as well as a selection from a more generic list of items for the entire group to take action on. For example, when I work with values in the virtual environment, I often find that it is useful to have group members complete a values checklist before the call, so we can use the call time to have discussion around the "So what? And now what?", rather than the initial exploration of what the values are.

In a team context it is likely that part of your time together will be spent working on creating an action plan with the team. Some weeks, different team members may have specific commitments in terms of moving the entire team goals forward, and any associated individual goals. Where skill development is important, such as in providing feedback or having difficult conversations, it may be useful to provide the team with a reading list or a series of tip sheets. Likewise, assessments may be required as a foundation for undertaking your

(Continued)

work together. Group members may be asked to complete field work, such as a strengths assessment (like VIA Strengths or StrengthsFinder 2.0) before the next session, and may be asked to bring it with them.

A reminder that the core competency associated with this is supporting action, where we may use a combination of:

- Coaching request
- Coaching challenge
- Coaching inquiry

Some ideas for field work could include:

- Reading lists
- Web resources
- Checklists (e.g., values checklist)
- Completion of assessments (e.g., VIA Strengths)
- Coaching request (for individuals or group/team), coaching challenge and coaching inquiry

Tips for Field Work

- In a group coaching context, have each group member identify his or her own field work and/or co-create it with you and others in the group.
- In a team coaching context, consider where field work may be more individually focused or team focused.
- Keep an eye on themes that emerge in conversation and you may not have time to cover. This might lead to some recommended resources or readings.
- Consider how it connects with the 30,000-foot view and the medium- and long-term focus and goals of the individuals, group or team.
- Consider what members find beneficial and motivating (watch for overburdening them with the field work).
- Field work may support taking action, deepening awareness around issues, or both.

As coaches, we have three main tools for supporting accountability and the action and awareness between sessions: inquiries, requests and challenges.

Inquiry: The inquiry is a "big question" for individuals, teams and/or groups to chew on, or think about between the calls. An inquiry is not just an open-ended, powerful question. It is often a powerful question "on steroids," which requires deeper thought and percolation over time. Examples of inquiries could include the following: *What's truly important here? What does it mean to pause and apply the gas?*

Request: In a coaching request, clients—whether individuals, teams or groups— are asked to take specific action in support of their goals and priorities. When working with teams and groups, inquiries may be individual for each group member or they may be collective. A coaching request with a group of new managers could be for them to schedule a series of one-on-one meetings with each of their team members. If the focus of your work together was on supporting the team leader to get to know their staff members better, or build stronger relationships, then this would be a good focus. A request for a team might be for them to decide on a structure of how they can see their team agreements every day. I have worked with teams who have decided to laminate their team agreements and have them visible in their offices, and other teams who review these at the start of their team meetings.

Coaching Challenge: A coaching challenge is designed to take the team's or group's breath away in service of expanding their comfort zones around goals. It is important to recognize that a challenge for one person may not be a challenge for everyone. An example of a challenge for a group of writers could be to have three chapters drafted by the next meeting. For some of the writers, this may be a real stretch point. For others, this may be well within reach, so we may need to work with them individually to find a challenge that will stretch them.

Trust and Intimacy Are Key

Building trust and intimacy is foundational within the group and team you are working with, and also with you as the team/group coach. Without trust and connection among the group, the coaching conversation may only reach the surface level. At the team coaching level, trust and a feeling of safety is even more critical when the stakes are raised, given that the conversation is around their livelihood.

Building trust and intimacy is a key theme of this book. In Chapter 7 you will explore strategies for building trust and intimacy in the virtual domain. Chapter 8 discusses different strategies for creating connection and engagement. The appendix includes additional activities for creating connection.

Keep It Simple, Not Simplistic

Everything should be made as simple as possible, but not simpler.
—Albert Einstein

With the myriad of relationships, personalities and agendas at play in coaching many, it is important to keep the design process simple. What might take 10 minutes to explore in an individual coaching conversation might take hours to explore through the team or group coaching process. Coaches can fall into traps by making it too complicated logistically, providing too much information or filling the time with too many questions, activities or focus areas. Keeping things simple does not mean keeping it simplistic.

Remain Flexible with Timing

Flexibility is key in any group or team coaching process. You never know what main focus needs may be uncovered in the check-in at the start of a coaching conversation. Likewise, you may not be aware of contextual changes that have occurred in the organization, changes that may now be bringing issues to the surface or changing the team's direction. As coaches we need to feel confident, as well as be skilled, at changing direction in the moment.

Have a Strong Focus on Process and a Light Touch on Direction

As coaches working with many (either teams or groups), it is very important that we have a strong focus on process. Creating a solid framework for the group or team to converse around sets the foundation for success. Once the team has the structure, it is important for us to fade back. This light touch on direction encourages us to be really focusing in on where the group or team wants to go.

Let the Group/Team Do the Work

A key perspective that successful team and group coaches adopt is letting the group or team do the work, and *trusting* them. As the group or team gets to know each other and develops their own capabilities, let them do the work. This may be having group or team members further influence focus areas, or even facilitating components of the process. As a coach, also watch for your stance in terms of "trying to fix things" when conflict arises. Your role as coach may include mirroring back or reflecting what you see happening, getting them to notice and name what is happening within the team, or asking the team to name the elephant in the room. Likewise, with reporting and other items, letting the group do the work in finalizing the action plan may be a key builder in terms of sustainability, and linking it back to their everyday processes.

It's not all about you. As coaches working with groups and teams our role can be seen to shift significantly. In an individual coaching conversation, our questions create the volley, the back and forth. In coaching many, we need to be comfortable in stepping back and not always being center stage. One of a team and group coach's best skills can be knowing when to step back and let the group do the work, and when to step in, ask a question, step back, and let the group keep rolling. Team and group coaches need to feel comfortable about checking their egos at the door, as well as confident about inserting themselves when it will be of benefit to the group.

Ensure that You Evaluate

Evaluation and measurement continues to be identified as a critical area of focus for coaches. This topic was identified as a key focus in the 2012 ICF Global Coaching Survey. In your group coaching programs you will want to consider what is useful to measure: is it only the program, or are there metrics that can be taken pre- and post-program? Several chapters in this book touch on measurement and evaluation. Taking the pulse of the group at the end of each session is also important. Be open to incorporating positive and constructive feedback throughout the coaching process.

Follow Up as a Value Add

Offering a follow-up group call two to six weeks after a weekend intensive, a six-week virtual program or a virtual intensive can be very useful in providing participants with a chance to reconnect as well as reflect on what they really learned in the bigger picture. It can also serve as a reminder about the commitments they made. In a recent group follow-up call to the two-day Group Coaching Intensive I offer, I heard from several coaches about the value of being able to reconnect and rearticulate the learning and action that had taken place. These follow-up group calls are also useful for longer-term evaluation and measurement of impact. Many coaches also consider how they keep the conversation flowing. For many years now, I have offered quarterly calls to my alumni community. It is a great way to stay connected with them, connect them to a wider community and continue the conversation.

Additional tips and best practices are included throughout this book, including some additional best practices in Chapter 8 (see Table 8.2: Pre-program One-on-One Worksheet). Most chapters have their own best practices highlighted.

Voices from the Field: Best Practices for Team and Group Coaching

Throughout this book you will meet a number of coach practitioners who have shared their insights about team and group coaching, along with examples of the work that they have undertaken. Coaches are often very curious to explore what the work looks like. The Voices from the Field sections are designed to provide you with examples and illustrations of team and group coaching in action. Many books only focus on the voice of the expert. Given the philosophical orientation and practical reality of our work, I feel it is very important to provide a variety of perspectives around the issues we work with through the insights of other coach practitioners.

One of the questions I asked coaches I interviewed was: "What do you see as a best practice in team or group coaching?" Here's what they had to say.

Best Practices for Team Coaching

Jacqueline Peters: Do a pre-assessment to benchmark the team's current state and then reassess in six to twelve months to measure progress and mark achievements.

Catherine Carr: Do a pre-assessment and consider coaching the team leader first to get the conditions in place to then work with the team. This pre-work is as important as the work with the whole team.

Sharon Miller: Look at what is happening in the system, what is trying to happen, what is being revealed. Work with each person as a voice of the system, and work with the system/relationship as a third entity. This can lead to perspective shift from a person as the client (e.g., a leader) to the web as the client.

Team contracts and the designed alliance are also important. This should include how we work together, how we live the values and how we engage with the purpose even when under stress and when we disagree. Then it is not dependent on each person's character or definition of integrity. Instead, the behavioral contract (what we will do and not do) is clear. All are expected to align with this and it may be woven into other HR systems (including hiring, performance reviews and development).

Phil Sandahl: In order to help the team move from where they are to where they want to be, it's important to know where we're starting. That's the benefit of starting with an assessment tool. I'm a little biased but the feedback we get from the field is that the Team Diagnostic is an ideal way to establish a starting point with teams. (Full disclosure: I am one of the developers of the tool and have used it with teams.) The Team Diagnostic treats the team as a whole, a system, and provides the team with a self-portrait and a pin in the map that says, "We are here." Coaching asks the obvious question: "Where would you like to be?" Because the model uses the everyday language of teams, it's easy to move quickly from seeing the results to conversation that leads to action.

Best Practices for Group Coaching

Renee Brotman: I like to end each coaching session with an evaluation of the session. This gives participants another tool for examining group process as well as taking responsibility for their own learning.

At the last session in a series of group coaching, I like to have some type of integrating activity—create their own leadership wheel, create a profile of their leadership journey, interview a leader they admire and report back to the group. . . . Also, create an activity that again links back to the overall learning objectives of the entire leadership development program and integrates classroom experience.

Shana Montesol: I always hold brief, 15-minute pre-program one-on-one calls with participants. I typically ask them what prompted them to sign up for the program, what they hope to gain from participating, what their learning style or group discussion style is, and what questions or concerns they have about the program.

This is a great way to establish the relationship with group members (most of whom I've never met before they register for the program), and

(Continued)

make sure that the program is a good fit for them. I can't imagine running a group without taking this important step.

Michael Cullen: There are a couple of best practices, including respect and making sure that the group has plenty of (time-limited) opportunities to (a) interact with each other and (b) complete individual exercises without feeling rushed.

Ray Rigoglioso: I would say it is facilitating a group discussion using a coaching approach. As a trained coach, I look for opportunities to ask powerful questions of participants. I set the working agreements so the conversation, to the extent possible, focuses on the "I." In the working agreements, I state that any member can invite another member to return to the "I." As I facilitate the group, I remind myself that this is not a casual discussion or conversation—it is an opportunity to help members learn about themselves, and to help members facilitate that discovery for each other. It is a skill set that is not explicitly taught, but one that comes in very handy.

In Coaching Many

Kevin Stebbings: For me, the best practice is the habit and technique of believing the best about those we are coaching. Demonstrate above all else that you believe the best about this group or team and want to see the best brought out in each individual. This belief in the potential of every individual needs to permeate through every word, attitude and action of the group coach. If it does not, the attitude of the coach will "leak out" to the group or team. From time to time, people will bring with them their cynicism, disappointment and frustration. The coach's response to these feelings will go a long way to making the group process a success. Demonstrating your belief in the group also builds respect and rapport, even when there is an initial reluctance from members. A coach can communicate his or her belief in the potential of the group by saying, "I don't have the answers for this group/team but this group/team has the answers for this group/team." The coach then needs to demonstrate that belief in every activity and conversation. A coach also demonstrates this best practice by getting out of the way so that the group or team can do its best work. A group coach does this by trusting the process of group coaching and not their abilities to perform miracles.

Ursula Lesic: Be a coach and use the ICF code of conduct as your guide. Remember that each group is going to be different. Work with a partner when you can.

Building on the framework of coaching many, this chapter explored the similarities and differences between team and group coaching, as well as different focus areas our work revolves around. We also explored 12 best practices for team and group coaching. These best practices will be further refined throughout the rest of the book.

End-of-Chapter Questions

Note the 12 best practices for team and group coaching. Which ones do you already incorporate?

Which new ones do you want to bring into your next program?

CHAPTER 2

THE FUSION OF APPROACHES, BENEFITS AND TRICKY ISSUES IN COACHING MANY

Fusion: a merging of diverse, distinct, or separate elements into a unified whole.
—Merriam-Webster Dictionary

Some of the most common questions I hear from coaches, leaders, and team and group members alike are: *How does coaching differ from other fields such as training or facilitation? How does group coaching differ from a workshop? How does team coaching differ from team building?* This chapter explores these foundational and fundamental questions.

What is apparent—in the context of organizations we work with today—is the need for varying approaches that practitioners can utilize with different groups. The disciplines of coaching, training and facilitation are often seen as distinct. In service to our clients and their goals, it is important that we consider what approaches will best support the teams and groups we work with. Sometimes this requires a mix of different modalities or approaches. At the same time, those entering into coaching work are often coming to it from related fields such as training, facilitation and performance management. This chapter explores some of the subtle yet important differences between these related domains.

Several coaches interviewed for this book pointed to how successful team coaches incorporate a number of different approaches in their work. For example, Team Coaching International's Phil Sandahl stated:

Part of TCI's perspective is that teams want help from us. This means that the art of the work draws in coaching, consulting and training. Every coach brings a specific experience or expertise and their own toolkit. We encourage coaches to become certified in other assessments such as DiSC, MBTI, etc. It helps the individuals in the team and gives them an understanding of who they are and how others are different. One of the Team Diagnostic measures is Values Diversity. We as a team become stronger as we take advantage of the variety of strengths. One reason teams are stronger is because they take advantage of these strengths *collectively*. Assessments can help raise awareness around individual differences and the unique contributions that come from Me and You. The Team Diagnostic provides the collective view, the view of the whole, who "we" are as a "team."

THE GROUP PROGRAM CONTINUUM

In *Effective Group Coaching* I introduced the concept of the Group Program Continuum to illustrate the gradients of approaches when working with groups. Figure 2.1 identifies some of the key distinctions of three approaches: coaching, facilitation and training. It is likely that most coaches working with teams and groups will find themselves working in one or across all three domains. In fact, while coaching, training and facilitation are all viewed as separate professions, each with its own competency frameworks, the world of our clients is not as "siloed" as these professions. What is critical to our work is that our clients' needs are being met, regardless of whether using a mix of approaches or a "pure" approach. I use the term *hybrid* to describe the need for weaving together different approaches based on the needs of our clients.

In my own work, and in speaking with other internal and external coaches about their work, as well as other allied professionals such as facilitators and trainers who coach, it is clear that it is increasingly useful to hold the idea of a continuum or gradients of needs of the group or team. From a positioning perspective in our conversations with clients and organizations, it is important to be able to distinguish the subtle but important differences among the three domains. The continuum is offered here to enable practitioners to be aware of the subtle differences among the approaches of training, coaching and facilitation. Over the years I have shared this with hundreds of coaches as well as other allied professionals. It can help us understand what we are bringing into our work, as well as what our clients may be looking for.

Figure 2.1: The Group Program Continuum

Coaching	Facilitation	Training
Core coaching competencies	Core facilitation competencies	Core training competencies
Powerful questions	Questions	Content
Goal setting	Focus on process and task	Training objectives are drivers
Action, awareness, accountability	Helping client group get from A to B	Trainer measured on "learning"
Unattachment	Coach may or may not be content expert	Often tighter timelines
Clients and their agenda are drivers		Trainer is expert
Client, not coach, is expert		Acquisition of KSAs
Integration of KSAs		
Focus on awareness and application		

Throughout my career I have found myself straddling the realms of these disciplines. My initial work with groups was in the training domain as a senior staff member at a summer camp, tasked with developing my staff teams around topics such as communication, performance feedback, leadership and other personal development issues. I also worked as an experiential educator, taking groups through intensive wilderness experiences, providing them a real-time backdrop for learning about strengths and themselves. As a graduate student in the early 1990s I studied process facilitation, adding this to my toolkit. As a former program director and manager within the United Nations and the international sector, some of my favorite work was in designing and training programs in the areas of leadership, train-the-trainer and security issues. Today, although the bulk of my work is in the realm of coaching, I do return to my roots in the areas of training and facilitation. My comments below stem from my experience in all three realms—coaching, facilitation and training.

Let's take a look at each one of these disciplines in turn, and the skills associated with each discipline. As you read through these descriptions, note for yourself where your skills and strengths lie.

Training

In today's context, training may take place through traditional classroom training, or virtually, through teleclasses or webinars. Training continues to be associated with supporting individuals to acquire new knowledge, skills and abilities (KSAs). Key to the training process is content. As a trainer we are seen as the expert. Even if content is delivered in a participatory way, the training process revolves around, and is measured by, how participants learn and absorb these new skills, knowledge and information.

As trainers, we are encouraged to undertake needs assessments to discover what our group members want to cover. Regardless, trainers often still hold the timeline very tightly and are guided by strong learning objectives. These learning objectives are what we are measured by. For example, a course for new leaders on relationship management may include objectives such as:

- Traditionally, training has been "left" in the classroom, with low rates of transfer back to the workplace. In recent years, more emphasis has been placed on the transfer or application of training. Note that it is not always the trainer who is responsible for supporting this, or tracking it.
- Training provides teams and groups with the information and skills needed to get ahead.

Questions to Consider

1. What skills are required to support the team or group in moving toward their goals? Will coaching alone be enough? For example, if a team has challenges with conflict, what additional skill building is required?

2. What else is required for the person to enhance their performance? In 1984, Robert Mager wrote *Analyzing Performance Problems*. A key message from this book is that training is not a solution to each performance issue. Sometimes teams cannot operate not only because of lack of skill, but also due to a lack of an enabling environment. Performance-related challenges can be due to the fact that compensation, reward systems, and key performance indicators do not support team-based goals. What other factors are creating blockages to the team's performance? As a coach, this is a question to ask the team. Note that this is in contrast to a consultant, whose role would be to identify the blockage.

Key components of the training process include:

- Rich content
- Focus on the acquisition of KSAs (knowledge, skills and abilities)
- Tight timelines (e.g., by 10:30 I should be at this point . . .)

- Utilization of group facilitation techniques to engage learners
- Learning objectives spelled out and measured against
- Trainer as expert

Different organizations have their own training competency models. You may want to refer to the ASTD competency model or the Canadian Society for Training and Development (CSTD) competency model, for more detail.

Training and performance, in general, are measured using four or five levels of evaluation. These levels are:

Level 1: Reaction. Level 1 evaluation is often referred to as the "Smiley Sheet" for the common practice of some facilitators asking participants to mark whether they liked the training (smile), did not (frown) or were indifferent. In level 1 evaluation we measure immediate reaction to the experience and ask our participants their thoughts about what they enjoyed in the coaching (or training) process.

Level 2: Learning. Level 2 evaluation looks at how much your learners increased their knowledge and capabilities during the training. This is often "tested" at the end of a training program. As coaches we may not be "testing" learning, but we should be asking what group members are "taking away in terms of new ideas, insights and learning." Group follow-up calls can be a good way to capture some of the learning that takes place in the more medium term.

Level 3: Behavior. This level of evaluation measures the learning and what changes are made to performance. Level 3 evaluation looks at the application of the new skills and knowledge into the participants' work. Post-calls, or ongoing team or group coaching calls after training, can focus in on this level of evaluation, asking participants to share what skills and approaches they have integrated into their work. Follow-up calls, or ongoing coaching calls, are also a way to continue the conversation and develop best practices around what does work, and what might not be "sticking" or transferring back. Coaches will want to work with partners to consider which metrics are best to track.

Level 4: Results Due to Training. Level 4 evaluation looks at the impact on behavior and performance, and can start with the group or team member being asked to identify what the impact has been on their work and/or personal realm. As coaches this is where follow-up contact weeks or months after your work allows you to look deeper at the results level.

Level 5: Return on Investment. Return on investment is still a very specialized measurement. Measurement in general has been identified as a key priority focus area going forward for the coaching profession in the 2012 ICF Global

Coaching Survey. For ROI measurement, coaches will want to look at the work of Jack J. Phillips.

Measurement is a key area of need for focus by team and group coaches. As Phil Sandahl from Team Coaching International says:

> In the last two years Team Coaching International has been encouraging graduates to ask the team, as part of the team debrief and action planning: How will you measure success in business terms? This should be something that the team measures in terms of its own indicators.
>
> Teams need to come up with the business case measurement for the team coaching engagement. That's where their attention will be. It makes it easier for the team to pay attention to it, and likely this is where they will be rewarded. It is also important so that the work feels relevant to their everyday work context.

Facilitation

The word *facilitation* comes from the Latin word *facilis*, "to make easy."

In facilitation we focus on supporting a group or team to move from A to B. The goal and endpoint are determined by the group or team, and these markers are often set out before the start of the engagement. Typical facilitation engagements may include strategic planning or process facilitation to support a group as they devise a plan or aim to increase sales.

As noted by the Office of Quality Management, "Your main task is to help the team or group increase its effectiveness by improving its processes. A facilitator *manages the method* of the meeting, rather than the content. Facilitators are concerned with *how decisions are made* instead of what decisions are reached."[1] A facilitator will use a wide variety of techniques to support groups in navigating an effective process toward their end result. Similar to coaching, facilitators will use core skills such as open-ended questions, and rely on an understanding of group process.

A key role of the facilitator is to clarify purpose and to record the progress of the group, capturing, just as coaches would, the insights of the participants.

---

[1] Nancy Thayer Hart, ed., *Facilitator Tool Kit: A Guide for Helping Groups Get Results*, Office of Quality Management, University of Wisconsin, 2007, http://oqi.wisc.edu/resourcelibrary/uploads/resources/Facilitator%20Tool%20Kit.pdf.

Facilitation as a profession has its own set of competencies guiding the practice and profession of facilitation. The facilitation competencies from the International Association of Facilitators (IAF) include:

A. Create collaborative relationships.
B. Plan appropriate group processes.
C. Create and sustain a participatory environment.
D. Guide group to appropriate and useful outcomes.
E. Build and maintain professional knowledge.
F. Model a positive professional attitude.

There are some key similarities between coaching and facilitation, particularly around the competency of "guiding the group to appropriate and useful outcomes." The IAF cites the following subcomponents:

a. Guide group with clear methods and process.
b. Facilitate group self-awareness about task.
c. Guide group to consensus and desired outcome.

Key to the success of a facilitator is his or her ability to have a range of facilitation techniques to draw out the knowledge of the group and facilitate their enhanced self-awareness about the task setup. Facilitators are not necessarily experts in content, but rather in process—note the term IAF uses, which is *guide*. Part of the role of team and group coaches is also to support the development of group or team self-awareness, and to support the group or team to their outcome.

Another similar competency is what the IAF calls "creating collaborative relationships." Key to facilitation is developing working partnerships, similar to the coaching agreement, that spell out the tasks and deliverables of facilitation, as well as the roles and responsibilities of different players. Likewise, facilitators are encouraged to design and customize approaches to meet various client needs. Facilitation is typically grounded in adult learning principles and incorporates an understanding of group dynamics (also reviewed in the digital chapter Group Coaching in Action at www.groupcoachingessentials.com).

What Makes Coaching Different from Facilitation?

Facilitation has a hard focus on supporting a group to a specific outcome, for example, the development of a strategic plan or a specific decision. Whereas the facilitator is engaged to support a group to get from A to B, the coaching philosophy is grounded in unattachment to the outcome. If the team or group decides midstream that the key priority is exploring values rather than creating a plan, then a coach needs to be ready to change course and move to this new realm of exploration. Key to the coaching process is a focus on deepening awareness around the issues at play.

Another key distinction is the coaching focus on goal setting and accountability. Coaching is a sustained process of conversation, with the goals forming the foundation of the series of conversations. Action is key in the coaching process, with coaches being on the sidelines as the team or group takes action. Facilitators may come in to work with a group or team to develop the plan, but usually are not present to check in and sustain the conversation around how the plan is being implemented.

Coaches will use the coaching skills of coaching challenges, inquiries and requests as a way to support clients into action as they move forward.

Facilitators will often draw out each group member to ensure balanced facilitation, and may also point to what is happening in the room. Coaches often take this "pointing out what is happening in the room" to one more level when working with teams, but holding up to the team a "mirror" of what they see, and also asking team members to connect what is going on in the room to how it is playing out in their own team.

Coaches can benefit greatly from becoming more skilled in facilitation techniques and approaches. As our client needs become more hybridized, it will be useful for coaches and leaders to have a range of facilitation techniques at their disposal, in working with teams and groups.

Key facilitation tools that coaches may also adapt or learn from are:

- Lewin's force field analysis
- Strategic planning (strengths, weaknesses, opportunities, threats)
- Strategic issues mapping

As well as processes such as:

- Dotmocracy (using colored dots for prioritization)
- Open Space
- World Café

TEAM BUILDING VERSUS TEAM COACHING

"Team building refers to the various activities undertaken to motivate the team members and increase the overall performance of the team."
—ManagementStudyGuide.com

Teams are large entities and change can take time. It is the small changes, sustained over time, that can have a tremendous impact on where the team ultimately gets to. This is one of the main benefits of the team coaching process. Team coaching is a process that is sustained over time.

Team-building initiatives often focus on enhancing trust, building stronger relationships by providing an opportunity to allow team members to get to know one another and focusing on topics such as communication and goal setting. Components of the team-building process may focus on:

- Getting to know each other
- Building trust
- Building skills: teamwork, communication, feedback
- Working together to achieve a common task, for example, Bridge Building or Tower Building (refer to the digital chapter Team Coaching in Action at www.groupcoachingessentials.com for a description of Tower Building)

A fundamental difference with the team-coaching process is the focus on accountability, as well as the sustained nature of the engagement, focus and conversation of the team. It is quite common for team coaching engagements to be six months in length, launched through a one- to two-day offsite retreat, and followed up with bi-weekly or monthly team coaching sessions, focusing on the goals and accountability items that the team has set for itself.

Team-building events may or may not be connected to corporate initiatives and priority areas. Many team-building initiatives are a "one-off" event, with little tie-back to the office. Great team builders are adept at supporting the group to make the link-back to the office. They may use a debrief process guided by the experiential "What? So what? Now what?" line of questioning to support team members to reinforce learning from the activity, its significance and how it may be applied going forward. (You will want to refer to the "What? So what? Now what?" text box found in Chapter 3.)

Developing teamwork skills may also be part of the work of a team builder. Some foundational teamwork skills include: Listening, providing feedback, sharing ideas, providing support to other teams, acknowledging and working through conflict.[2]

Team coaching, in contrast, as we will see in Chapter 6, is a sustained process of conversation, skill development, application and revision with a team. The focus for coaches should be on supporting the goal setting, action and awareness of a team, within an accountability framework. Part of the value of the team

---

[2] Sharon Boller, *Teamwork Training* (Virginia: ASTD Press, 2005), 2.

coaching process is also the focus on helping the team develop deeper insight into their strengths, roles and the patterns that support and sabotage them.

Even if coaches are working in the team-building context, coaches can bring in as many coaching tools and approaches as possible (for example, a Wheel of Leadership, Workaround Roles). The appendix includes a number of specific coaching tools you may wish to incorporate. You will see this comment reflected by many of the coaches highlighted throughout the book.

Coaching

Coaching has evolved as its own profession with a focus on:

- Core coaching competencies (refer to Chapter 3)
- Client, not coach, is expert
- Support for the integration or application of knowledge, skills and abilities
- Powerful questions
- Goal setting
- Action, awareness, accountability
- Unattachment by the coach in terms of direction or outcome (this should be grounded by the success measures created by the clients)
- Clients and their agenda or priority areas are drivers of the process

Other chapters in this book go into great depth around the skills and focus areas of coaching. On a final note, a key distinction between coaching and the other modalities is the ongoing focus and support to the teams and groups we work with on the integration or application of the knowledge, skills and abilities they are uncovering. It is this emphasis that makes coaching different from other modalities.

Activity: The Group Coaching Continuum

Using Figure 2.2 draw a symbol of where you naturally fall along the continuum.

Where do your clients want you to be? Draw a different symbol in terms of what your clients are looking for.

What do you notice?

What impact does this have for your work—in terms of design, positioning, marketing and implementation?

Figure 2.2: The Group Program Continuum

Coaching   Facilitation   Training

THE BUSINESS CASE FOR COACHING MANY

The 2009 Global Coaching Client Survey found that people who had been coached—our coaching clients—described coaching as "forward thinking," "focused," "structured," "direct" and "an experience that forced clients to address 'the BIG questions.'" The ICF described it as a "tool to help clients meet their goals and objectives through the action plan." Self-esteem and self-confidence were identified as the number one sphere where coaching affected clients positively.

Other benefits identified by people being coached included:

- Improved ability to relinquish control and delegate responsibility
- Enhanced ability to focus
- Improved listening skills
- Enhanced ability to apply past learning to assist them in new situations
- Improved ability to evaluate and take calculated risks as opposed to "snap decisions"
- Improved planning skills (corporate strategy)

How do these benefits translate to the group and team coaching contexts? As you will note from the different case studies throughout this book, different engagements lead to different results. No surprise here, given the highly tailored nature of the coaching relationship, where each team or group will have a different set of goals, focus areas and priorities they are working around.

In *Effective Group Coaching*, I identified the following benefits for group coaching from the vantage point of the clients or participants of the group, the coach and from the organizational level. (Refer to Table 2.1.)

At the organizational level, the benefits of being able to involve more employees in a coaching process is a key advantage. Providing these services at a lower per-capita price has definitely been an initial selling point for organizations, as is the time factor. Scalability is also seen as a real advantage—being able to roll this out to many people at one time, leading to the potential for a greater cascade effect.

As organizations start to roll out this work, the added advantages of the cross-functional fertilization that happens among parts of the organization, through

Table 2.1: Benefits of Group Coaching[3]

Client	Coach	Organization
Collective wisdom Multiple perspectives Less didactic (back and forth questioning) Less "on the spot" Enables people to connect across geographic and industry boundaries	Leverages time and resources Economies of scale Effects change Harnesses the collective wisdom of groups Scalability	Time Money Scalability Effects change more readily Cross-functional fertilization Culture change Enhanced retention of learning

the relationships and conversations that happen among peers, becomes an even more important advantage of the group coaching process. This can lead to culture change over time.

From a group member's perspective, the collective wisdom and insights that are created in group setting are often seen as most valuable. For individuals who enjoy a group process, group coaching is a natural fit for them. They often do not mind that the focus of coaching is wider rather than deeper. The depth can be provided by offering a hybrid of individual and group coaching interventions. For those who enjoy a collaborative learning experience, group coaching provides the opportunity to build stronger peer relationships, often across distance. The group coaching process also provides clients with multiple perspectives they might never be connected with in an individual coaching conversation, simply by listening to their peers.

Dorothy Nesbit writes the following about the additional benefits of group coaching:

> Group coaching offers some of the benefits of good training. Group members learn in a safe environment away from work and often feel less alone when they learn that others face the same challenges. In addition, it is highly tailored, helping group members identify the questions they want to address and providing support as they find new ways forward. Over time, trust builds and group members risk more, benefiting both from the personal coaching they receive and from observing the coaching of their colleagues. They also build relationships of trust that continue after the coaching has finished: this

[3] Britton, *Effective Group Coaching.*

can contribute to a changing culture in an organization and increase the willingness of group members to collaborate with colleagues.[4]

Coach Lynda Monk has noted that in addition to the more specific individual benefits group members have accrued through her writing group coaching, group members have indicated in their evaluations about "being inspired through peer support, dialogue and shared learning."

Benefits of Team Coaching

The benefits of a team coaching process can be to the team, the individuals involved and the organization. Table 2.2 outlines team coaching benefits. As you read through this list, note which ones are beneficial to the team, which to the organization, and which to both.

As we will explore in later chapters, a best practice for team coaches is to have team members identify their success measures and metrics. As you consider a team coaching engagement, what might be the benefits for the team? What would they identify as possible benefits?

Table 2.2: Benefits of Team Coaching

Benefits for the Team	Benefits for the Organization
Alignment around where the team is going (vision) and what is important	Higher productivity
Enhanced relationships within the team	Stronger results
Understanding of strengths and values	Clearer goals, with link to the business
Shared agreements of how to work: what's acceptable and what's not	Stronger relationships within the team and sometimes with internal and external partners
Enhanced goal clarity and focus	Greater alignment
Ongoing/sustained focus on what's important, what's working, and what's not; support for adjustments along the way	Clearer vision
Team members rowing in the same direction	More committed and engaged employees

---

[4] Dorothy Nesbit, "Coaching in Hard Times," *Training Journal* (May 2012): 65–69, http:// www.training journal.com.

TRICKY ISSUES IN TEAM AND GROUP COACHING

Tricky issues can occur at all phases of the team and group coaching conversation. Key to a successful team or group coaching process is being proactive and mitigating, or reducing, the possible impact of tricky issues. What follows are common tricky issues that can emerge in the group or team coaching context. Additional tricky issues specific to team coaching are listed in Chapter 6. As we have said earlier, the team coaching context can be even more complicated, due to the relationships among the individuals, the history of the grouping, the culture in which the coaching takes place, and the link to group members' livelihood.

Many coaches new to this work ask, "What can I do to avoid tricky issues and what do I do in the event that they happen?"

Remember that some of the reasons why participants become "difficult" is that they do not feel that they are:

- Being heard
- Being valued
- Made comfortable
- Made safe

Take a look at your program and ask yourself, "How am I creating a safe space for everyone to participate?"

Trust is a foundation of a successful coaching conversation. Without trust, group and team members may not be willing to engage in the coaching conversation. It goes back to the expectations you set from the start of the program. How much are people expected to show up and be ready to engage and participate with others? Key in establishing trust is to consider whether there is enough connection among participants. In a group and team coaching context, the connection between participants can be just as important as, if not more important than, the connection with the coach. Have we created enough time for the group to get to know each other, and has trust been advanced with us as coaches?

Another area to consider is whether people will value some reflection time before they speak. Likewise, some groups may prefer to have smaller group conversation rather than larger group conversation. If your group size is in the eight to fifteen range, you may find that a majority of conversations take place in the smaller group realm.

There are five main areas where tricky issues can surface in a group coaching process, as follows.

Tricky Issue #1: The Personalities in Your Group

Every group will have its own unique personalities. They can include the Talker, the Challenger, the Quiet One, the Joker, or the Super-achiever. As you work from group to group, you will likely see a wide variety of personalities show up, time and again. There are simple things you can do to develop the trust and rapport so it is about a conversation and people are aware of the impact they have on others in the group.

The Talker: Talkers love to have all the airtime. In a group and team coaching process it is important that we hold equal space and time for each participant. If you are faced with someone more verbal, it is important to have some discussion with them. A proactive way in creating the space for equal airtime is to work with the group to create ground rules, or how your group wants to operate. As well, at the start of call one or session one, introduce the skill of bottom lining, sometimes called the skill of head lining or the skill of laser speak. It is simply the ability to condense a story to its key elements. An essential communication skill today is getting to the core of conversation—zooming into the content and guts of the story. Bottom lining facilitates this. If you are undertaking work in person you may want to create a gesture around this.

Many of the tricky issues that show up will have a flag. They can show up in the pre-program one-on-one call. I often find that I will encounter tricky issues if I do not have a touch point or pre-program contact with each group member. As we have seen already, one of the best practices for group coaching, and some team coaching engagements, is to meet with each participant for a pre-program call during registration or later. During this call it is important to share information so expectations are clear. You will also get a clear sense of who each person is. I often pose the question, "What should I know about how you learn best?" Often I hear from people who are very talkative that they are talkative. This feedback gives me the opportunity to indicate that as a coach I will likely "intrude" at times and cut them off in service of the group. It provides an opportunity to get permission from them. This becomes a proactive, rather than reactive, conversation.

The Challenger: Challengers may show up in your room; however, they are quite rare in my experience with groups that I organize ("public groups"), simply because we have the chance to meet before the program starts. If I sense the program is not a good fit, I will let the person know before the start. Challengers may be more common in corporate groups, where people are possibly mandated to attend. Key to working with a perceived Challenger is building rapport and relationship. We also need to check our assumptions as well. You may want to consider if one of the four needs above is not being met.

The Quiet One: It is likely that you will have more introverted processors in your groups. This may be surfaced in the pre-program one-on-one, where they may tell you that they are quieter than other people. During the first session with the group it is important to grow your understanding of the group members as a grouping. It is useful for group members to share a little about their own learning preferences at the start of the program. So, for example, a quiet person may indicate that they are generally more quiet. Certain group or team members may need more time to process, or may prefer to communicate in writing. Be aware of putting people on the spot when it is not comfortable. If they are quieter, get their coaching permission to put them on the spot.

The Joker: Fun and humor are important, but not appropriate in every context. Humor can also be a flag that something may be happening below the surface. This can be an interesting coaching conversation to have individually with the Joker.

Super-achiever: You may have group members that just take off and are totally running. This can have the positive impact of raising the bar. It may also demotivate others who feel as though they are not "getting it" or moving as quickly.

In terms of dealing with any tricky issues, it's always a question of whether you address it during sessions or privately. In the case of the Super-achiever, you may address it only if it is having a negative impact on the group. Nine out of ten times others get excited by others "walking the talk."

If there are deeper issues at play I don't like to call them out in the venue, especially if it is an early session. It is better to raise tricky issues or curiosities in a one-on-one call, rather than in front of the group, if the relationship is not established. The strength of your relationship will be key in determining how you raise tricky issues.

The issue of comparison is a real one that can show up in a group coaching process. Continue to stress throughout a group coaching process that each group member will be moving at a different pace, undertaking different actions, and achieving goals at a different pace. It's about how we want to continue to improve. If individual group members are expressing the motivation to meet their goals, ask: "What do you need to do to amp it up for yourself?"

Developing trust and rapport within the groups and teams is one of our core coaching competencies. Group and team coaching is a conversation. Spend time to leave space for people to share and build relationships.

Questions to Consider

Which of these personalities or issues would be trickiest for you to address? What do you need to do before, or during, your group coaching process to mitigate these tricky issues?

Tricky Issue #2: Preparation

The second tricky issue revolves around us as coaches and preparation. What can we create for ourselves in terms of preparation and running a coaching program?

As coaches ourselves, we need to step back and let the group do the work. As facilitators we will want to give the group a framework and tools and then step back and let them do the work.

As a coach, trust yourself and the skills you bring. Take stock of the tools you have at your disposal.

One of the traps may be to throw too much into a session (recall the best practice of "less is more"). Coaching is all about the conversation. Leave space for the group to engage, and keep listening for what they value.

Some coaches may feel that they don't bring enough to the session. The Design Matrix (Chapter 4) as a structure provides a road map of possibilities, options for where you may go with the group depending on their needs and agendas. In the Design Matrix you can identify the different approaches you have for core topics such as values or vision, and it will also help you have "back pocket" ideas or sets of questions to bring into the discussion. As coaches we want to remind ourselves that it is important to step aside, trusting ourselves and the coaching we bring. Note that there is a fine balance between preparation and being present to coaching in the moment.

As coaches, our stance and presence can also become a tricky issue. The tone you set is infectious. Notice your voice, the way you are speaking, how much you are speaking, your body language, what you are saying and not saying. It is important that we use the skill of intuition, as many times in a team and group coaching context the most important things are not verbalized.

Personal Preparation for the Event

Do a walk through and speak through: talk it out loud.

Consider what will support you. For some it is having a matrix prepared. For others, it is thinking through powerful questions that may be pertinent.

Get a good rest.

Be present and focused on the experience.

Remember, it's all about the team and group experience!

Questions to Consider

What will make you feel confident and prepared before your session?

What key preparation activities do you want to undertake before the program? As you move forward with the group?

What is the tone you want to set with your group?

What will move you forward in terms of the feeling of preparation and confidence?

Tricky Issue #3: Logistics

There are generally three logistical areas coaches can stumble into. These may seem very simple, but when we forget to do something it can become a big issue. In team and group coaching, business systems—or lack thereof—can create undue challenges.

In phone-based programs, the most important resource is your **conference calling system**. You will want to make it a habit of calling in early, one to make sure there are no glitches, and two, to be able to welcome people as they arrive. Make sure that you have a bridgeline that works, and a backup. Have these back-up details with you for that alternative. A number of coaches have flagged logistics and bridgelines as key tricky issues.

Another area coaches will want to look at is the **systems** to ensure that people can easily and effortlessly find you and undertake business with you. How do you want to accept payments? What barriers exist in your registration process? We need to make it easy—some people may not even call because they are so frustrated. Some prefer to do everything offline: Do you want to become a Visa, AmEx or MasterCard merchant through your bank?

Think through your business and what is going to be appropriate for each client you work with. If you are working with organizations, ask them what they use in terms of bridge lines, specific teleconferencing solutions, or webinar applications. Tap into the organizational systems that exist. You don't have to reinvent the wheel; work with what they have. A key concern if using organizational systems is to ensure that calls are kept confidential, and that others in the organization cannot access the calls.

Another key area of systems is support for group communication. How will you get information out to the group? How will you sustain the conversation? Later chapters go into different options for supporting group or team conversation between touch points, including private Facebook pages, JournalEngine and others.

Questions to Consider

On a scale of 0 to 10, what is your comfort level around the different systems listed in the text box Systems to Support Your Team and Group Coaching Work?

What is one thing you can do in the next week/month to boost or shore up your logistics support?

Systems to Support Your Team and Group Coaching Work

- Registration and payment (online, offline)
- Ongoing communication: blog, newsletter (e.g., Constant Contact, AWeber)
- Teleconferencing/webinar systems, including recording facilities
- A way to support group/team member conversation/touch point between sessions
- Program material: Word, Publisher, graphic designer, printer
- Promotional material: speaker page, program descriptions
- Proposal templates for Requests for Proposals (RFPs)
- Past client lists and/or testimonials from past clients
- Information kit: program overview, frequently asked questions

Tricky Issue #4: Marketing

Marketing is often the Achilles heel for coaches. We can be the best coach, but if we don't have a group or team to coach, our skills atrophy. The topic of marketing is of such importance that a digital chapter is dedicated to it. Something as simple as the date and time of day can influence client availability. Start listening to what your individual coaching clients are asking for; keep noticing the times that are most convenient for them to get together. We need to give ourselves enough time for marketing and ensure that we don't put all our eggs in one basket. Coaches interviewed indicated that the marketing context continues to shift for our work.

Tricky Issue #5: Tricky Issues in the Virtual Domain

For those who are going to be undertaking programming in the virtual domain, a number of common tricky issues can emerge, which are outlined in Table 2.3.

Table 2.3: Tricky Issues in the Virtual Domain

Tricky Issue	What to Do
No one talks	Be directive in asking participants for input. Have clients check in at the start of a call and sit themselves down at the virtual table.
Everyone talks at once	Establish a process or "order," particularly for larger calls. Call on group members specifically.
Bridge line does not work	Have a backup bridge line. Provide callers with explicit instructions at the start of the program for the process of moving to an alternative bridge line. For example, I might provide the following instructions to callers by email: "In the event of a massive bridge line quality problem, I will send out an email if we are going to switch. So, please check email if you are having problems getting on and/or no one is there."
One person dominates the call	Set boundaries/be directive in asking for input from everyone. Ask, "What are some other perspectives?" Remind callers about bottom lining and hogging airtime.
One speaker goes on and on	Talk about the skill of bottom lining during your first call. Have the group create a structure/code for bottom line.

Silence seems to drag	Silence is good, in moderation. Create a "silence is golden" rule so that people know that after 10 or so seconds when you say this, that you will be moving on, unless someone adds something else.
Calls seem too rushed	Go back to design: either take content or exercises out, or look to elongate the call.
Participants don't feel they are going deep enough around issues	Consider a hybrid format call—a mix of group and individual calls. Consider the mix of your group: is there enough common ground? Leave space for individuals to consider what is similar and different between themselves and others.

THREE TIPS FOR MITIGATING TRICKY ISSUES

In closing, here are three things coaches can do to mitigate the tricky issues that may arise:

1. **Preparation and Presence:** As coaches we always want to ensure that we are coaching in the moment and being fully present with what we are hearing and observing with our client group. At the same time, pre-program/session preparation can be invaluable in getting to know your clients, their needs, agendas and preferences. Preparation may include holding pre-program one-on-one calls with each participant or having a menu of exercises you can select from related to that weekly theme.

2. **Systematize:** Having systems allows you to replicate your work more quickly and enable you to have the bandwidth to address tricky issues as they arise. Systems such as registration forms, payments and bridge lines can make the work easier. Refer to the text box on systems (above) for a list of ones you may wish to create for your business.

3. **Practice:** Great group and team coaching is an art. Even the most seasoned coaches and facilitators will get rusty when they are not in front of a group. Practice, practice, practice, is an important part of mastery as a team or group coach. As you grow in your work, ask yourself, "What are the edges to my learning?" "What activities will help me stretch and grow?" "What opportunities do I have, or can I create, to get in front of groups?"

One of the key messages of this chapter was for coaches to consider the key approaches their clients will benefit from. In practice, masterful group and team coaches will always lead from a coaching approach and our foundational coaching competencies. Our work will benefit from the inclusion of training and facilitation approaches, as appropriate. We also looked at some of the benefits to team and group coaching. Finally, the chapter explored some of the tricky issues that can emerge in any process of coaching many.

Our next chapter takes a deep dive into the skills of masterful team and group coaches. We explore all 11 of the core coaching competencies of the International Coach Federation, in light of team and group coaching work. The chapter will provide further insights into the subtle but important distinctions with team and group coaching.

End-of-Chapter Questions

Where do you stand on the group program continuum?
Where do your clients want you positioned?
What do you see as the benefits of this work for your clients—team or group?
What do you see as the biggest tricky issue you might face?
What other tricky issues might pop up in your program?
What are you going to put in place to mitigate tricky issues?

CHAPTER 3

CORE SKILLS FOR TEAM AND GROUP COACHING

For the things we have to learn before we can do them, we learn by doing them.
—Aristotle

As a discipline, coaching is grounded in a series of core coaching competencies. These skills distinguish our work as coaches. Inherent to the discussion of coaching many is an exploration of the core skills and approaches needed for team coaching. This chapter helps to further delineate coaching from other related fields such as training, facilitation and consulting.

The core coaching competencies make group and team coaching what it is. This chapter explores what the core coaching competencies are, and how they play out in the team and group coaching conversation. Whether you are an internal or external coach, a leader or a peer coach, these skills will be important to build upon throughout the coaching process.

THE ICF CORE COMPETENCIES

This chapter explores the 11 core caching competencies from the International Coach Federation (ICF) in depth. Related competency frameworks exist for coaches, namely those of the IAC (International Association of Coaches) and the Board Certified Coach (BCC) competency framework. It is interesting to note that most coaching models (at least those recognized by the ICF) will be grounded in these 11 competencies.

The following table summarizes the 11 core coaching competencies, their definitions according to the ICF, and core approaches and techniques utilized in team and group coaching.

Table 3.1: ICF Core Coaching Competencies and Team and Group Coaching

Competency	Definition from the ICF (www.coachfederation.org)	Core Approaches/Techniques Used in Team and Group Coaching
A. Setting the Foundation		
Meeting Ethical Guidelines and Professional Standards	Understanding of coaching ethics and standards and ability to apply them appropriately in all coaching situations	Ongoing focus on ethics
Establishing the Coaching Agreement	Ability to understand what is required in the specific coaching interaction and to come to agreement with the prospective and new client about the coaching process and relationship	Pre-program one-on-ones or team meeting Team assessment Questionnaires Design in the first session: key focus areas, themes, priorities
B. Co-creating the Relationship		
Establishing Trust and Intimacy with the Client	Ability to create a safe, supportive environment that produces ongoing mutual respect and trust	Ground rules/ways of working Team agreements Pre-program one-on-ones
Coaching Presence	Ability to be fully conscious and create spontaneous relationship with the client, employing a style that is open, flexible and confident	The being of the coach Intuition Risk taking Humor
C. Communicating Effectively		
Active Listening	Ability to focus completely on what the client is saying and is not saying, to understand the meaning of what is said in the context of the client's desires, and to support client self-expression	Levels of listening Emotional field Bottom lining/head lining/laser speak Listening for what is said and not said ("elephant in the room") Noticing body language

Powerful Questioning	Ability to ask questions that reveal the information needed for maximum benefit to the coaching relationship and the client	Powerful questions "What? So what? Now what?" Learning style differences
Direct Communication	Ability to communicate effectively during coaching sessions, and to use language that has the greatest positive impact on the client	Adaptation of language, words, to meet the diverse needs of the group Listening for what is said, and not Metaphor
D. Facilitating Learning and Results		
Creating Awareness	Ability to integrate and accurately evaluate multiple sources of information, and to make interpretations that help the client to gain awareness and thereby achieve agreed-upon results	Perspectives Inquiry Metaview/30,000-foot perspective and the microview or view at the ground ("in the weeds") Listening/body language Synthesis/mirroring back Normalizing Diversity of collective wisdom
Designing Actions	Ability to create with the client opportunities for ongoing learning, during coaching and in work/life situations, and for taking new actions that will most effectively lead to agreed-upon coaching results	Request Challenge Field work: pre- and post-work Do it now
Planning and Goal Setting	Ability to develop and maintain an effective coaching plan with the client	SMART-E goals Iterative nature Bookends: check-ins and end-of-session check-outs
Managing Progress and Accountability	Ability to hold attention on what is important for the client, and to leave responsibility with the client to take action	Bookends: check-ins and check-outs Mutual accountability

The ICF has laid out 11 core coaching competencies that underpin the work of the coach. We will look at all 11 competency areas from the perspectives of both team and group coaching. As we will see, these competencies are interrelated, with touch points throughout. Coaches are encouraged to review the Minimum Skill Requirement Documents for the level at which they are coaching. The Minimum Skill Requirement Documents were created by the ICF, including the subcomponents of skills. The documents also spell out what coaching behaviors are expected at each of the three levels: Associate Certified Coach (ACC); Professional Certified Coach (PCC); and Master Certified Coach (MCC).

Competency #1: Meeting Ethical Guidelines and Professional Standards

The first competency focuses on the ethics and professional conduct of the coach. All professional coaches who are members of the International Coach Federation adhere to the ICF Code of Ethics. The ICF Standards of Conduct cover our professional conduct at large, conflicts of interest, professional conduct with clients and confidentiality/privacy. All coaches are encouraged to make themselves familiar with the Code of Ethics and Standards of Conduct at the ICF website.[1]

As we explore throughout the book, there are some ethical gray areas that emerge in the team and group coaching processes. One key issue in the team coaching context is the conflict of interest a team coach may face if he or she is coaching both the leader and the team. The gray areas around confidentiality can be averted by keeping the relationships clean, and engaging a separate coach to work with the team.

Competency #2: Designing the Coaching Agreement

The International Coach Federation defines the second competency as the "ability to understand what is required in the specific coaching interaction and to come to agreement with the prospective and new client about the coaching process and relationship."

Establishing the coaching agreement with team and group members is an essential part of the coaching process, and sets the foundation for success. The clearer the coach and group or team client are on the agreement, the more easily tricky issues can be mitigated down the road. As we will see throughout the book, tricky issues

---

[1] The current ICF Code of Ethics can be accessed at http://www.coachfederation.org/includes/media/docs/Ethics-2009.pdf. Accessed April 9, 2013.

often emerge when expectations are not clearly co-created at the start. In the group and team coaching processes, with multiple players involved, shared and co-created agreements around what the coaching process will entail is critical for success.

Key components of this competency include having a discussion with teams and groups you are working with about what coaching is (and is not), what people can expect from the coaching process and what the coaching process is going to look like (scheduling, number of sessions, participation, etc.).

Many teams and groups may be used to team-building initiatives and training, and may be surprised at how team coaching is different. The sustained nature of the coaching process is a key distinction with other modalities such as training, as is the confidentiality of the process. Group and team coaching conversations delve into deep topics, where it is common for individuals to expose their vulnerabilities, real feelings and sentiments. Confidentiality warrants discussion, shared understanding and commitments around what it means to the group or team. Some teams opt to define it as "what is said in Vegas stays in Vegas."

Designing the coaching agreement often starts pre-program and extends into your first touch point with the group or team. In general, it is about clarifying expectations and identifying those key areas group and team members want coaching around.

Key components of establishing the coaching agreement include:

- Pre-program meetings, questionnaires or assessments
- Pre-program communication and administration
- The first session itself

Pre-program Meetings, Questionnaires or Assessments

It can be very useful to host pre-program meetings with each member to circulate questionnaires to participants. This provides an opportunity for individuals to think about their involvement prior to the program (priming), as well as an opportunity to start building the relationship.

In terms of other pre-program communication, even before the official "first session" it will be important for coaches to put in place the following:

1. A welcome email to team members, welcoming them and discussing what they can expect in terms of length of engagement, touch points and pre-work (i.e., assessments). You may also want to highlight some of the differences between coaching and other modalities such as consulting, and counseling.
2. For group coaching, a written coaching agreement.

Approaches that can be used to establish the team or group agreement in the first session include:

Development of "ways of working" or ground rules: Agreements around what is acceptable for the team and group in terms of behavior and what will make the learning process a positive one. Chapter 8 includes sample group ground rules/agreements and suggestions for working with groups for in-person and virtual sessions. Chapter 6 discusses team agreements.

Identification of key focus areas for the coaching process: A facilitation technique such as using dots (outlined in Chapter 5) can be an engaging way to get everyone involved in identification of the key coaching topics. Chapters 5 and 6 provide process outlines for team and group coaching.

Competency # 3: Creating Trust and Intimacy

This competency is defined by the ICF as the "ability to create a safe, supportive environment that produces ongoing mutual respect and trust."

Trust is essential for an effective team and group coaching process to take place. Without the foundation of trust it is very difficult to enter into the depth of the coaching conversation. Pre-program contact is an important way to start establishing the terrain between coach and team/group members. We must also be cognizant of creating trust and intimacy between members as well.

The terrain in team coaching can be fraught with high risk for team members who are asked to be transparent and engaged, and divulge their true feelings. Where job security issues may be at play, and a person's career or livelihood is on the line, it can be extremely risky for the team member to verbalize problems and challenges facing the team, point to dysfunctions and advocate for change in doing things a different way.

As Douglas Riddle from the Center for Creative Leadership writes, "Full team member engagement won't occur unless each member of the team can trust that the conversation will not result in harm to their objectives or to their future prospects."[2]

A focus early on in connecting with team and group coaching members is a critical success factor. It also can support the recommendation of bringing in a co-facilitator when working with teams and/or larger groups. Co-facilitation is addressed in Chapter 11.

Practical activities that group and team coaches can use to establish trust and intimacy are:

---

[2] Douglas Riddle, *Senior Leadership Team Coaching* (White Paper), Center for Creative Leadership, 1998, 5, http://www.ccl.org/leadership/pdf/research/SeniorLeadTeamCoaching.pdf.

1. Hold pre-program one-on-one calls with individual participants prior to the program start. A short 15-minute call can help you to start developing a bond with each participant/client and get to know them. Find out what brought them to the program, what they want to learn, what's unique about their own learning style preferences. This call can also provide an opportunity to answer any questions, and also check out whether the program is going to be a good fit for them. This pre-program contact can be an important step in building rapport with each group member.

2. Leave time at the start of programs, particularly phone-based programs, for participants to introduce themselves and get to know each other. Knowing "who is who" is an important part of the group coaching process.

3. Discuss group expectations/develop ways of working. What are the ground rules for group participation? Behavior? What can people expect? Spend time discussing this as a group, including key ground rules such as confidentiality.

4. If pre-program one-on-ones are not possible before your first meeting, leave time and space to discuss expectations, hear from each participant about what they want out of the process and what has brought them there.

5. Walk your talk: Follow through as you have promised. Circle back to check in on commitments. Check in with the group regularly throughout a session to see what's working and what changes may be needed. Chapter 8 explores the topic of engagement.

The topic of trust in teams is an important topic for team coaches. An entire book could be dedicated to this topic. There is no one specific approach that is the "magic bullet" to building trust in teams. This, in fact, can become one of the foundational themes of our work.

As a starting point, as coaches we will want to ask teams about what their level of trust is. Certain team assessments, such as the Team Diagnostic from Team Coaching International, may also measure a team's level of trust. Discussion about trust is a tricky issue for teams today, particularly if trust has been broken.

A foundational coaching philosophy is that our clients are "creative, resourceful and whole." This too extends to teams. As the ICF writes, coaches "seek to elicit solutions and strategies from the client; they believe the client is naturally creative and resourceful. The coach's job is to provide support to enhance the skills, resources, and creativity that the client already has."[3]

As a coach I believe that teams have the answer and capability to rebuild trust. One, or more, of your coaching conversations may be spent exploring this rich area.

---

[3] International Coach Federation, "Coaching FAQs", accessed April 3, 2013, http://www.coachfederation .org/clients/coaching-faqs.

Competency #4: Coaching Presence

The ICF describes coaching presence as the "ability to be fully conscious and create spontaneous relationship with the client, employing a style that is open, flexible and confident."

Coaching presence is all about how a coach "shows up" in the coaching conversation. This is often referred to as the *being* of the coach. Group and team coaching is infused with the tension of not knowing what will show up for the group or team in response to the coaching conversations and issue exploration. This requires a level of comfort, confidence, and trust by the coach in his or her ability to react to and be with whatever emerges in each and every moment. Being able to take risks in service to the client is also a key.

Many coaching models and even the ICF competency framework use the term *dancing in the moment* to describe a coach's ability to be flexible in approach, tone and stance according to what shows up in the moment. Masterful coaches have a variety of tools and approaches to bring to their work with teams and groups. The ICF articulates this in that a coach "sees many ways to work with the client, and chooses in the moment what is most effective."

Masterful team and group coaches are very aware of what they bring to the coaching process, their biases, strengths and blind spots. The atmosphere we create within our groups is critical. Coaching presence is also expanded by having a variety of tools and approaches to draw on, in service to what needs and preferences show up.

Given the multiplicity of people we are coaching in both modalities, coaches need to rely on the relationships they have established with the individual clients, and the knowledge they have acquired about different persons' learning styles, preferences and approaches. This points to the subcomponent of "seeing many ways to work with the client, and choosing in the moment what is most effective."

The Triad of Communication Competencies

Communication is the oxygen for the coaching conversation. This umbrella, or triad, includes the related coaching competencies of:

- Active listening
- Powerful questioning
- Direct communication

Competency #5: Active Listening

The ICF defines this as "the ability to focus completely on what the client is saying and is not saying, to understand the meaning of what is said in the context of the client's desires, and to support client self-expression."

Great group and team coaches focus in on listening at many different levels. Key to successful team and group coaching is a hard focus on listening for the client's needs as well as "concerns, goals, values and beliefs" (ICF). Active listening is also an area where coaches can provide the teams and groups some training around the topics as well.

Beyond using skills such as "summarizing, paraphrasing, and mirroring back," coaches with mastery in this competency area will also be aware of:

1. Levels of Listening

Most coaching models make reference to listening at different levels in the coaching conversation. The Co-Active Coaching Model[4] explains that in any coaching conversation there are typically three levels of listening in which clients can engage:

- Level 1 listening: Internal listening
- Level 2 listening: Focused listening
- Level 3 listening: Global listening

Level 1 listening is all about listening to your internal dialogue. As a client this is where we want to be, but when we are listening to peers, it is important to shift to level 2 listening or what is also known as focused listening.

Level 2 listening means taking a hard focus and really listening deeply to the person talking. In focused listening we want to notice the tone, pace and pitch of the person speaking: What does this say? What is being said and not being said? Great team and group coaches will want to spend their time at level 2 and level 3. There is also benefit for us to "train" the teams and groups that we work with around level 2 listening, and checking in with them throughout the coaching process, to see how they are doing with level 2 listening. Throwing out a question such as "On a scale of 0 to 10, where are you with level 2 listening?" can help focus or reorient group members in listening.

---

[4] Laura Whitworth, Karen Kimsey-House, Henry Kimsey-House and Phil Sandahl, *Co-Active Coaching: Changing Business, Transforming Lives* (Lanham, MD: Davies Black Publishing, 1998).

Level 3 listening is all about listening to what surrounds you or the environment you are coaching within. Perhaps it is a bell ringing just when you get to someone who really looks like they do not want to share, or it may be a bridge line that drops. It means tuning in, and pointing the group or team to notice the environmental cues, which can also provide some important information and meaning.

For example, you may be in the midst of a call and the bridge line disconnects. As coach Shana Montesol shared with me in an interview, a key bonding process for a group she worked with happened when she herself was dropped off the bridge line. It created an opportunity for the group to connect without her on the line. When she was able to get back onto the call several minutes later she was pleased to see that the group had continued the conversation without her.

The third level of listening is an important level for team and group coaches to incorporate into their work, and share as a concept with the team.

2. Emotional Field/Temperature Check

Coaches working in the team and group coaching domains should become skilled in reading the emotional field, and working with the group or team to take the pulse or temperature of the environment. Many teams find it a fun and less risky way to identify what's going on in the room. Asking each team member to identify the weather pattern—sunny, stormy, cold, hot—can all provide information and perspectives on where each team or group member is.

Coaches play a key role in creating non-judgmental spaces for teams and groups. There may be the need at times for team or group members to "vent" or clear things before they can fully step into the coaching conversation.

3. Listening for What Is Said and What Is Not Said (The Elephant in the Room)

As Peter Drucker once wrote, "The most important thing in communication is to hear what isn't being said."[5]

Many coaches interviewed indicated that a core skill for team and group coaches is in listening for what is said, and also in listening for what is not said. We often call this the elephant in the room. This elephant can be stepped over for months, even with the coach prodding the team to uncover what is at the core.

---

[5] http://www.goodreads.com/quotes/254861.

Sometimes the elephant is apparent and can be surfaced early on, and other times it may be deeply buried.

One team engagement I was involved with did not uncover the elephant until the fourth month of a six-month coaching process. While the team was making process in working through difficult conversations, it was apparent that there was still something below the surface. Getting to the elephant requires a deep level of trust in each other and the coaching process. As coaches we need to make sure we are leaving space for the elephant to surface, and also be curious in asking the team what's happening.

4. Bottom Lining

Central to the team and group coaching processes is getting to the core of the message. We often talk about the importance of teaching the skill of bottom lining to ensure all voices are heard. Bottom lining is also known as "head lining" and "laser speak" in other coaching models. Sharing this concept of getting to the core of a message is a key skill in today's environment. Coaches may want to create a gesture with the group or team they are working with, so that they can take this forward into their own contexts. In *Effective Group Coaching* I wrote about how the skill of bottom lining was essential with a group of women business owners I worked with years ago. It is a skill I find many teams embrace and start bringing into their meeting processes.

Capacity Development Skills

Skills to pass onto teams you are working with:

- Levels of listening
- Emotional field/temperature check
- Elephant in the room: what's not being said
- Bottom lining

Competency #6: Powerful Questions

The ICF defines this competency as the "ability to ask questions that reveal the information needed for maximum benefit to the coaching relationship and the client."

Powerful questions are open-ended questions that are geared to deepen or expand awareness and promote action around the focus area(s) of the coaching conversation. In different coaching models, powerful questions may also be known as evocative questions, etc. Powerful questions are usually short (five to six words in length) and to the point. In a team or group coaching context it is important to keep the following in mind with questions:

Questions That Meet the Diverse Members of the Group

In a team or group coaching context, coaches should be aware of the fact that there may be diverse learning styles in the room. Some group members may have a more visual preference and may respond better to a question such as "What does it look like?" An auditory learner may respond better to "What does it sound like?" and a kinesthetic learner may respond better to "What does it feel like?" Unlike in an individual coaching question where coaches are encouraged to ask only one question at a time, given the diverse styles in the room it may be appropriate to ask a question in different ways to have resonance for the different group members. Coaches should still avoid "stacking" questions, that is, asking a couple of different questions at the same time. The approach above is more about rephrasing the questions in different ways.

Develop a Selection of Questions

Coaches can benefit by taking stock of the types of questions they regularly ask. As so many new coaches are hungry for powerful questions, the appendix includes a variety of questions for team and group coaching. You may also wish to check out the questions contained in these books:

- Laura Whitworth, Karen Kimsey-House, Henry Kimsey-House and Phil Sandahl, *Co-Active Coaching: Changing Business, Transforming Lives* (Lanham, MD: Davies Black Publishing, 1998).
- Sara L. Orem, Jacqueline Binkert and Ann L. Clancy, *Appreciative Coaching: A Positive Process for Change,* (Hoboken, NJ: Jossey-Bass, 2007).

Watch What Your Questions Start With

As new coaches we are often encouraged to stick to "what" questions. Questions that start with a "why" may put people on the defensive. Likewise, "how" questions may lead people to drop into process or problem-solving orientations.

Teaching Powerful Questions

Teaching the art of asking powerful questions is an important skill for leaders, managers and peer coaches today. This is a skill area you may wish to explain and model for the groups and teams you work with.

"What? So What? Now What?" Questions

My roots with groups extend back several decades to the late 1980s, to my first work in the experiential education field, working around youth development issues. Thinking back to these formative experiences for me as a university student spending summers working in Algonquin Park, I recognize how influenced my work has been as a trainer, coach and consultant by experiential models.

A set of questions that continue to stand out for me from these early learning days are the powerful questions of "What? So what? Now what?" For those of you who are reading as a coach, you will notice how these three questions are so grounded in many of the coaching models we use.

What?

These questions are designed to stimulate thinking about what significant experiences clients/group members have gone through. Common questions you may incorporate include:

- What was your most significant achievement this week?
- What has been your biggest hurdle?
- What key milestones have been achieved?
- What was significant for you/the team this week?
- What have been key activities/experiences?

So What?

"So what" questions encourage clients to look at what the meaning and importance is of an issue/experience they have faced. Building on to any of the learning points/experiences which a client(s) has shared, so what

(Continued)

questions help to "deepen the learning" (a core coaching competency). So what questions may include:

- So what was important about that?
- So what did you learn?
- So what is significant about this?
- So what do you know about how this is a pattern?

Now What?

"Now what" questions help group members and clients look forward/ahead. Based on their experience and new insights, now what changes do they want to make, what actions do they want to take going forward?

"Now what" questions may include:

- Now what are you going to do (differently)?
- Now what changes are you going to make?
- Now what are you going to keep an eye on?

How do you incorporate these types of questions into your work? How may these be useful?[6]

Competency #7: Direct Communication

The third part of our communication triad is direct communication, which the ICF defines as the "ability to communicate effectively during coaching sessions, and to use language that has the greatest positive impact on the client."

Providing Feedback and Clarity regarding Process

One part of this competency is about sharing and providing feedback to our clients. Just as in an individual coaching conversation, it may be very appropriate to point out things that we notice about the team or group, as it relates to

---

[6] Jennifer Britton, "Powerful Group Coaching Questions: What? So What? Now What?", adapted from Group Coaching Ins and Outs blog, May 26, 2011, http://groupcoaching.blogspot.ca/2011_05_01_archive.html.

their goals. Team and group coaches also need to continually keep an eye on the process, and share with the client what they are doing, and where they are going.

Adapting for the Style of the Groups You Work With

Coaches in the team and group coaching environment will want to adapt their language to meet the needs of different audiences. I continue to work across industries in my work—from health care, to chemical, to pharmaceutical and the international sector. The language I use needs to adapt to meet diverse needs. Part of this competency is about avoiding our "coach-ese." *Language is extremely important in the team and group coaching context and coaches should observe and listen for the different preferences present.*

Focus on Metaphor

Another component of this competency is around metaphor. Metaphor can be a rich area for exploration with teams and groups, and may become an anchoring theme for them. Two of the activities that tap into metaphor are Personal Logos (see the Field Journal that follows) and the use of visual cards (refer to Chapter 10, Renee Brotman's Voices from the Field).

Field Journal: Personal Logos

As I shared in *Effective Group Coaching*, one of my favorite kick-off activities is "personal logos." It is a great activity for groups that are new, teams that know each other, and can be used at the start, mid-point or end of a program. Very simply you ask each individual to draw a logo that represents what they uniquely bring to the team or group. I give about one minute for each group member to draw this—giving them enough time to complete a rough draft, but not too much time to overthink it. The time pressure prompts people into action.

Have each individual share their logo with the larger group. You may point to the different themes that are emerging, or ask the group what they notice about synergies. The logos presented can lead to some interesting work around metaphors and can also be a point to return back to and evolve from.

(Continued)

For example, I included this activity in the first of several sessions with a leadership team. The statement given to the group at the start was, "Draw a logo that represents what you uniquely bring to the team." The leaders pointed out how this activity allowed them to quickly capture what made them each unique. This will feed into our next conversation around strengths.

This activity can also be done over the phone or web with each individual verbally sharing his or her logo and/or taking a photo and sharing it. The question can be adapted for different groups. For example, if you are working with a group of new managers, the request may be, "Draw a logo that represents who you *are*, or what you take a stand for, as a manager."

Competency # 8: Creating Awareness

This competency is described by the ICF as the "ability to integrate and accurately evaluate multiple sources of information, and to make interpretations that help the client to gain awareness and thereby achieve agreed-upon results."

Creating awareness is one of two levels in which the coaching conversation takes place. It may be useful to think about the two levels of creating awareness and supporting action. In creating awareness coaches are working with groups and teams to expand their understanding around the issues and goals of importance. Key to this work is exploration of:

Perspectives

What are the perspectives the team or group are rooted in individually or collectively? How is this perspective supporting the client, or not? What alternative perspectives are possible? Undertaking work around perspectives is a rich area in a team coaching context at the individual and team levels.

Strengths versus Learning Areas

The coaching process also helps teams and groups identify their strengths as well as their learning areas or "edges." Just as we look at the balance of leveraging strengths and working on growth areas with individual clients, team and group coaches will need to be attuned to the balance for each individual, and the collective level.

Ongoing Patterns within the Team

This competency also encourages us to look at what are ongoing patterns of behavior and thinking, versus one-off events. This can be a rich area for coaches to foster communication around, and also mirror back to the group what they are noticing. What are the recurring behaviors of the team/group/individual? This competency encourages coaches to identify the patterns that are "trivial versus significant." Identifying patterns in the coaching process can be a real eye opener for teams and groups at multiple levels.

> *"Assumptions are the termites of any relationship."*
>   —Henry Winkler[7]

Assumptions the Team/Group Is Holding

Assumptions and assumption busting are critical in any team coaching process. Sometimes individuals within the team, or the entire team, are carrying assumptions that are below the waterline. For example, a team may believe that they are the "underdogs" of an organization, when in fact they are highly regarded. Throughout the coaching conversations it may become apparent how this assumption is holding them back from their full potential.

The Use of Inquiry

An inquiry is a large question that provokes deeper thought and conversation. In a group coaching process, it may be common to have an individual inquiry out of each session. For example, in working with new managers, an inquiry might be, "As a new leader, what is the stand I want to take?" It is likely that this question has multiple layers, and cannot be answered in the moment. Teams may hold an inquiry at the collective level. For example, in working with a health care team, an inquiry might be, "What would exceptional focus on service provide for our clients?" Note that the inquiry is designed to expand awareness around the issue.

---

[7] http://www.goodreads.com/quotes/41593.

Diversity of Collective Wisdom

One of the key benefits of the team and group coaching processes is the collective wisdom that shows up and the diversity that is present in a grouping. Hearing from and being in conversation with peers opens up new perspectives, and normalizes things so people do not think, "It's just me." As coaches, we play a powerful role in mirroring and pointing to themes, similarities and differences that have emerged with the groups and/or teams we work with.

Metaview versus "In the Weeds"

A rich area for exploration in team and group coaching is to support the participants to look at the issues and goals from multiple levels. One level is the 30,000-foot, big picture view, or metaview,[8] which is different from what can be seen at the ground level. Supporting your groups and teams to explore issues at both zoom levels can be very significant. Looking to the metaview/30,000-foot view allows us to get to the strategic issues, versus the microview or "weeds" perspective, which takes us down to ground level and may be more tactical. This too can be an area for skill development with teams and groups.

Key Components of Creating Awareness

- Perspectives
- Strengths versus areas for learning
- Assumptions
- Inquiry
- Patterns: trivial and significant, patterns versus one-off
- Diversity of collective wisdom
- 30,000-foot metaview versus the microview ("weeds") perspective

---

Competency # 9: Designing Actions

Action is the other realm of the coaching conversation. We can work with our groups and teams to develop awareness about significant issues; however, coaching is not complete without taking action.

---

[8] Many coaching models use the term *metaview* to include the big-picture view, including the Co-Active Coaching Model (Whitworth, Kimsey-House, Kimsey-House and Sandahl).

The ICF defines designing actions as the "ability to create with the client opportunities for ongoing learning, during coaching and in work/life situations, and for taking new actions that will most effectively lead to agreed-upon coaching results."

Application Opportunities

Fundamental to the coaching process is the action that comes from the conversation. As we saw earlier, coaching is a conversation with intent. What action is the group or team inspired to take? Application of the new learning is key in the group and team coaching process. Coaches may make a coaching request or issue a coaching challenge. A coaching request is designed to support clients into action. In a group, each member may receive a different coaching request.

For example, in working with new business owners, Sandy may have identified her ability to procrastinate around sending follow-up emails to warm leads. A coaching request would invite Sandy to put a focus on sending five emails that week. As a coaching request, the person (or entity) is always given a choice. They can say yes to it (*"Yes, I'll send out five emails"*), no (*"No, that's too much, I'll email two"*), or provide a counteroffer (*"No, but I will phone them personally instead of emailing them"*).

In a team coaching context, coaching requests are significant in moving the team into action, and taking responsibility for the action. A request may be for the team to revisit the team agreements in an upcoming meeting, or to bring the skills of bottom lining or temperature checks into their next meeting. Again, the team is at choice to say yes, no or make a counteroffer.

A coaching challenge is designed to take a person's breath away, stretching their comfort zone. Again, at the group level, the context is more individual. At the team level, it may be more geared to developing new habits that members have shied away from.

Brainstorming and Other Approaches

A foundational coaching philosophy is that our clients are naturally creative, resourceful and whole—or, in non-coachese, that our clients have the ability to discover and devise their own action plan. Through the design and use of facilitation processes, group and team coaches can support their clients in identifying new options. It is this ongoing *active experimentation and self-discovery through the sustained conversations that leads to learning*. Teams may find it difficult to meet on a regular basis but it is critical to do so to sustain the process of change.

Do It Now!

Many group members in a group coaching process join the group to create an accountability structure. As you can see in the online chapter Group Coaching in Action at www.groupcoachingessentials.com, in different approaches for working with groups, some modalities of group coaching such as virtual retreats are more suited for this "Do it now!" approach. It is common for all of us to have something we have put off, and put off. When we are given an opportunity to focus and take action, surrounded by peers (whether live or virtual) those short bursts of action can create significant breakthroughs.

Stretch and Super-Stretch

At the same time, one person's comfort zone is going to be different from another's. What is a stretch for one may be a super-stretch for others. A coach needs to be comfortable with the peaks and valleys of the work as well as the strong emotions that may show up as comfort zones are expanded.

Opportunities for Celebration

Groups and teams need opportunities to pause along the way and notice learning that is being applied, and new habits that are becoming second nature. When working with a team for extended periods of time, it is important to provide these pause points regularly (e.g., every few months).

Field Work Is Also a Key Part of the Process of Sustaining the Learning

Coaching is not always about content, yet group and team members may be eager to read or explore more on a topic. Field work can provide options for different team and group members to explore. Recall the discussion of field work in Chapter 1.

Key Components of Designing Actions

- Application
- Brainstorming and other approaches
- Do it now!
- Stretch and super-stretch
- Opportunities for celebration
- Field work

Competency #10: Planning and Goal Setting

Planning and goal setting is defined by the ICF as the "ability to develop and maintain an effective coaching plan with the client."

Working with clients to specify goals is key to the coaching process. The 2009 Global Coaching Client Survey found that goal setting is one of the key distinguishing features of the coaching process. The goals set out early in the coaching plan should become a breathing, living plan that should be referred back to throughout the coaching engagement. Part of goal setting is also identifying success measures for the work together.

In terms of goal setting and planning with a group, it is likely that each group member will have their own individual set of goals that they are working on throughout the coaching process. In a team, the development of a team action plan, with associated individual action plans, will likely be a more useful approach. Techniques for working with a team in planning and goal setting may be:

Identifying Additional Resources for Learning

Sub-component four of this competency points coaches to "help the client identify and access different resources for learning" (e.g., books, other professionals). This is a reminder for coaches to consider how additional resources can supplement the coaching process, without requiring that those resources be brought into the coaching conversations directly. Team and group coaching processes provide an opportunity for field work, whether as reading lists proposed for a team or group to select from, or the collaborative generation and sharing of resources from peer

Nice to Know, Need to Know, Where to Go

A trick that I picked up from master trainer Bob Pike more than a decade ago was the instructional design tip around "Nice to Know, Need to Know, Where to Go." The tension between coaching and client's need for content is one of the challenges in working with teams and groups. As you think about all of the items/materials/focus areas for your upcoming work with a team or group, it may be useful to apply the mantra of Nice to Know, Need to Know, Where to Go.

Nice to Know: What are the things that would be nice, but are not essential, to cover or explore in the time you have together?

Need to Know: What are the pieces/information areas people need to know or definitely want to explore?

Where to Go: Where can people go to find out more information? This can be a coach's best friend. Given that we are not content driven, like trainers (refer to the continuum in Chapter 2), coaches can support the learning and content needs of groups and teams through weblinks, reading lists and also tip sheets. One of the best practices identified is to use the coaching time to focus on conversation.

to peer. Additional resources may span the gamut from books, to podcasts, audio books, web sites.

SMART-E Goals

The ICF competencies point to the need for creating SMART goals with our clients, that is, goals that are Specific, Measurable, Achievable, Realistic and Timebound (or Timely). In my work with teams and groups I usually introduce them to the concept of SMART-E goals, adding the important category of motivation, or E for Excitement. This addresses the realm of internal motivation. If goals are not exciting to us our motivation to undertake them may decrease.

Planning for Short, Medium and Long Term

In supporting our clients in planning it is important that we develop short-, medium- and long-term plans, the definition of which is determined by the client. For some teams *long-term* means the next year; for others it is the next strategic cycle (e.g., three to five years).

Focusing on a Limited Number of Goals

Marshall Goldsmith, a well-known executive coach and author of *What Got You Here Won't Get You There*; often talks about the importance of setting a limited number of goals to ensure a focus.[9] In team coaching situations, part of the action planning process should include a prioritization of these key goals.

Iterative Nature of Goals

In working with goals, it is important to provide opportunities for group and team members to adapt the goals as they go. The check-in around goals may become part of your standardized check-in and check-out process.

Key Components of Planning and Goal Setting

- Identify additional resources for learning
- SMART-E goals
- Short term, medium term, long term
- Limited number of goals
- Iterative nature of goals

Competency #11: Managing Progress and Accountability

The hard focus in coaching on accountability is a key differentiator of the coaching process from other related modalities. Team and group coaches can play a key role in working with teams and groups to develop this skill, expressed this way by the ICF: the "ability to hold attention on what is important for the client, and to leave responsibility with the client to take action."

Accountability is key to the coaching process for teams and groups. As Darcy Hitchcock and Marsha Willard write, "research indicates that holding people accountable for their results has very positive effects: greater accuracy of work, better response to role obligations, more vigilant problem solving, better decision making, more cooperation with co-workers, and higher team satisfaction. (For additional information on this kind of motivation, see 'Why Self-Direction Works: A Review

---

[9] Marshall Goldsmith, *What Got You Here Won't Get You There: How Successful People Become Even More Successful* (New York: Hyperion, 2007).

of Herzberg's Concepts')."[10] Accountability should link back to the coaching plan, which will be revisited throughout the coaching process. Team and group coaches may choose to redeploy assessments at key stages, for example, mid-point.

Bookends

Throughout the book you will see me writing about the concept of "bookends." In fact, each coaching conversation I hold with groups typically starts and ends with a focus on accountabilities and commitments. What's been done? What successes and learning have people had? At the end of the conversation the fundamental question becomes, "What are you committed to (doing, thinking, reflecting on)?"

When Things Don't Get Done

There is often a rich area for exploration when things don't get done. Just as in an individual coaching conversation you may pose the following questions: "What was the value of not doing it? What did you learn from this? How might you want to change future commitments and accountabilities?"

In a group coaching process the stakes may be raised by their peers for people to follow through on the public commitments they have made the week before.

Mutual Accountability

The focus of accountability in a team and group coaching process is slightly different than in the one-on-one coaching environment. Accountability looks different in a team and group coaching process. In working with teams it becomes *team accountability*. Who does what, and how do they hold themselves accountable? It will be important to consider the culture of the organization around accountability.

In a team coaching process, writes Peter Hawkins, the team members and leaders are "mutually accountable." He goes to say that coaches need to "ensure that the responsibility with the team is not left just with the nominal team leader,

---

[10] Darcy Hitchcock and Marsha Willard, "Accountability a Sticky Subject for Teams," Teambuildinginc .com, accessed August 23, 2012, http://www.teambuildinginc.com/article_team_accountability.htm. Peter B. Grazier, "Living with a Self-Directed Work Team & Why Self-Direction Works: A Review of Herzberg's Concepts," Teambuildinginc.com, accessed May 1, 2013, http://www.teambuildinginc .com/article_selfdirected.htm.

but is collectively held and all team members are actively held accountable for their colleagues."[11]

Connecting the Client's Actions into Their Other Structures

In a team coaching process it is very important to connect the clients' actions to their own processes such as team meetings. This is key for the sustainability of the work that you do together.

Sustainability

Every coaching process has a beginning and an end. What will happen after the coaching process is over? How will the team, or individual group members, sustain its learning, insights, action and accountability in its own context? As the external or internal coach it is very important to keep an eye on the issue of sustainability and ultimately working ourselves out of a job. Chapter 9 looks at the topic of capacity building, which addresses sustainability in the larger picture.

Key Components of Managing Progress and Accountability

- Bookends
- When things don't get done
- Mutual accountability
- Connecting the clients' actions with other structures
- Sustainability

Voices from the Field: Key Skills in Group and Team Coaching

One of the key areas I continue to get questions around is, "What are the most important skills a coach can bring?" I took this question to the coaches I interviewed. Here are their responses. You may wish to check off those skills you already bring, and highlight ones that you would like to further develop.

---

[11] Peter Hawkins, *Leadership Team Coaching: Developing Collective Transformational Leadership* (Philadelphia: Kogan Page, 2011), 25.

Table 3.2: Key Skills for Group and Team Coaching

Key Skills for Group Coaching	Key Skills for Team Coaching
Michael Cullen: • Powerful questioning • Setting and maintaining the "ground rules" of interaction • Ability to "dance in the moment" • Providing pertinent exercises and examples at the right time and at the right frequency	**Jacqueline Peters:** • Assessment • Coaching • Program development • Workshop design • Facilitation • Process leadership • Giving courageous feedback • Training skills for specific skill development components (e.g., peer coaching skills)
Catherine Carr: The group coach is creating a group field that usually doesn't exist until the members come together. In group work, there is more of a focus on building momentum and synergy from individuals authentically sharing and their week-to-week successes. Individuals have their processes and goals witnessed and supported by the group, get inspired and motivated by one another and are shaped toward success by the momentum of the group.	**Catherine Carr:** In team coaching versus group coaching I use more interviews and assessments, focus on team and organizational goals and might use a team 360 tool to get outside-in feedback about the team as a whole. In both team and group coaching, the coach needs to have systemic thinking and group facilitation skills. In group coaching you typically build the culture, or at least witness it as it develops. In team coaching you typically observe an existing culture and see how the members interact.
Kevin Stebbings: For group coaching, the focus is still on the individual learning and discovery. Therefore the important skill needs to be juggling the balance of group dynamics while still allowing time for individuals to gain insights for themselves.	**Kevin Stebbings:** The key element for me when coaching a team has been the need to zoom out from an individual focus and to view the team as a system. This has proved to be both an art and a science. In particular, viewing the team as a system has really helped shift my perspective so that I do not overly focus on individual voices but listen to the collective voice of the system. Asking the question, "What is the system saying?" has been very helpful in drawing out insights and helping a team create awareness.

Renee Brotman: • Active listening • Probing questions • Facilitation of group process • Educator as presenter of new models and sometimes mentor	**Sharon Miller:** Coaching, process/facilitation, workshop design, understanding systems, ORSC concepts such as Relationship Systems Intelligence self-management (confidence and fear about being in the front of the room), virtual coaching with a team (over the phone, etc.), listening for what's going in the system versus what one person may or may not be saying or focusing too much on getting through the design. Understanding toxic communication styles and how these exist in a team (John Gottman's work). Other Skills: • Intuition • Courage • Intellectual horsepower to understand systems and manage multiple lines of thinking (parallel processes) • Emotional intelligence—managing own triggers (need to get out of the way of the team) and understanding how others can be triggered
Shana Montesol: The skills I use as a group coach are a combination of coaching skills (e.g., many of the core competencies defined by the International Coach Federation, such as active listening, powerful questioning, creating awareness, etc.) and group facilitation skills (e.g., paraphrasing, moving the discussion along, creating a safe space for sharing, helping the group to move through the forming/norming/storming phases, etc.)	**Phil Sandahl:** Key skills for team coaching include: • Reveal the system to itself. • Notice/name the energetic field. • Highlight diversity and the value to the team. • Listen for the undercurrent of change. • Reinforce co-responsibility. • Increase positivity/decrease negativity.
Kim Ades: I bring the group together in a variety of platforms throughout the coaching term including phone calls, daily group journaling and sub-group exercises. The more contact, the more engaged they are and the more impact they receive through coaching.	

(Continued)

Table 3.2 (*Continued*)

Group Coaching	Team Coaching
Ray Rigoglioso: The most important skill is to be able to facilitate a group discussion using a coaching approach. It is not something I have been taught per se, but it is what makes the difference between a discussion and a coaching conversation. Intrinsic to this is the ability to acknowledge what I'm hearing, to gently redirect conversation when it strays off topic or too far from the "I" and the ability to challenge people's sabotaging statements or judgments as they arise. This latter skill is the one I find the most challenging.	

In closing, this chapter explored the core coaching competencies in light of team and group coaching work. As we have seen, exceptional team and group coaching is grounded in a solid coaching foundation. Readers are encouraged to use the end-of-chapter questions and undertake the self-assessment to consider areas of strength, as well as areas for exploration, in your own skill development.

The next section, Part II, explores group and team coaching in greater depth. We will be focusing on the process behind team and group coaching, as well as exploring several examples of team and group coaching in action through the provision of case studies.

End-of-Chapter Questions

Undertake the self-assessment that follows. Around the core coaching competencies, consider the following for yourself:

Which competencies are you strongest at?
Which ones do you want to further develop?
What specific actions can you take?
What resources can you tap into?
Who do you want to be accountable to?

Self-Assessment: Core Coaching Skills

On a scale of 0 to 10, rate yourself in terms of your level of confidence and skill in each of these areas. Which are your strengths? What can you do to leverage these? Which may be a learning point for you?

Table 3.3: Self-Assessment—Core Coaching Competencies

Competency	Definition from the ICF (www.coachfederation.org)	Level of Skill and/or Confidence; Focus Areas
A. Setting the Foundation		
Meeting Ethical Guidelines and Professional Standards	Understanding of coaching ethics and standards and ability to apply them appropriately in all coaching situations	
Establishing the Coaching Agreement	Ability to understand what is required in the specific coaching interaction and to come to agreement with the prospective and new client about the coaching process and relationship	
B. Co-creating the Relationship		
Establishing Trust and Intimacy with the Client	Ability to create a safe, supportive environment that produces ongoing mutual respect and trust	
Coaching Presence	Ability to be fully conscious and create spontaneous relationship with the client, employing a style that is open, flexible and confident	
C. Communicating Effectively		
Active Listening	Ability to focus completely on what the client is saying and is not saying, to understand the meaning of what is said in the context of the client's desires, and to support client self-expression	
Powerful Questioning	Ability to ask questions that reveal the information needed for maximum benefit to the coaching relationship and the client	

(Continued)

Table 3.3 (*Continued*)

Competency	Definition from the ICF (www.coachfederation.org)	Level of Skill and/or Confidence; Focus Areas
Direct Communication	Ability to communicate effectively during coaching sessions, and to use language that has the greatest positive impact on the client	
D. Facilitating Learning and Results		
Creating Awareness	Ability to integrate and accurately evaluate multiple sources of information, and to make interpretations that help the client to gain awareness and thereby achieve agreed-upon results	
Designing Actions	Ability to create with the client opportunities for ongoing learning, during coaching and in work/life situations, and for taking new actions that will most effectively lead to agreed-upon coaching results	
Planning and Goal Setting	Ability to develop and maintain an effective coaching plan with the client	
Managing Progress and Accountability	Ability to hold attention on what is important for the client, and to leave responsibility with the client to take action	

PART II

TEAM AND GROUP COACHING FOUNDATIONS AND IN ACTION

Part I of this book looked at the skills, best practices and tricky issues of "coaching many." In this section, we take a look at team and group coaching, the foundations, processes, as well as case studies "bringing to life" group and team coaching initiatives.

Chapter 4 looks at design principles and practices for creating outstanding team and group coaching programs.

Chapter 5 takes a look at group coaching best practices and processes. A digital chapter entitled Group Coaching in Action (www.groupcoachingessentials.com) covers approaches for working with groups and includes several Voices from the Field to illustrate the diversity of group coaching approaches.

Chapter 6 looks at team coaching best practices and processes. A digital chapter, Team Coaching in Action (www.groupcoachingessentials.com), explores tricky issues specific to team coaching, four Voices from the Field, and several activities coaches may wish to incorporate into their team coaching work.

Increasingly team and group coaches are rolling out this work in virtual channels, some phone based, others using a web platform as a foundation. Chapter 7 explores the topic of virtual design and delivery.

Chapter 8 explores the topic of connection and engagement. As we have already explored, the coaching conversation requires a deep connection among group or team members. The chapter explores varying approaches and techniques to boost engagement and interaction of different group and/or team members in virtual and in-person environments.

CHAPTER 4

DESIGN PRINCIPLES AND PRACTICES FOR COACHING MANY

Good design begins with honesty, asks tough questions, comes from
collaboration and from trusting your intuition.
—Freeman Thomas[1]

A whole book could be devoted to designing effective team and group coaching programs. In general we want to lead from adult learning principles and consider active engagement throughout the process. Specific distinctions around virtual programs are made in Chapter 7.

I find that coaches are hungry for practical tools to do their work better. In *Effective Group Coaching*, I introduced some of the core tools to support you with your program development. These tools are foundational in *both team and group* coaching work:

- MindMapping initial program ideas
- Knowing your client
- Creating a Design Matrix
- Undertaking checklists for program preparation (virtual or team)

These steps are illustrated later in the chapter.

---

[1] http://www.brainyquote.com/quotes/topics/topic_design4.html#XIYyOHKgoLbZxitQ.99.

Design in the context of team and group coaching is a creative tension of creating a strong framework for the group or team to engage with—grounded in their needs, preferences and priority areas—and stepping back and letting the group do the work. Where you stand along the group program continuum will influence the balance between how much a program design is created by the coach or facilitator, and the level of co-creation with the team or group.

This chapter explores the topic of design. Whether you are running a virtual or in-person program, coaches will benefit from undertaking some initial pre-work prior to the start of the program. As we will explore in this chapter, key pre-program activities such as MindMapping, pre-program one-on-one calls and using the Design Matrix, create a foundational design structure.

As with any coaching process we need to take the lead of "where our clients are in the moment" at the start of any coaching conversation. This requires flexibility, and leads to the tension of being prepared before the coaching conversation, and also being ready to adapt the design during the coaching conversation to meet the client needs.

BEST PRACTICES FOR PROGRAM DESIGN

- Focus on the conversation.
- Start with the end in mind.
- Modularize.
- Bookend each session.
- Select tools with intent.
- Build it as you go.
- Be ready to let it all go/be flexible.
- Vary approaches (large group, small group).
- Consider linkages with themes.

Focus on the Conversation

As Robert Hargrove writes, "The backbone of any conversation involves finding out who people are, not just in terms of their jobs but who they are in terms of what they passionately care about."[2] Whether we are working with teams or groups, it is all about the conversation.

---

[2] Robert Hargrove, *Masterful Coaching Fieldbook* (San Francisco: John Wiley & Sons, 2003), 107.

Start with the End in Mind

A key tension that team and group coaches find themselves in is how much they design themselves, and how much is co-created with the group. The balance will vary from group to group and according to the stance or philosophy you bring as a coach.

Ask yourself, *"What is really important for this group/team to take away? What are the key priorities of this group?"* This will help you in determining the best mix for your approach. We want to remain open in what we do. Keeping the end point or outcome in mind gives us flexibility in terms of how we get there.

Modularize

Building group and team coaching programs using a modular approach can be highly effective and will enable coaches to repurpose their materials quite easily.

A great metaphor for building programs in a modular approach is the Lego or building block approach. Imagine that each topic area can be a standalone building block. For example, you may have modules on strengths, leadership, values and vision. They can be combined in different ways for different clients. Later in this chapter you will be introduced to the Design Matrix, which is foundational to the concept of modularizing.

Bookend Each Session

Even though the macro processes of group and team coaching are slightly different, at the session or conversation-process level greater similarities may be seen. I often talk about the bookends of the start and close. Typically I will start a coaching conversation with a check-in to hear from each group or team member. Check-in questions might include:

- What did you accomplish this week?
- What was most interesting or important about your week, as it relates to your goals/focus?
- What key success would you like to share with the group?
- What one focus area is going to give you some momentum today?
- What would you like to get out of today's call/conversation?

At the end of every team or group coaching session I want to leave anywhere from 10 to 30 minutes to hear about learning, commitments and next steps. Some common closure questions are:

- What do you want to remember from this activity/conversation?
- What's standing out for you from this conversation?
- What are you going to commit to doing no matter what?
- What's the action you are going to take (individually or collectively) before our next session?

Checking In and Checking Out

Draw up a list of five opening and five closing questions for your next group or team coaching conversation.

Select Tools with Intent

What is the purpose of the tools, questions and activities you bring in? Given that coaching is a conversation with intent, anything we bring into a group or team coaching conversation should have intent behind it. Rather than just throwing in any exercise, consider the purpose of the activity. As you will see in the appendix, exercises can serve different roles. Some activities or exercises are better at building connection, while others are geared to build individual awareness, or support goal setting.

What's in Your Toolbox?

Make a list of the tools and resources you already have to draw on.

Build It as You Go

Coaches often feel that they need to have everything complete before they start the work. There is a great perspective of "creating as you go." As you develop new materials consider how it can be repackaged or recombined with other material to serve another group or purpose. Perhaps you have developed a tip sheet for one client about emotional intelligence. How could that be shared as a support resource for others?

On the specific group or team program level, you may build each session week to week to integrate themes as they emerge. The value of the Design Matrix tool (which we will see later in this chapter) is that as the team and/or group needs become more clear, you can select, pare down and prioritize these areas based on what you are learning of the group (their priorities, learning styles, preferences and pacing).

On a wider level, coaches may benefit from adopting the mindset of taking action every day on key business and program issues to build their foundation as you go. Over time you will notice how pieces do come together.

Be Ready to Let It All Go/Be Flexible

Recognize that groups and teams will have different paces and preferences. As coaches we need to feel very comfortable with throwing any design work "out the window" if this will best serve the client, based on their focus at the time, or what they prefer. We can use the metaphor of throwing spaghetti against the wall and seeing what sticks.

It is important for coaches and leaders to recognize that time is critical. You cannot rush emotion or process. As team and group coaches, we need to be agile with time. It may mean that the end point does not have a "nice neat bow." Not everything may be completed in the time that you have together. A foundational coaching principle for most models is that the people we coach are creative, resourceful and whole. It is important for coaches to trust the group and team members that they will be able to take their learning and insights forward into their work and conversations.

A significant focus for coaches to keep an eye on and adjust around is: "What's the agenda/focus item for the group/team? What's happening in the room/over the phone? Where is the energy?"

Vary Approaches (Small Group, Larger Group)

Chapters 5, 6 and 7 go into detail about different ways coaches can work with groups and teams. Some groups may flourish with the larger or smaller group dialogue, whereas others may benefit from working in pairs. Refer to

Table GC1 in the digital accompaniment on Group Coaching in Action (www
.groupcoachingessentials.com) for a listing of the various approaches coaches
may wish to incorporate when working with groupings in teams and groups.

Consider the linkages between themes and how they might build on one
another. Sequencing is very important in design work. In considering the flow of
your structure, you will want to keep in mind:

- Level of trust and relationships among the group members
- Level of comfort zone
- Self-awareness
- Progression of topics
- Amount of risk

Usually we want to work from low risk to higher risk, building onto topics, as
the level of trust deepens.

THE DESIGN PROCESS FROM ONE TO MANY

One of the most common questions I get asked is, "How do I create this work?"
This next section is an overview of the design process for both team and group
coaching. The process is very similar with both approaches.

To bring it to life, I will walk through these tools using the example of one
of my programs, the 90 Day BizSuccess Program, a group coaching program
designed for business owners. Note that the same steps can be used in designing
a team coaching process.

Figure 4.1 outlines the typical stages in any design process (note that
design may not always follow a straight line and sometimes you may jump
stages).

Step 1: MindMap/Brainstorm

Brainstorm all the ideas you have for an upcoming program based on the needs you
know. What follows in the next section is a sample MindMap (Figure 4.2). MindMaps
are a right-brained tool, originally conceptualized by Tony Buzan. MindMapping
is a free-flowing, very visual approach to brainstorming. The MindMap found
in Figure 4.2 is actually based on the 90 Day BizSuccess Program I have offered
since 2008, which coaches now license to deliver themselves. If we were working on

Figure 4.1: A Typical Design Process

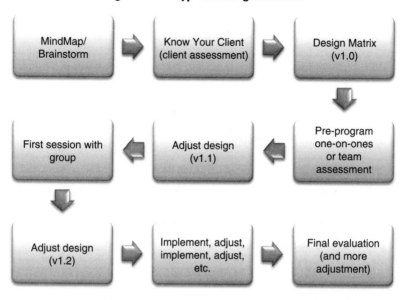

a team coaching engagement the initial brainstorm would include ideas based on initial discussions and/or requests from the sponsor.

Step 2: Know Your Client

Critical to the process is knowing who your client is. Again, we'll work through the example of the 90 Day BizSuccess Program. If you are working with a team, initial meetings with the leader, team and sponsor may provide this level of detail of who your client really is, and what their priorities are.

Step 3: Create a Design Matrix, Version 1.0

The Design Matrix is a great tool to start fleshing out what an actual session may look like. At this stage coaches will start to identify initial components of a program, and will want to move between the Design Matrix and the MindMap. The MindMap will include the potential ideas, topics, and exercises that may get incorporated into the design. Note that this is version 1.0 or the first draft. It will change as you have more conversation.

Step 4: Pre-program One-on-Ones

One of the key best practices we have seen already is the pre-program one-on-one. These conversations will further infuse our design. In a team coaching context the pre-program one-on-one may also include a team or individual assessments such as the DiSC, or Team Diagnostic.

Step 5: Adjust the Design Matrix

Based on what you have learned through the pre-program one-on-ones or the team assessment, adjustments will be made to the Design Matrix.

Step 6: First Session with Group

Here is where we find out how the design really fits. It is only when we are finally with the group or team that we know what is needed in that moment. It is critical for team and group coaches to really notice what works for each team and group they are working with, and adjust accordingly. Of particular note, keep an eye on pace, preferences, etc.

Step 7: Adjust, Implement, Adjust

The feedback you receive from your group or team members during each session will help you to adjust and make changes as you go. One of the core coaching competencies is coaching presence. This skill area is about how coaches "show up" in the moment and adjust accordingly.

Step 8: Final Evaluation

Coaches are encouraged to undertake a final evaluation—written and/or verbal—at the end of the coaching process. This feedback will be useful in pointing to additional areas of need for your group or team members, as well as valuable feedback about the coaching process, and the skills, components and resources you have used.

Note that these steps are iterative and may cycle backward and forward at times. The creative process is not always a smooth path.

Field Journal: Walking Through a Sample Design Process

To bring to life some of these design tools I am going to use my sample design for a group coaching program for small business owners as an example: the 90 Day BizSuccess Group Coaching Program.

We are going to walk through three of the key design steps, including: Step 1 (MindMap/Brainstorm); Step 2 (Know Your Client); and Step 3 (Create a Design Matrix).

Step 1: MindMap/Brainstorm

The first step I undertake in the development of any new program is a Mind-Map. Refer to Figure 4.2, which illustrates initial ideas around the 90 Day BizSuccess Program.

Figure 4.2: MindMap

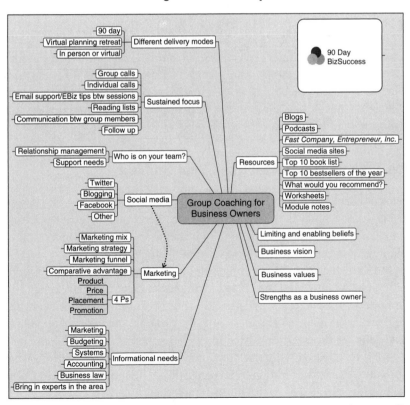

(Continued)

MindMaps are a great starting place for designing both group and team coaching engagements. Whether you draw freehand or use a computer software program or app, MindMapping allows you to get all your ideas out onto one piece of paper. You will be amazed at what emerges in 10 or 15 minutes of brainstorming. MindMapping is an iterative tool. I will continue to add to my MindMap as new ideas emerge. As my program ideas evolve, I will often assign these a different version (for example, 1.0, 1.1, 1.2, as well as a date).

Activity

Set aside 10 to 15 minutes for brainstorming or capturing all your ideas for your upcoming program. On a blank piece of paper, flipchart or computer screen, MindMap all of your ideas about an upcoming program. When you exhaust your ideas, take a look at what emerged as possible topic areas (for example, strengths, vision, values, relationship management, limiting beliefs, etc.), as well as ideas for delivery, venue, activities, keeping the conversation going (sustained focus), marketing and other informational needs (which will be covered by others, not by me as coach).

For professionals who do not find the MindMap process works well, you may wish to use a set of index cards or Post-it Notes, and capture each one of your ideas on a separate card/Post-it. After you have exhausted all your ideas, lay them out on the floor, a large table or wall and notice the common themes that emerge.

Now we have done some initial thinking about our program, we can move to Step 2: Know Your Client.

Step 2: Know Your Client (the Client Profile)

Clients—the people we work with—should be the driving force of any design process. In coaching, the focus is set by the client, not the coach. Getting to understand who your clients are, what they want and value, is critical to designing an effective team or group coaching process.

The Knowing Your Client profile helps us think through and start to connect with what our clients are really looking for. A great program design will be infused by their needs. Depending on your background and current connection with the niche you are designing the program for, you may be able to quickly answer the questions listed in the left hand column, and some may need a bit of research. Other sections may not be applicable (n/a) to what you want to create. In addition to being useful for design, the Knowing Your Client profile can also be useful for the marketing process.

In design we have a fine balance between "driving the bus" and determining what is going to be incorporated, and stepping back and letting the group or team determine it. Note that you may be working with Knowing Your Client at the high level, or 30,000-foot view. As you get to know your group in pre-program calls you will start learning more about their specific needs and focus areas.

The conversations you have, and research you do about Knowing Your Client, will likely lead you to add more ideas to your MindMap. You can download a blank Knowing Your Client template at GroupCoachingEssentials.com.

What follows is a completed Knowing Your Client Profile for the 90 Day BizSuccess Group Coaching Program.

Client Profile: Knowing Your Client

Overall Description of Client

Service-based solopreneurs or business owners (coaches, consultants and trainers)

Key takeaways they are looking for from the coaching process

- Clarify business vision and goals for the next year
- Space to set goals
- Be held accountable: get it done!
- Peer support: learn and connect with others
- Resources to support them to grow their business

Table 4.1: Knowing Your Client Profile

Client's Needs (in no particular order)	Create a vision for their business
	Space to set goals for their business: 12 months as well as medium and long term
	Accountability around key business goals
	Exploration of company brand
	Identification to key strengths as a business owner
	Systems to support their work
	Hearing about what works as a small business owner/solopreneur
	Navigating marketing: social media, traditional marketing

(Continued)

Client's Main Goals	To develop their business plan
	To identify marketing approaches, pricing, promotion
	To learn about what works, and what I can do on a budget
	To set up my business so it works for me
	To get into action
Age Range	Varied: different programs can tap into different age ranges
Gender	Both
Socioeconomic Status	n/a
Geographic Location	Virtual program; can support business owners globally
Employment/ Professional Status	Solopreneur ("one-person show") or small business owner
Spending Patterns	Be aware of tax submission times. Also take into account times which may be start and end of fiscal. Business owners may want to spend more money before year end.
Associations/ Organizations They Belong to	Local chambers of commerce
	Business networking groups
	National/federal small business services—also at provincial/state level
	Professional associations—e.g., ASTD/CSTD, ICF
Availability	Varied—end of week may be more attractive to some. Evenings may be popular depending on schedules. May need more time to clear schedule. Need to consider what happens if they miss a call.
Preferred Format	Phone, with possible web support

Marketing Approaches—consider preferences around:	
Newspapers/ Magazines/ Publications They Read	*Inc., Forbes, Entrepreneur, New York Times*
Internet Sites	Fast Company, Local Business Network
Blogs They Read	Duct Tape Marketing, Go To Guides
Radio Stations They Listen to	More research needed into Internet and regular radio shows that may apply to business owners
Venues that Would Reflect Their Preferences	Online or creative venues
Other	Opportunity to connect around special events such as small business week

Activity

Complete a Knowing Your Client Profile for your client group or team. Notice which areas are clear. Which are not? What conversations do you need to have to learn more? What is your next step? What needs to be added to your MindMap?

Step 3: Create a Design Matrix

The next step of the process is to start drafting out what some of your sessions might look like. The tool I use is the Design Matrix. I consider the Design Matrix a drafting tool, providing me with some possible options depending on what the group needs in the moment. It can be very valuable in helping me think through different possible exercises or questions to bring into the work with the team or group. It also provides an opportunity to start mapping out what the session might look like. This mapping out can help us avoid the danger of being overwhelmed, when we are trying to fit in too much.

Note that some coaches will prefer, and feel more confident, going into the session with lots of details in hand; others may wish to have a list of focus areas

(Continued)

along with potential coaching questions and activities that they can choose from in the moment, and adapt based on the group or team members' needs.

To illustrate the template, a potential draft of a first session Design Matrix for the 90 Day BizSuccess Group Coaching Program looks like the following on paper. Note that it is a combination of "speaker's notes," facilitation tips and other notes on timing and process. Coaches should adapt the information in terms of what is useful in support for their style.

Table 4.2: Creating Your Business Roadmap

Time	Component	Potential Coaching Questions
5 min	**Welcome and Introduction** Introduce yourself and provide a quick overview of the format of the course to participants: • Dates and content of group calls • Individual calls • E-biz tips	
15 min	**Introductions** Round Robin: Who are you? What do you want to share based on the introduction questions? Have them write it out on Post-it: collect if in person, scan if virtual. Point out common themes. *Need to bring Post-it Notes*	What is your intention for the program? 90 days from now, what do you want your business to look like? 90 days from now, what do you want to have accomplished, or to be in progress?
5 min	**Ways of Working** Develop a list of how we would like to work together as a group; post or send out after the call. Round Robin: Hear from all. Make sure we address confidentiality, respect, focus, etc. *Need flip chart if in person, paper if not; to send by email*	What are the group agreements we would like to set to make this a powerful learning process?

10-20 min	**Creating a Business Roadmap** Either: Walk through the visualization on the phone or need to develop a list of vision questions. Give yourself 15 min to read through this, and give participants a few minutes to capture notes as you go or at the end. Have participants comment on/share these. Assign as fieldwork and focus on the 1 Percent Rule to Business Development.	
5-10	**Action Planning** You may want to share this quote with group members: "Vision takes a purpose and starts to turn it into specifics. What specifically will you do, when will you do it, and how will you accomplish it?" – Stephen Covey Without action, information is just information. Talk with group about the importance of creating an action plan for the next 90 days. Have them complete an action plan based on their most important goals. This will likely be a piece that is completed as homework.	What action steps will you commit to taking in the short, medium and long term?
10 min	**1 Percent Rule to Business Development** (if time or shift to next week OR Incorporate with action planning piece) Successful business owners are those who are clear in what they want to achieve and take regular, consistent action. Business owners often fall into the trap of feeling overwhelmed with everything they have to do, or overwhelmed at how big the tasks are.	What is the area you would like to focus on for applying the 1 percent rule?

(Continued)

Session #1 *(Continued)*

Time	Component	Potential Coaching Questions
	The 1 percent rule encourages us to break things down into daily, actionable steps.	
	If you took action on a daily basis of 1 percent toward a goal, how much would you have achieved by the end of the month? (Answer: 30 percent)	
	Ask participants to identify for themselves one area they want to take action on, and identify and share with the group the 1 percent of actions they will take over the next two weeks.	
5 min	SWOT—Strengths, Weaknesses, Opportunities and Threats	
	Introduce the group to the SWOT and talk about how it is used. Complete as homework. Walk group through how they can use the tool and what to look at for each step.	
5 min	Weekly assignment/field work to deepen learning:	
	Confirm that this week's field work is the SWOT (Strengths, Weaknesses, Opportunities and Threats). Reminder that the impact of coaching happens in between the calls.	
	Assign: • Book one-on-one call with coach. • Point to references for this week.	

10 min	**Call Wrap-up**	
	Wrap up call using a selection of the following statements and questions: 1. As a result of today's call I will . . . 2. I will focus on the following 1 percent rule. . . . 3. What are the top two things you will commit to doing? How will we know? You may also wish to use this time asking the group to comment on: • What worked well for your learning today? • What are you taking away? • What should we do differently next time?	

Note the emphasis that this is a draft. In practice, the first session rolls out differently each time I work with a different group. As a coach I hold the matrix much more fluidly, ready to put things aside if group members' interest is not there. For example, a recent group wanted to spend the bulk of the time getting to know each other and setting goals for the entire coaching work. We also looked at part of the vision. Their preference was to complete the bulk of the exercises offline between sessions one and two. They all came to session two with a great deal of deep individual work done during those two weeks. Their preference, when we moved into week two, was to be "laser coached" around some of the key interest areas that surfaced with their vision work. In laser coaching, a coach will coach one individual on a specific issue for a short amount of time. This brevity, and emphasis on a very clear topic, gives it the name of *laser coaching*. Given the small size of the group we were able to incorporate this request, as well as move into the next connecting theme of relationships.

The great thing with the matrix is that it provides a place for your ideas and possibilities. It is very common to have similar requests come from different client groups or teams. The matrix allows you to start fleshing out your ideas, and build a bank of resources you can draw upon. As we discuss the best practice of modularization in design, the matrix allows us to easily package different modules in different ways, leading to an entirely new program.

(Continued)

The matrix can be as detailed as it is above, or it can be just a few lines to provide you with more of a laundry list to select from during the session, based on the energy and interest of the group. Notice how I have laid out some options in Module 1 above, spending more time on the visualization rather than the 1 percent rule of business. Depending on how much structure you want in your programs you may choose to leave the timeframes in or take them out. I find that time ranges help me think through the possible flow of the program. More often than not, in a first draft, there is too much I want to incorporate rather than too little. Recall the best practice of "less is more" from Chapter 2.

The matrix shown above actually comes out of the 90 Day BizSuccess Program that I license to coaches. There is space for flexibility in terms of where the group needs and energy exist.

Activity

Draft out a Design Matrix for each of your sessions. As we have seen, these three steps (MindMap, Know Your Client and Design Matrix) are important for preparation. Doing this pre-work often allows coaches to be more focused and present on the issues that emerge with the team and/or group, enabling them to quickly draw on questions, tools or activities they have listed earlier as options in the design matrix.

Voices from the Field: Other Perspectives on Lessons Learned in Designing and Implementing Team and Group Coaching

One of the questions I asked coaches I interviewed was what they considered their biggest lessons learned in designing or implementing team and group coaching. Here are their responses. Take note of any lessons you will want to incorporate into your work.

Designing and Implementing Team Coaching

Jacqueline Peters and Catherine Carr:
Designing: Have a plan but be fluid.

Implementing: Really talk about the need for a broader program than a one- or two-day event. Ask them what the team really needs to step up to, what they need to get them there, how long they think it will take, and then offer to partner with them on the journey.

Analogy: It's not enough to buy a membership to a gym and go hard for a day. If you want to be fit, you need to participate in the gym experience more regularly.

Sharon Miller: Don't do it alone—get a partner. The work becomes a better product, and a better experience for participants and for you. Also note that in team coaching there is more unsaid than said because of safety and trust issues. This is very different from the one-on-one coaching context. Don't believe you're getting the full story.

Phil Sandahl: Most organizations and most teams are not clear about what they want or need; they are often buying familiar solutions because that's what they know or what their peers do.

Teams don't really care what "hat" the coach is wearing—the team wants results. Sometimes that means acting as a consultant with valuable experience and advice; sometimes it means providing skills training; sometimes it means interacting as a facilitator in a group process. The art of the work is deciding what will serve the team the best in each moment.

Designing and Implementing Group Coaching

Kevin Stebbings: Group coaching has taught me the lesson of juggling the group process while still focusing on individual discovery for group members. Learning to "dance in the moment" seems to be amplified in a group setting. It requires the group coach to continually zoom in and out from the level of the individual to the level of the group. What has helped me in the midst of this dance is to remind myself that "group coaching is about each individual's discovery and action in the context of a group process."

The perspective that has helped me implement effective team coaching is the fact that the team is the client. I do this is by shifting my language in the coaching conversation. Instead of highlighting an individual and saying, "Mary, I have noticed you have not spoken up yet," I would say, "I notice that some members of the team have not yet spoken up. How does this impact the team?" Learning to view the individuals through the lens of a team keeps the focus on the bigger picture and the needs of the team as a client.

(Continued)

Renee Brotman: Biggest lessons: The need for close coordination with the overall program managers to routinely validate learning objectives and to obtain up-to-date group issues that surface within the group during other aspects of the program. Also very important to have consistency and reinforcement of classroom learning principles by linking how principles play out in the real work environment.

Shana Montesol: Lessons learned in designing group coaching programs: When I design the program, I keep in mind the "accordion" approach to content. This is a terrific concept that I learned from group coaching expert Jennifer Britton in her Group Coaching Essentials course: You can prepare to cover a variety of topics, questions and exercises, but if there is more interest in one particular component, one can squeeze the accordion and condense the content. Conversely, if there is less energy than expected on a specific piece, one can expand the accordion to lengthen the content. The trick is to first identify which pieces of content are "anchor points" that I want to be sure the group covers.

Lessons learned in implementing group coaching programs: It's not your program or group—it's the participants'. When I have taken this approach, I have seen groups flourish. Participants have gained so much from hearing the experience and insights of others, people have jumped in to support and help each other and group members have been spurred to take action (and make changes they probably would not have done without the group).

Michael Cullen: To deliver what was promoted and promised, to create a "safe" environment, to mix individual and small group exercises in equal measure (if not more) to what I talk about, to be really prepared such that the participants have no doubt that you are what you say and do—so be sure to do (and time) all the exercises, etc., yourself beforehand!

Kim Ades: There must be a high degree of interaction in the coaching experience and between the coaching calls or meetings.

It's crucial to design a journey that all members can follow that enables them to share themselves safely.

Frequent contact points are important.

One-on-one contact between the coach and the client is also important over and above the group calls.

There must be a methodology for them to support one another and provide valuable coaching to one another beyond just the calls or meetings.

Ursula Lesic: In implementation, creating a safe, supportive environment that takes people out of their day-to-days to focus on the group topic or team.

Word use is an important consideration when marketing or describing the program: *enhancing* versus *improving, stretch* versus *perfection, fieldwork* versus *homework*. In designing, spend the time on designing the alliance and ground roles.

Design is always an iterative process, one that will continue to emerge and evolve right into the time we are with our groups and teams. As important as pre-program preparation is, as a coach it is essential that we are present and open to whatever emerges in our work with the group or team, anchored by their key focus areas. In this chapter we used a group coaching example to illustrate these design principles. All of these tools can be utilized in the team coaching context as well as in the peer coaching context, and with the leader as coach.

End-of-Chapter Suggestions

Consider an upcoming team or group coaching program you have. Undertake some initial drafting of your next program working through:

1. MindMapping
2. Knowing Your Client
3. Creating a Design Matrix for one or more of the sessions

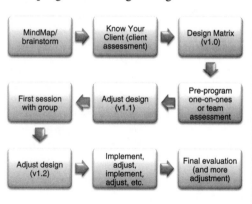

Note the best practices for design. Which ones do you already incorporate? Which new ones do you want to bring into your next program?

CHAPTER 5

GROUP COACHING FOUNDATIONS

Many ideas grow better when transplanted into another mind
than the one where they sprang up.
—Oliver Wendell Holmes

This chapter explores the foundations of group coaching, including:

- The context of group coaching
- What group coaching can look like—different models and approaches
- Group coaching process overview
- Positioning group coaching as a support to organizations
- A reminder of best practices for group coaching

As group coaching becomes more prevalent with groups in the public domain and with organizations, what has become apparent is that there is continued expansion of the different types of approaches or models that can be used in a group coaching process. Depending on client needs, coaches are using a variety of approaches in the work including laser coaching, reflection and peer coaching processes. Coaches are offering "pure" group coaching programs as well as integrating group coaching approaches into their own group programs such as workshops and teleclasses.

In the public domain, group coaching ranges from groups for business owners, to parents, to those in career transition, to writers. Group coaching has also taken root in organizations, being seen as an opportunity to sustain the conversation after training, as a standalone intervention or as part of a larger learning strategy.

This chapter offers an overview of the group coaching process, as well as what are typical components of any group (or team) coaching conversation. The chapter also explores five ways group coaching can be positioned in organizations. A reminder of group coaching best practices wraps up this chapter.

THE CONTEXT

Group coaching is a sustained conversation among members of a small group which focuses on goal setting, conversation to deepen awareness around issues or to support action around key themes, goals and issues. The group coaching conversation is typically bookended by a check-in and check-out process (commitments, insights and actions). The check-in focuses on group members' insights and actions undertaken around the commitments they have set, as well as taking stock of where interest lies for the coaching conversation. The check-out process includes individual and collective commitments, insights and actions.

Key principles that distinguish group coaching from other group modalities include:

- a focus on goal setting, action and accountability
- a sustained conversation and action space
- an intimate conversation space (15 people or fewer)

Group coaching is truly an intimate conversation space. It's about the quality of the conversation and relationships—not the numbers. The International Coach Federation indicates that for a group to be considered group coaching for credentialing purposes, it needs to include no more than 15 persons. In *Effective Group Coaching*, one of the questions explored with other pioneers and practitioners of this work was, "What is an optimum group size?" Many coaches responded that their groups were in the lower range (four to eight people per group) for virtual programs, and slightly larger for other groups.

As we saw in Chapter 2 with the continuum, coaches may deliver more "pure" group coaching programs, or incorporate a group coaching approach as part of their retreats, workshops or teleclasses. In the digital chapter Group Coaching in Action (www.groupcoachingessentials.com), you will meet four group coaches whose work illustrates a number of varying approaches: virtual groups, in-person groups, intensive programs and also corporate groups.

The Group Coaching Litmus Test

I use the following as a litmus test to determine whether a group is taking a group coaching approach:

- Is the participant setting the direction and agenda of the focus of the conversation?
- Is there a focus on goal setting and/or action planning?
- Is the conversation geared around deepening awareness of the participants' key goals/focus areas?
- Is the conversation geared around taking action on issues of importance?

Groups may form in different ways. First, group coaches may offer "public" programs that they develop and market to the wider public. In many of these programs, themes provide the anchor point by which individuals decide to join a specific group. Certain individuals may be drawn to a group that is working around business issues, whereas another may want to look at time management issues. The themes or focus areas for the BizSuccess program include topics such as business vision, business values and focusing on strengths. These theme areas provide potential group members with a better understanding of what the program will be focusing on. In most of my programs I often leave one or two sessions "open" to meet the emerging needs of specific group members. For example, a group of business owners I recently worked with really wanted to explore social media. We were able to incorporate this into one of the "open sessions."

Groups that are already formed may invite coaches to work with them. For instance, a group may be a group of friends who want to engage a coach and enjoy each other's company, but want to work on different themes. For example, one person may want to focus on relationship issues, while another may want to look at financial issues. In contrast, it may be a professional association that invites a coach in to undertake work with an established group around one core topic area such as leadership strengths. Chapter 2 identified some of the benefits of the group coaching process. From a group member's standpoint, the cost effective nature and opportunity to connect with others is a common response I hear when I ask group members who sign up for my programs. Review the benefits listed in Chapter 2 and consider which ones are likely to apply to your programs.

In Group Coaching in Action, an accompanying digital chapter at www .groupcoachingessentials.com, you will meet four coaches who undertake their own group coaching work: Michael Cullen, who describes his group coaching work around re-employment; Shana Montesol, who delivers group coaching programs to international professionals; Ray Rigoglioso, who has designed programs for nonprofit leaders as well as gay men; and Lynda Monk (who was also highlighted in *Effective Group Coaching*), who works with writers. Note the benefits their participants have identified.

WHAT GROUP COACHING CAN LOOK LIKE

What falls under the umbrella of group coaching in terms of approaches is increasingly diverse. As coaches roll out this work around the world, what is apparent is that different approaches work better for different types of groups. Coaches will want to recall the best practice of "knowing your client" to consider what group members' preferences are. Some of the potential program designs coaches are rolling out under the umbrella of group coaching include:

- Ninety-day group coaching programs bringing groups of the public together to explore common themes (e.g., work/life issues, time management).
- Group coaching programs geared toward professionals facing similar issues (e.g., new leaders, lawyers, health care professionals, educators). These programs may meet intensively, monthly, over the course of three to six months or even quarterly over the span of a year or more.
- Groups that are formed around key themes and interest areas for a one- to two-year process where group members remain the same.
- Rotational groups meeting regularly. Membership may change, and key components of the coaching approach such as goal setting action or awareness may be present. Examples of rotational groups include patients who are dealing with cardiac care issues or issues after bariatric surgery.
- Hybrid groups where group coaching calls are supplemented by individual coaching calls.
- Group coaching conversations supporting corporate training initiatives (e.g., leadership development training programs or post-360 feedback groups).
- Virtual retreat or intensive format: groups coming together for intensive bursts virtually. The benefit of this approach is that it brings a "retreat to your home or office." Check out my field notebook (below) for more information.

Field Journal: Virtual Retreats

I started offering virtual retreats years ago when my son was an infant, as it gave me the flexibility to continue facilitating retreat processes without leaving home. On an annual basis I continue to offer a number of public virtual retreats and intensives—one series for business owners, and one for professionals looking to create their own group programs. I have also offered virtual retreats in the past around getting organized and work/life balance issues.

Unlike an elongated group coaching process, a virtual retreat provides the advantages of intensive bursts of focus for retreat participants, all held by phone, Web or Skype. Typically held over a three- to six-hour (or more) period, over one or more days, my virtual retreats have hourly focus areas. We meet as a group for the first 15 to 20 minutes of each hour for group dialogue and discussion, with the remaining part of the hour focused on individual work offline from our homes, offices or even hotels.

This offline time provides participants with individual reflection time. For a business owner the focus may be on planning, reflection or taking action, whereas in a work/life balance retreat, the focus may be more on self-reflection about strengths and rejuvenation. As the coach I am typically available and "on call" during this time if anyone wants individual laser coaching.

For busy professionals looking to "get away" but not really wanting to travel, this is a great option. It also provides the mix of individual reflection and immediate accountability (to really get things done!), as well as group dialogue, support and connection.

The same model can be adapted for virtual team retreatants who are not able to get away and meet face to face. For virtual teams the focus in this instance would be on individual development and team sharing. As such, the online and offline time would need to be balanced differently.

Question

What would be appealing for your client groups or teams with a virtual retreat format?

Other authors have also included these approaches as part of the modality of group coaching:[1]

- Coaching circles
- MasterMind groups
- Action learning groups

Let's take a quick look at each one. You may wish to consider how these could work for your client context and groups.

Coaching Circles

Many coaches may explore the opportunity to create coaching circles within their program offerings. Charles Brassard outlines the following four focus areas of a coaching circle process in his 2008 Worldwide Association of Business Coaches (WABC) article.[2]

In its simplest form, there are typically four elements to each airtime:

1. The presentation by the client of his/her issue or challenge
2. A period of collaborative inquiry designed to help the client apprehend this challenge in new ways
3. Solo time to reflect on what was learned from the exploration
4. A period during which each member voices his/her insights and where the client highlights what has shifted in his/her perspective and what he/she intends to do next

Brassard notes that coaching circles usually include four to six people and meet every six to eight weeks. He states that coaching circles "marry the principles of practices of action learning (pioneered by Reg Revans) and those of integral coaching (pioneered by James Flaherty)."[3]

MasterMind Groups

The term *MasterMind* is often attributed to Napoleon Hill, author of *Think and Grow Rich*, in which he defined it as a "coordination of knowledge and effort, in

---

[1] Hawkins, *Leadership Team Coaching*, and Christine Thornton, *Group and Team Coaching: The Essential Guide* (London: Routledge, 2010).
[2] Charles Brassard, "The Point of Coaching Circles," *Business Coaching Worldwide* 4, no. 3 (2008), http://www.wabccoaches.com/bcw/2008_v4_i3/get-the-edge.html. Used with permission.
[3] Ibid.

a spirit of harmony, between two or more people, for the attainment of a definite purpose."

MasterMind groups usually bring people of a similar interest together, such as business owners, to share, learn and grow. The benefits of the MasterMind process include peer learning, the development of new wisdom, in an environment that focuses on peer sharing and peer accountability.

Unlike a pure group coaching process where the coach coaches group members, or in a coach-led coaching circle, in a MasterMind group each group member is peer coaching others. In a MasterMind process the strength comes from the connection within the group. There is typically no coach leading the process. This is one of the key distinctions with a MasterMind. MasterMind groups are very common in the entrepreneurial sector. One great go-to resource for more information on the topic of designing and developing MasterMinds is Karyn Greenstreet of Passion for Business.

As Hill wrote back in the 1930s, "No two minds ever come together without, thereby, creating a third, invisible, intangible force which may be likened to a third mind."[4]

Action Learning Groups

As a graduate student in the early 1990s, I explored many different models of learning, including action learning. One of my professors, David Morely, a master facilitator, wrote the following about action learning: "learning stems from reasonable experience, and is reinforced when that experience is shared with others . . . learning is . . . enhanced by the coming together of people in the same boat to work on live problems of common concerns."[5] Twenty years later, action learning is a component of many learning initiatives. As David Clutterbuck writes, "Action learning is a well-established process that relates learning to current, meaningful tasks, on which learners receive the benefit of support, criticism and ad hoc coaching from each other."[6] In action learning, the role of questions is essential. Key to the process of action learning is Reg Revans' equation:

$$L = P + Q$$

---

[4] Napoleon Hill, *Think and Grow Rich* (Radford, VA: Wilder Publications, 2008), 134.
[5] Reg Revans (1982) quoted in David Morely, Susan Wright and E. L. Trist, *Learning Works: Searching for Organizational Futures* (Toronto: The ABL (Adapting by Learning) Group, Faculty of Environmental Studies York University, 1989), 178.
[6] Clutterbuck, *Coaching the Team at Work*, 180.

The equation means the following: learning equals programmed or expert learning plus insights from inquiry or a powerful question from experience.

Depending on where you stand on the continuum, there may be a challenge to "programmed or expert" learning on the part of coaches. Both Christine Thornton and Peter Hawkins expand upon action learning in the group coaching context in their books.

COMPONENTS OF A GROUP COACHING PROCESS

Regardless of whether you are offering a pure group coaching process, incorporating it as a follow-on to a training program, or bringing a group coaching approach to a workshop, there are several key components of any group coaching process. These elements will be present whether you are running a 90-day program, a virtual retreat or even an in-person weekend "retreat" using a group coaching approach. See Figure 5.1: Components of a Group Coaching Process.

In general there are five main phases to any group coaching process:

1. Pre-program
2. First session
3. Ongoing sessions/conversations
4. Final session
5. Group follow-up (optional)

Figure 5.1: Components of a Group Coaching Process

Pre-program	First Session	Ongoing Sessions	Last Session	Group Follow-Up (optional)
• Pre-program one-on-ones (telephone, web, email) • Materials out with relevant details	• Ways of working/team or group agreements • Introductions • Expectation setting • Validation/setting of topics for coaching	• Themes to be determined • Bookends —check in and check out • Coaching exercise related to theme • Field work to deepen learning & support action	• Next setps, accountability, future goals • Closure and celebration • Set up follow-up: evaluations, post group calls, or one-on-one calls	• Discussion of actions undertaken since last call, celebrations and challenges • How are they sustaining learning and action? What's worked? What hasn't?

Phase 1: Pre-program

Connecting with your group members is important even before the start of the program. Before the group comes together, coaches will want to hold a pre-program one-on-one call with each participant. This pre-program call is critical in learning about your group members, answering any questions they may have, and going over logistics. (Refer to Chapter 8 for questions you may want to incorporate.)

In the pre-program calls you will want to note learning styles group members bring, key focus/interest areas, goals participants have mentioned and anything else of significance, such as a person being a very verbal processor (refer to Tricky Issues in Chapter 2).

As you get to know your group, you will uncover key themes they are looking for coaching around, which may be added to the core themes they have been attracted by.

Any pre-program materials should be circulated in advance. I usually aim to get materials out a week in advance for a virtual program. Key materials at this stage include:

- A welcome email (refer to text box)
- Module notes or worksheets for each session
- Any pre-work, e.g., assessments, materials people should have on hand

---

Writing the Welcome Letter/Email

A welcome letter/email should be sent out to group members in advance of the program. Items you will want to include in a welcome letter are:

- When the program is being held
- Where the program is being held (physical location, virtual bridge line)
  - Who is responsible for costs such as long-distance expenses, etc.
  - Any considerations for call quality, such as recommendations to use a landline, or call from a quiet room
- What is included in the program (group calls, any individual time, etc.)
- What to expect: pre-work/touch points

(Continued)

- Preparation required before the first call
- Link to any frequently asked questions
- Coaching agreement (see below)
- Outline of the program
- Your contact details
- What to have on hand; i.e., materials
- Weekly assignments/homework/fieldwork/commitments
- Time zone converter for programs with participants in different locations (I use www.timeanddate.com)

Written Coaching Agreements

Using written coaching agreements has been a best practice for coaches in the individual realm for many years. It is becoming a best practice for group coaching contexts as well. Coaches are strongly encouraged to consider what is appropriate given the context, and jurisdiction, in which they coach. You are encouraged to discuss this at your local ICF chapter level and/or with any legal professionals you work with. Coaching agreements are one topic area I explore in the Group Coaching Essentials teleseminar.

Phase 2: First Session

The first session really creates the foundation for successful group coaching. The purpose of this first session is to:

- Create connection
- Develop ways of working
- Explore and share expectations for the program
- Establish or confirm topic areas for coaching (either pre-set or using colored dots)
- Discuss logistics, meetings, etc.

The first session sets the tone of the engagement and is critical in connecting people with each other. Remember that groups at this stage are in the forming process (refer to Chapter 10). Group member needs at this stage are "safety," connection between you and other group members, as well as discussion around expectations and where the group is going.

Key to the discussion in this first session is to develop some ways of working for the group. These may also be called "terms of engagement" or "group ground rules." The ground rules serve as a co-designed agreement as to how the group wants to operate. They should be captured and posted on a flip chart if you are in person, or sent out in a follow-up email after the group call. You will want to remind group members of their agreements regularly. These agreements can be supportive if there are any challenges down the road.

If you are marketing a group coaching program to the public it is likely that key themes have been set for each week. You will want to validate this or review these with the group.

If themes have not been set, then you will want to work with the group to identify and prioritize themes. One of the techniques I use is an adaptation of the Dotmocracy method, which I was introduced to years ago during some facilitation work I did in Europe. Note the Field Journal entry Using Dots to Identify Core Themes in Coaching.

Field Journal: Using Dots to Identify Core Themes in Coaching

Setting key themes to work around in your first session with new groups is key. In much of my organizational work I may be brought in to work with a new group of managers or leaders for six sessions over a three- to four-month period. Sometimes session topics are set; other times there is some flexibility. This method works in both instances.

First, brainstorm with the group the list of all topics they might want to explore. You may come up with a laundry list of a dozen or more. Write these on a flipchart, or have each person identify key themes they want to look at, on a Post-it Note (one item per Post-it). If you are using Post-its, make sure that you have sufficient wall space to have each participant come up and share their idea, posting it on the wall. Similar topics should be grouped. Once you have your entire list, and have exhausted all options, give each group member a number of colored dots. Depending on the number of topics you have listed and numbers you want to pare it down to, you may give each member several

(Continued)

dots (two, three or more). Have each group member place a dot beside the topics they are interested in.

Very quickly, and very visually, you will see where interest lies. This will enable you to identify the themes for the remaining sessions. Further dialogue may be required if there is no clear consensus on the topics.

Phase 3: Ongoing Sessions

The structure of your ongoing sessions may include the bookends of check-in and check-out and time for exploration around one of your key themes each session. As you will note in the section "Different Approaches to Working with Groups" in Group Coaching in Action at www.groupcoachingessentials.com, you may incorporate a number of different styles in each session. Key is to ensure that each person has the opportunity to be coached. You may incorporate laser coaching opportunities (where one individual is "laser" coached for a short amount of time), individual reflection, large or small group discussion, peer coaching, assessments or more standard coaching activities (such as a Wheel of Leadership/ Health/Life) or values work. (You may also wish to refer to the appendix for a selection of activities and exercises.)

To support you in mapping out what your session might look like, use the Design Matrix. Refer to the completed Design Matrix in Chapter 4 for an example. Note in that example that the first session was made up of 75 minutes, in which the first 15 to 20 minutes were planned as a check-in, and the last 10 minutes were planned for commitments, action planning and feedback, leaving only 35 minutes for core exploration of that week's topic.

One of the best practices we have highlighted throughout the book is "less is more." Don't try to fit too much in. This is reflected in the successes and challenges from the field.

At the end of each session, individual or collective commitments can be established by each person. This may include an inquiry, coaching challenge or coaching request.

Refer to the Team and Group Coaching Process Overview (Figure 5.2) for a high-level overview of components that will usually be in each group and team coaching conversation.

Note the components that are included in each touch point during a team or group coaching conversation. I see five distinct focus areas in each conversation.

Figure 5.2: Group and Team Coaching Session Process Overview

Check-In

- Updates on commitments
  - Celebrations, challenges/roadblocks
- Focus areas for conversation that day, including measures of success (What are your burning questions? What do you want to get out of our conversation today?)

Areas for Exploration

- Coach and group identify areas for exploration for that session—may also have been predetermined (Dotmocracy, themes)

Coaching Conversation

- Key focus area for that week—i.e. values, vision, difficult conversations

Action and Accountability

- What are you going to commit to doing before our next call (may be on the *being* or *doing* realm)
- For teams: What will you do? How will this connect with your own structures? Who will be responsible? How will the rest of the team know?

Check-Out

- Closure and evaluation:
  - What worked well? What are you taking away? What should we do differently next time?
  - What is the energy/focus you are leaving our conversation with?
  - What was your biggest learning or "aha" today?

These include:

- Check-in
- Areas for exploration
- Coaching conversation
- Action and accountability
- Check-out

How much time will you have to spend on each one of these areas with your team or group?

Phase 4: Final Session

Key components of a final session with the group will include a check-in and review of key learning and insights throughout the program, and key actions each group member has undertaken. This may in fact form the bulk of the first part of the session. Another key area to explore with the group is their next steps. What are their action plans going forward? What accountability do they want to create? What future goals do they want to keep in mind? How do they want to stay connected?

A main focus of the final session will likely be around closure and celebration for the group. Remember to leave ample time for closure. We often place great emphasis on the start of things, but not enough focus on the end. You may wish to refer to the appendix for exercises you can incorporate into the final session. You will want to leave space for individuals to reflect on what they have learned, and achieved, as well as share their thoughts and insights with other group members.

You will also want to set up any follow-up for the group. This may include final evaluations, and post-program group or individual calls.

Phase 5: Group Follow-Up (Optional)

Holding a group follow-up call two to six weeks after your last group coaching call is a great way to bring together the group members. It often serves as a prompt for group members to take action on the commitments set at the end of the process. This will give you an idea of the impact of the program beyond the immediate impact.

POSITIONING GROUP COACHING AS A SUPPORT IN ORGANIZATIONS

Coaches, leaders and human resources professionals are often curious as to how group coaching can be brought into the organizational context. In the corporate world, group coaching can be positioned in five ways:

1. as a standalone program to support individuals exploring common issues
2. as a follow-up to a current training initiative
3. as part of a learning design, positioned as a follow-on or way to sustain the conversation and support the transfer of learning
4. integrating a coaching approach into traditional training, presentations and workshops
5. as a standalone to facilitate conversation across the silos that exist within an organization

This section of the chapter explores these five ways and provides different examples.

1. As a Standalone Program to Support Individuals Exploring Common Issues

Some examples would be new managers, or work/life issues. The standalone program has the advantages of being able to bring together individuals from across the organization and foster conversation.

In *Effective Group Coaching*, Maureen Clarke was spotlighted for her group coaching work around work/life balance. Post-program results from the eight-week phone-based work/life program in the pharmaceutical field indicated the following results for participants:

- 84 percent felt their productivity had increased.
- 86 percent agreed that they had developed concrete strategies to balance work and personal lives.
- The number of participants who felt they had the opportunity during the previous two months to perform their jobs without work/life conflict increased by 25%.

There were the following impacts on stress indicators:

- 28 percent increase in healthy habits
- 22 percent decrease in overall stress
- 14 percent increase in psychological wellbeing

As I wrote, "Clarke notes that the changes identified with group coaching clients translate to an average annual savings of $6,000 per employee. This amount was calculated using the Johnson and Johnson formula that determines a saving of more than $4 for every $1 spent on work-family programs."[7]

2. As a Follow-Up to a Current Training Initiative

A group coaching call or series of calls can be held as follow-ups to an already established training program. Many times training is left in the classroom, with little or no follow-up after the workshop. A group call held several weeks after a workshop can provide an opportunity for participants to refocus on what they have learned, what they are using and what changes they may need to make. These calls can also provide an opportunity for the creation of a list of best practices.

---

[7] Britton, *Effective Group Coaching*, 41, 42.

Benefits of adding a group coaching component to an existing training initiative is that this taps into something which is established, and may not be having the optimum impact. Group coaching has a main benefit of supporting the transfer of learning from the training process.

Here is what Shana Montesol notes about her experience in offering group coaching as a follow-up to a current training initiative:

> Organizations can leverage the power of group coaching to increase the return on their training investments. I regularly facilitate a 2.5-day soft-skills training at an international organization (on topics such as effective workplace communication, how to manage your boss, and how to work cross-culturally). Part of the design of the program is a two-hour group coaching session that takes place three months after the 2.5-day workshop is completed. It's a great chance for the participants to cement their learning, revisit the course content and be coached in areas where they have gotten stuck. It's also an important additional data point in terms of evaluation. Trainings often end with a written evaluation form, but the true test of an effective learning experience is whether skills are applied outside the classroom. This group coaching session is a way to get a glimpse into that.

3. As Part of a Learning Design, Positioned as a Follow-On or Way to Sustain the Conversation and Support the Transfer of Learning

A third way coaches may position the work is as part of a new learning design, as a way to sustain the conversation and support the transfer of learning. My Field Journal highlights some work I did that incorporated a group coaching process to sustain the transfer of learning: the Coaching and Mentoring Skills Training Program.

Field Journal: The Coaching and Mentoring Skills Training Program

An international organization operating in West and Central Africa wanted to boost internal capacity by developing and enhancing their internal coaching and mentoring skills. The HR team brought together 25 staff members, representing 21 offices across West and Central Africa, for a five-day Coaching and Mentoring Skills ("Train the Trainer") Program. My company, Potentials Realized, was engaged to custom-design and deliver the five-day training in Senegal, West Africa.

The training and materials were provided in French and English, focusing on skill acquisition and practice of foundational and advanced coaching and mentoring skills. Activities also focused on the adaptation of the skills and tools for their own program contexts. New coaches returned back with the task to share these skills with their colleagues at the country office (national) level, in addition to designing their own internal coaching and mentoring programs as appropriate for their local-level realities.

We knew that one of the key challenges field-level personnel would face would be the transfer of skills, as well as the adaptation of the skills for their local contexts. In addition to having each individual partner up with another coach, we also put in the design of the initial program five months of follow-up group coaching, and virtual training support.

During the five months that followed the training, country office teams were supported with twice-a-month group coaching calls and two virtual training sessions. The group coaching calls were designed to check in on progress, share experiences among the participants and identify common bottlenecks as well as successes. Throughout this five-month period, the new coaches designed and rolled out initial educational sessions on coaching with their country office teams and identified local coaches to be trained.

Impact

- 25 staff trained in coaching and mentoring skills, becoming "internal coach resource persons"
- 21 country offices impacted
- Dozens of staff members coached and mentored as a result of the training

Key Challenges with the Project

Diversity of local-level realities: Working across 21 countries was a key challenge. Each country office team had its own unique cultural context and organizational context. The adaptations needed to the coaching process

(Continued)

became a key part of our discussions during the in-person training and throughout the entire project. Adaptations were widely encouraged.

Ensuring that all participants could access the group coaching calls: Initially it was suggested that we use WebEx as a platform for all the follow-up conversations and training by HR. We recommended going low-tech with a regular bridge line to reduce technical challenges to getting on the line. Even this posed challenges. Calls were recorded and those not able to attend were encouraged to let the group know about their progress and questions.

Rotational nature of posts: Each participant was in the role for only a fixed amount of time. This necessitated that conversation from day 1 focused on transfer of skills to others within the office.

The local HR person who participated in the training became an important resource person in taking this work forward.

4. Integrating a Coaching Approach into Your Training and Workshops

A fourth way to infuse group coaching may be to bring a coaching approach into your training and workshops. As many coaches who were interviewed indicated across the team and group coaching realms, organizations and individuals may not be looking for a pure group or team coaching process. We can, however, integrate more of a coaching approach into the work we do in a training or workshop environment. Refer to coach Lynda Monk's Voices from the Field about integrating a coaching approach into your training and workshops.

Voices from the Field: Tips for a Coaching Approach to Training and Workshops, by Lynda Monk, CPCC

I offer a coach approach to everything that I do—whether I am offering a group coaching program, speaking at an event, facilitating a wellness workshop within a workplace or guiding a virtual journaling retreat. I am often integrating a blend of coaching, facilitation and training all at once. It is this integrative blend that I consider to be at the heart of this coach approach to my work.

As a registered social worker, I have been facilitating training workshops for many years across a wide range of topics related to the health, well-being and burnout prevention needs of "helping professionals," including social workers, counselors, healthcare providers and caregivers. That being said, my work really evolved and shifted when I became a certified coach. I started to see my work in a whole new way and this began informing both my program development and facilitation.

My workshops and programs seemed to take on a whole new life and became infused with coaching elements. I learned to "dance in the moment," for example, and allow content-driven curricula to be replaced with a much more process-oriented coaching style that created the space for participants to co-create the agenda for the learning and our time together.

Three tips for new coaches who are embarking on offering a coach approach to workshops:

1. Create a clear focus for your event—have an agenda, design your session—and be open to having it shift and flow as a result of the intentions and goals of your clients/participants. This allows for a number of key coaching elements to emerge:
   a. Client owns/contributes to the agenda.
   b. Dance in the moment, allowing the heart of the group to appear.
   c. Listen deeply to what wants/needs to emerge in the group.
   d. Powerful questions become the foundation to learning, new insights, growth and change.
2. Let clients know that the event will be highly interactive—training and workshops with a coach approach are less about transferring knowledge (though this is still part of it) and more about creating transformative learning experiences.
3. Develop what I call "principles for success" to help give your event the tone you desire. For example, here are the principles for success for my Journaling to Heal Stress workshop that I have offered to a number of teams and working groups in various human and social service organizations:
   a. Compassion for self and others
   b. Confidentiality
   c. Open heart/open mind
   d. Focus on what matters
   e. Contribute your thinking
   f. Listen for deeper insights and learning
   g. Give yourself permission to play, be curious, and be fully present

(*Continued*)

As a registered social worker and life coach, I always work from a whole-person perspective wherein I am mindful of the multiple dimensions of well-being, including the physical (body), psychological (mind), emotional (heart) and spiritual (spirit) aspects that allow for healing and growth for individuals in the group. I also honor a person-in-environment model of health, wellness and personal transformation—meaning that the context of peoples' lives and work environments impact who they are and how they are doing. We must look at the whole to understand the parts of a situation.

I love bringing a coach approach to my work with individuals, groups, teams and organizations. This work is values based, respectful, inspiring and always collaborative in nature. I am always asking myself this question: "How can I set this up so that we can be together honestly and with integrity to advance the individual goals and shared agendas that are present?"

Lynda Monk, CPCC, CreativeWellness.com

5. As a Standalone Initiative to Facilitate Conversations across the Silos that Exist within an Organization

In today's era of rapid change, silos continue to be prevalent challenges in organizations. Group coaching can be positioned as a modality to start connecting employees from across different departments and divisions. By starting to build connection and conversation between people from different parts of the organization, individuals start forming relationships. It is these relationships that can start opening doors or being resources in solving more complex issues, or working across distance.

Geographically siloed and departmentally siloed organizations may wish to consider how group coaching could start to build greater connection and cross-fertilization in change initiatives, planning and other endeavors.

This chapter explored several foundational topics to group coaching including process components of any group coaching program, as well as typical components of any group (and team) coaching conversation. We also looked at how group coaching can be positioned in organizations. You are invited to review the chapter with the end-of-chapter questions in mind.

The book is accompanied by a digital chapter on Group Coaching in Action at www.groupcoachingessentials.com. In it, we explore different ways coaches may choose to work within the group coaching process, and successes and challenges in group coaching. We also explore four separate Voices from the Field, illustrating the range of this work with public groups, organizational groups, in person and with virtual groups.

End-of-Chapter Questions

What do you want your group coaching programs to look like?
What do you want to incorporate at each stage of the group coaching process?
If you work with organizations, how do you want to position group coaching?

CHAPTER 6

TEAM COACHING FOUNDATIONS

Teams outperform individuals acting alone or in large organizational groupings, especially when performance requires multiple skills, judgements and experiences.
—Jon Katzenbach and Douglas Smith[1]

This chapter explores the foundations of team coaching. We will explore:

- What team coaching is
- Who is involved and what team coaching is all about
- The types of issues that may get incorporated into our work as coaches
- The team coaching process
- Why team coaching can fail

Team coaching is related to, but distinct from, the fields of process facilitation and team building. Reflect back to the discussion of the continuum in Chapter 2 and reflect on where you would place these related domains.

Foundational to team coaching are these characteristics:

- **Conversationally based**.
- **Sustained conversation**: typically coaching takes place over multiple touch points.

---

[1] Jon Katzenbach and Douglas Smith, *The Wisdom of Teams: Creating the High-Performance Organization* (New York: HarperCollins, 2003), 9.

- Incorporates strengths work, key focus areas, goal setting and action planning.
- Establishes, and revisits, team **agreements**. These team agreements become accepted ways for the team to operate.
- May include some **skill development** so teams can achieve their goals or become more effective. For example, teams may struggle in having difficult conversations. Providing teams with a model, and some skill practice in this area, can be useful.
- Optimally focused on **relationships and results**.
- Focused on outcomes including **action and accountability**.
- **Deepened awareness** around issues facing the team in the interpersonal and productivity realms.

As we saw in Chapter 1, in a team coaching process all members become mutually accountable for the goals, work plan and results of the team. This includes both the leader and team. Hawkins writes that to be "mutually accountable" is to "ensure that the responsibility with the team is not just left with the nominal team leader, but is collectively held and all team members are actively held accountable for their colleagues."[2] This mutual accountability is often a foundational premise of team coaching work. We explore one specific activity, entitled "Team Action Planning," at the end of Team Coaching in Action, a digital chapter at www.group coachingessentials.com.

A major question for coaches and clients alike is, "What exactly does team coaching entail?" Note how the following definitions of team coaching are varied:

- ". . . regular meetings between a leadership team and a trained facilitator, designed to produce enhanced performance and/or positive changes in business behavior in a limited time frame. . . . The intent of team coaching is the same as with an individual: to guide the team to realizations about their behavior or performance, to enable them to make their own improvements and to make those changes sustainable over time."[3]
- "Team coaching is coaching a team to achieve a common goal, paying attention to both individual performance and to group collaboration and performance."[4]
- "High performance team coaching is a comprehensive and systemic approach to support a team to maximize their collective talent and resources to effectively accomplish the work of the team."[5]

---

[2] Hawkins, *Leadership Team Coaching*, 84.
[3] The 7th Annual 2012 Executive Coaching Survey from Sherpa Coaching.
[4] Thornton, *Group and Team*, 22.
[5] Catherine Carr and Jacqueline Peters, "The Experience and Impact of Team Coaching: A Dual Case Study," Dissertation for Doctor of Philosophy, Middlesex University, London, 2012. Used with permission.

In his book *Leadership Team Coaching*, Peter Hawkins distinguishes between many different forms of team engagements, and offers this description of systemic team coaching: "Systemic team coaching is a process by which a team coach works with the whole team, both when they are together and when they are apart, in order to help them improve both their collective performance, and how they work together, and how they develop their collective leadership to more effectively engage with all their key stakeholder groups to jointly transform the wider business."

Similar to group coaching, it is important for the team coach to co-design with the team and other players, such as sponsors, what type of team coaching engagement is going to be of greatest support for the team, and how it interfaces with other initiatives in the organization.

As Douglas Riddle writes, "Good team coaching also helps the group take charge of their key team functions: setting direction, creating alignment throughout the organization, and building the commitment of everyone needed to accomplish organizational objectives."[6]

As we will see through this chapter and the next, team coaching practically is rolling out in many different ways, and can incorporate a variety of activities, ranging from working with a small team subset of three or four members to a larger virtual team grouping. Team coaching engagements may range from the more traditional six-month model[7] to a series of intensive, virtual touch points.

Coaches will find the Team Coaching Process outline included in this chapter a useful guide regardless of the length of engagement. Most, if not all, team coaching engagements will incorporate similar processes or components.

Another key distinction that occurs in many team coaching engagements is the fact that this work is often led by more than one team coach. The topic of co-facilitation is covered in Chapter 11.

WHO IS INVOLVED WITH TEAM COACHING?

As team coaching continues to evolve, our work is being expanded out to increasing diverse teams.

Common types of teams coaches may be called on to work with include:

- Project teams
- Matrixed teams

---

[6] Riddle, *Senior Leadership Team Coaching*, 5.

[7] Phil Sandahl, "TCI Grads: Trends and Opportunities," webinar, Team Coaching International, November 7, 2012.

- Teams with new leaders
- Teams after a merger and acquisition (M&A)
- Teams during the organizational change process or during downsizing
- Global teams
- Virtual teams

Each one of these types of teams has its own unique nature and challenges.

Project teams: Project teams come together for the spn of a project, either for the whole or during part of the project cycle. Team members are likely from different backgrounds and may be supported through matrix management structure. As a coach you will want to consider who is involved in the "coaching" and how team members share learning and tools with others in their matrix.

Teams with new leaders: These are increasingly common in today's environment. Teams with new leaders may benefit from the support of a team coach in working together to identify strengths and gaps within the team, to set a new vision for their work together, or to come up with a team contract or a standardized set of agreements of how to work together. Teams with new leaders may also benefit from exploring the strengths of each individual member of the team.

Global and virtual teams: These provide unique challenges, as well as opportunities. As a former global virtual team leader myself, I've seen that some of the key issues global and/or virtual teams may want to explore include synergies and differences due to position, location or culture. This is on top of the standard layers of a standard team coaching conversation. Given their geographic scope, what is essential for these virtual teams is an opportunity for team members to get to know each other and to create touch points for people to connect with—anchors that they can latch onto and evolve in their own ways. Face-to-face meetings, even if only once a year, help to develop understanding and relationships at a deeper level, which is invaluable in the changing business environment. As Sharon Miller states, "Business is done through relationships." Creating these bonds and connections is critical when most, if not all, your work will be by phone and/or Web.

Teams after a merger and acquisition: Teams forming after a merger and acquisition (M&A) are often challenged by different cultures—sometimes those that conflict. In working with these teams, coaches may wish to place an emphasis on exploration of the multiple perspectives at play, the creation of shared values, and envisioning a new and common future. There is likely a need for team members to undertake reflection on what has been lost, and have the space to consider and dream about what is possible.

Teams in an organizational change process or after downsizing: Increasingly common in today's environment are teams that are made up of "survivors" following organizational change or downsizing. In fact many of these members may have been part of several rounds of cuts. In addition to being enveloped by doing more with less, there may be significant trust issues at play.

Questions to Consider

What are the types of teams you are working with/want to work with?
What will be some of the key issues they may want attention around?

Figure 6.1: The Coaching Approach with the Team as a System or a Collective of Individuals

Team as an Individual

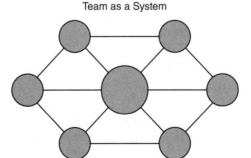

Team as a System

Regardless of what type of team you are working with, a key consideration for team coaches is to identify *how* you are working with the entity. Is the team coach working with the team as a system, or is the team coach working to support the development and growth of each individual member within the team context? In working with the team as a system, imagine a spider's web. A change in one part of the web will have impact in another. In coaching the team as a system, the focus is on making explicit and building onto these webs of relationships and results.

Knowing that we are working with the team as a system is critical, as it will impact:

- The design of the work we undertake.
- How we structure conversations. In working with a team as a system the focus is on the web of relationships among the group members.
- Who else we may bring in to support the coaching process. Part of the stance of our work may be around transparency. Coaches can run into some ethical gray areas if they are working with one or more member of the team (for example, the leader), as well as coaching the entire team, particularly when information is divulged about specific individuals. This is where an additional coach who works with individual group members may be of value. It should be considered on a case-by-case basis.

Not every coach will work with the team as a system. Coaches may work with the team to boost individual as well as collective capabilities. Working with a team by building individual capabilities may be more prevalent when coaches are engaged for shorter periods of time.

FOCI OF TEAM COACHING

Team coaching processes should be as holistic as possible. Most engagements will focus on the interpersonal, the relationships within the team, as well as the performance, business or productivity, measures. With the coaches interviewed it was very common to hear them speak about the importance of both relationships as well as results. This is evident in some of the leading assessments for team coaching, such as Team Coaching International's focus on 14 productivity and positivity strengths in the Team Diagnostic assessment. The assessment helps a team measure its strengths in the realms of both productivity and positivity. A case study is included in the Team Coaching in Action digital chapter (www.groupcoaching essentials.com) from Team Coaching International.

The team coaching process needs to factor in team design, structures and business needs for maximum results. As Dr. Catherine Carr and Dr. Jacqueline Peters state:

> Working only on interpersonal team dynamics can be for naught if elements such as having the right talent, team size, roles and responsibilities, alignment of values, purpose, goals, and working agreements are not in place. It's a little like pouring water into a hole in the sand. Because the sand structure is not solid, the water doesn't stay in the hole for long. That's what our research showed as did Hackman and Wageman's team effectiveness studies and Beckhard's earlier model called the GRPI (goals, roles and responsibilities, processes and procedures, and interpersonal relationships). Hackman uses an effective analogy. He says that working with teams is equivalent to a space rocket launch—once it leaves the ground, the best you can do is make minor adjustments to the trajectory. It is far more powerful to design the rocket well to begin with.

As Carr and Peters continue, Ruth Wageman's research revealed six conditions for team effectiveness, comprised of three essential elements and three enabling conditions (summarized in Table 6.1):

Table 6.1: Six Conditions for Leadership Team Effectiveness[8]

Essential Elements	Enabling Conditions
1. Real team, defined as having clear boundaries, interdependent goals, and clarity of membership (who's on the team)	4. Solid team structure including clear roles and responsibilities, and working agreements or norms
2. Compelling direction with a purpose	5. Supportive organizational context (e.g., the team has, or will have, access to the information and resources they need)
3. The right people on the team; all team members add value to the team and have the skills and knowledge to achieve the purpose	6. Competent team coaching (delivered by a person from inside or outside of the team)

1. Is it a real team with clear membership and interdependencies?
2. Is there a compelling purpose and direction? Is the purpose clear, consequential and challenging?

---

[8] Adapted from Ruth Wageman, et al. (2008), "Senior Leadership Teams: What it Takes to Make Them Great," quoted in Catherine Carr and Jacqueline Peters, "The Experience and Impact of Team Coaching." Used with permission.

3. Do we have the right talent to deliver on the purpose with the requisite leadership, functional or technical skills, and teaming skills?
4. Do we have a solid structure? This includes clear roles and responsibilities, accountabilities, and levels of authority, etc. People also need to be explicit about how to work together effectively (e.g., working agreements/norms).
5. Do the organizational context and resources support the effective functioning of the team? Does the team have sufficient time, money, people and information? This can also include the policies and procedures that enable the team to perform.
6. Is there access to competent team coaching from someone inside or outside of the organization?

In designing team coaching interventions coaches will find these six factors useful to keep in mind. The six factors are also a discussion point to share with the team. David Clutterbuck indicates that team effectiveness issues include decision quality, innovation, psychological safety, communication about task, using skills and knowledge, mutual support, managing interfaces outside the team, and using diversity.[9]

As Catherine Carr and Jacqueline Peters note, "Team coaches need to make sure that we are not only dealing with symptoms but getting to the root cause. Many team interventions have typically had poor results—team members leave with a 'feel good' quality but it does not create sustained performance." Consideration of these six conditions will help to enhance sustainability of the work undertaken.

WHAT TYPES OF ISSUES ARE IMPORTANT IN TEAM COACHING?

"High performing teams keep goals at the top and never lose sight."
                                                          —Leslie Bendaly[10]

It is the behavioral agreements, coupled with goal setting, that can bring some of the greatest benefits to teams. Team coaches will find themselves working around a variety of topic areas, grounded by specific goals for the team. Team coaches provide support for these new behaviors over time.

---

[9] Clutterbuck, *Coaching the Team at Work*, 125.

[10] Leslie Bendaly and Nicole Bendaly, *Improving Healthcare Team Performance: The 7 Requirements for Excellence in Patient Care* (Toronto: John Wiley & Sons, 2012), 43.

Team coaches may not be involved only in coaching. There may be a need for some KSA (knowledge, skills and ability) development on the part of teams. Michael Stevens and Michael Campion's work identified five KSA areas for team-work.[11]

Three interpersonal KSAs include

- **Conflict resolution:** The ability for a team to resolve conflict, and the skills associated with this.
- **Collaborative problem solving:** The ability for a team to problem solve collaboratively.
- **Communication:** Knowledge, skills and abilities in the area of communication.

Two self-management KSAs include

- **Goal setting and performance management:** Knowledge, skills and abilities in setting goals and managing performance.
- **Planning and task coordination:** Knowledge, skills and abilities to support planning as well as co-ordination of the work, or tasks, that need to happen.

It is likely that team members may need support in establishing a common framework, and developing skills in any one of these five areas.

Some common team coaching focus areas may include:

- Priorities
- Roles within the team
- Styles (leadership, communication, conflict)
- Vision (at the team, individual, organizational levels)
- Values (at the team, individual, organizational levels)
- Strengths
- Communication(ranging from meeting management to styles to feedback and virtual team issues)
- Difficult conversations

---

[11] Michael J. Stevens and Michael A. Campion, "The Knowledge, Skills and Ability Requirements for Team Work: Implications for HR Management," *Journal of Management* 20, no. 2 (1994): 503–530.

- Feedback
- Trust and respect
- Conflict (styles, navigating conflict)
- Working synergistically and working across differences
- Goal setting and action planning
- Alignment of goals, roles, etc.

The Team Coaching in Action digital chapter (www.groupcoachingessentials .com) and the appendix provide a number of illustrations of how team coaches are working around these issues, as well as descriptions of how some activities can be facilitated.

THE VALUE OF A TEAM COACH

In today's era of cost cutting, the conversation around the value add of team coaching is critical. What do team coaches bring to the table that the team cannot do for themselves?

In today's busy world of doing more with less, with little space to pause and reflect, the team coaching process can provide teams with:

Space for the team to pause and reflect: In today's busy environment it is very easy to let reflection moments become swept away by immediate issues. A team coach sometimes provides the only reason why teams will stop: "We know that they are coming in" or "We know that we have scheduled it."

Prioritizing the need for focus: By bringing in team coaches (whether internal or external), there is now pressure to make this a priority. It is not an issue that can slide as easily as if the leader or team members were tasked with this.

A non-judgmental sounding board/space for dialogue: Coaches provide the non-judgmental sounding board and space. It may be the only safe place for team members to "air their dirty laundry." The confidential nature of the conversation can help to surface the "elephants in the room." One team I worked with indicated that they had failed to address the elephant for two years because they did not feel safe in divulging it, nor did they have a confidential forum in which to raise it. Once the issue was raised it enabled the team to make a significant change in terms of the types of difficult issues they were communicating and addressing.

Ability to mirror back to the team what is going on: Coaching provides an opportunity for the team to see itself in the mirror. What do they notice about how communication happens, or persistent patterns play out day after day?

Mirroring provides an opportunity to really "see" what is happening in the team, its processes and its relationships.

Strong focus on the outcome: Team coaching holds the space for the team to create a deep focus on the issues that are important for the team, as well as identify key outcome measures. *What is important to us? What will the outcome be? What will success look like?*

Accountability focus: One of the greatest benefits I hear from team coaching clients is that it holds the entire team responsible for taking the action, and making the changes they have committed to over time, through sustained conversation and check-ins. If the team has operated in a culture of creating action plans but not following through, having an external accountability partner such as a coach can have a big impact.

Voices from the Field: Team Effectiveness

Jacqueline Peters and Catherine Carr recently completed their doctorates in the area of team effectiveness and coaching. I asked them, "What's really important with team coaching?" Here's what they said:

> A critical aspect of team coaching is the ability to engage leaders in the ongoing communication and work required for the team to be successful. Team coaching is like fitness. We know it's not a one-shot deal but a lot of people fall off their fitness schedules and commitments when they are self-directed. Similar to creating health and fitness, our bodies don't necessarily look different from just one or two days of workouts. It takes time. A key challenge in the team coaching process is how to keep people moving and engaged in the team development journey throughout the time frame required to deliver on their compelling direction and goals. The coach helps to build capacity and helps the team members stay connected to their direction and goals by focusing not just internally, but also on external stakeholders' needs and feedback, as this is who relies on the team's work. Too many coaches focus only on interpersonal skills and not enough on stakeholder requirements. This includes attention to the required business outcomes and outputs, and the success measures that help team members know how they are doing along the way.

(Continued)

Key questions for team coaches to ask leaders include: "Are you getting the results you want to get?" and "Are you stepping up to what it will take for you to be a top performing team now and also in a year's time? Would your stakeholders agree?"

Everyone can lead from where they are. Team coaching is really about building leadership capacity so that every member can effectively contribute to the team's success. Sometimes it is about the relational element too—we know from the Gallup Q12 Survey that having a best friend, or someone you can personally count on at work, is key to engagement. We also know from the literature and our own research that team coaching helps create more openness, safety, trust and connection so that the team interacts more effectively and achieves better results.

Another key element of team coaching that has been underused is peer coaching. It is most effective if team members can find a way to link up their individual goals with the team goals. Peer coaching helps team members effectively do their day-to-day work in service of these goals and creates team camaraderie. This is strongly supported by recent research by the Corporate Executive Board company, which lists peer coaching as an increasingly important driver of employee engagement.

The role of the team coach is to catalyze performance and also work on the structure within which the team can develop. If team coaches don't address the structure, there is risk of failure for the team—it's like treating only the symptoms, not the causes of team ineffectiveness or team dysfunction. To be clear, it's not that interpersonal dynamics are not important. In fact, we think that team safety and trust are so critical that we put this concept in the center of our newly developed High Performance Team Coaching system. When we talk about structure in the team coaching context, it means ensuring that teams identify the right organizational structure, reporting relationships and explicit working agreements that guide their team interactions.

We found in our research that the discussions about working agreements were critical to set the stage for team performance, and team coaching sessions were great opportunities to check in with the team to see if they were following the agreements. If they were not, we could foster a discussion about what was getting in the way. We provided an opportunity for the team members to hold themselves accountable and make refinements to their agreements if needs. Clear working agreements can provide a safe way to support a team to delve into the "elephants in the room" and help people to name them. It is during these tricky discussions and in the implementation of the working agreements that the role of the team leader becomes critical. The leader needs to walk their talk and show support for the team coaching and chosen team directions.

The team coach models new behaviors, such as responding with clear listening and checking for understanding. The coach also observes the team as a whole and can support members to see things they don't because they are immersed in the system being observed. The team and the leader may not be used to this level of support or accountability. During ongoing team coaching sessions, the team coach supports the team to adjust to new norms, and have genuine and effective conversations, ensures inclusivity and diverse views, invites innovative ideas and ensures reflective learning processes. This allows the team members to experience and see a role model that allows them to eventually develop and take on the coaching themselves within the team.

In creating successful team coaching engagements it is really important to talk about what team coaching is and what team coaching is not. The team coach is not a business advisor, a counselor, a replacement for the leader or a group therapist. The team coach is a resource and support to the team who strengthens and empowers members to do their own work, not do it for them.

Team coaching provides an opportunity for a team to grow and perform at a whole new level. Most team members don't sit back and look at lessons learned or consider their team from a meta-perspective. Team coaching is exciting and progressive work, although demanding when done well. In our research on team coaching, the teams we worked with saw sustained changed one year later, emphasizing that team coaching can make a substantive difference to team performance.

Dr. Catherine Carr and Dr. Jacqueline Peters

SKILLS FOR MASTERFUL TEAM COACHES

Masterful team coaches should continue to leverage all the skills of a masterful group coach, in addition to utilizing the coaching skills of:

- **Mirroring:** Reflecting back to the team what you notice, patterns and roles.
- **Listening:** Listening for what is said and what is not said. What's the elephant in the room that everyone is skirting?
- **Surfacing:** Pointing out what's not being said or the elephant in the room.
- **Commitments:** Leaving time for the team to provide a check-in and check-out around their commitments, individually and collectively.
- **The ability to "fade in and fade out":** In a team coaching process, masterful team coaches are able to fade back and let the team have the dialogue.
- **Action planning:** Action planning in the team coaching process may include collective and individual action plans. It is important to leave sufficient time to identify significant individual and team action plan items. Are they SMART-E (Specific, Measurable, Achievable, Realistic, Timebound and Exciting) for everyone?
- **Noticing the layers:** In a team coaching process, just like in a group coaching process, coaches must become adept at picking up what's happening at the different layers of the experience. This includes reading the emotional field or energy of a group, noticing body language, observing how team members relate, and groupings that form, as well as picking up the culture of the team.
- **Understanding the context** and business environment the team operates within.

Douglas Riddle identifies the following key skills for team coaches:[12]

1. The ability to read in the moment the multiple levels of dynamic occurring in the team and raise only the productive elements to the surface for conscious consideration.
2. An awareness of power and its movement within groups and comfort at intervening to influence the ways power is used in the group. Who has what kinds of power and how are they using it?
3. An ability to put into simple, jargon-less language what is observed and the stature to raise any issue with the team or its members at the right moment.

---

[12] Riddle, *Senior Leadership Team Coaching*, 6.

Figure 6.2: The Team Coaching Process

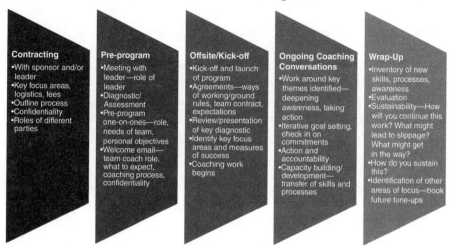

Contracting	Pre-program	Offsite/Kick-off	Ongoing Coaching Conversations	Wrap-Up
•With sponsor and/or leader •Key focus areas, logistics, fees •Outline process •Confidentiality •Roles of different parties	•Meeting with leader—role of leader •Diagnostic/Assessment •Pre-program one-on-ones—role, needs of team, personal objectives •Welcome email—team coach role, what to expect, coaching process, confidentiality	•Kick-off and launch of program •Agreements—ways of working/ground rules, team contract, expectations •Review/presentation of key diagnostic •Identify key focus areas and measures of success •Coaching work begins	•Work around key themes identified—deepening awareness, taking action •Iterative goal setting, check in on commitments •Action and accountability •Capacity building/development—transfer of skills and processes	•Inventory of new skills, processes, awareness •Evaluation •Sustainability—How will you continue this work? What might lead to slippage? What might get in the way? •How do you sustain this? •Identification of other areas of focus—book future tune-ups

4. A firm grasp of the ethical and practical dangers of working with a group and the individuals on it.

5. A keen sense of business acumen, of how businesses make money. Coaches gain the trust of client leadership teams because they know group and team process, but more because they understand the business of that leadership team.

THE TEAM COACHING PROCESS

Stages of a Team Coaching Process

In general, there are five main stages of a team coaching conversation. The stages will be very similar regardless of whether the process is held over one month, six months or a series of touch points over an extended period. The five stages, as illustrated in Figure 6.2, are:

1. Contracting
2. Pre-program
3. Offsite/kick-off
4. Ongoing coaching conversations
5. Wrap-up

Stage 1: Contracting

Team coaches will typically have been brought in by the leader, or by HR or a senior leader. At the contracting stage it is important to understand the context in which the coaching will occur and to ensure that an understanding of what team coaching is, and is not, is understood at the macro level.

Table 6.2 offers a basic overview of what team coaching is and is not.

During the contracting stage, key areas that are discussed and negotiated are:

- Logistics and fees
- Confidentiality
- Roles of the different parties (sponsor, HR, team leader, team members, coach)
- Exploration of the link to the wider processes going on in the organization

An understanding of key corporate goals and priorities, as well as the culture in which the team coaching is taking place, are important for the coach, or

Table 6.2: What Team Coaching Is and Is Not

What Team Coaching Is	What Team Coaching Is Not
Conversationally grounded	Only experiential processes such as high rope courses or trust falls
Strengths-based	Remedial in nature, trying to fix what's wrong
Focused on goals, alignment, action	A band-aid solution
Mutual accountability structure	Up to the leader or just one person to implement
Co-created and owned by the team	Imposed on the team
About the entire team	About just one member of the team
One of several solutions to support the team	Therapeutic in nature or business advising
Focused on relationships and results	Only about results or relationships
Focused on goals and the business	Disconnected from the work you do every day
Sustained: a process of change that happens over time	A one-off intervention

coaches, to understand. *Team coaching sometimes fails because of the context in which the team operates.* For example, if the organization is naturally hierarchical, some of the changes the team is striving to make in terms of each team member having an equal voice may not be sustainable. Likewise, if the culture of an organization rewards individual performers, what impact will this have as the team moves to more of a team-based performance approach? Will the compensation structure hold back the impact of the changes the team is making? These are real considerations for coaches to look at and explore with sponsors. The sponsors may or may not have influence over these more "systemic" issues internally, but should be aware of the impact and potential limitations to the overall success of the work with the team.

Confidentiality is important to discuss with sponsors as well. In a team coaching process the "client" is the team. As such, in terms of reporting that may be required, the coach will only be able to validate the number of meetings that have taken place but not the specific content areas. This is up to team members to share. Some teams may opt to make the theme areas they are working on public. For example, the team members may give approval to share with sponsors that they are exploring four topics over the course of their work including a focus on styles (learning, communication), strengths, holding difficult conversations and feedback. This does not mean that the specific content of the coaching conversations are made public. Only the theme areas become information for the public domain.

Stage 2: Pre-program

Once the coach has been engaged, the following activities are recommended pre-program:

- Meetings and discussion with the team leader
- Welcome email or initial presentation
- Pre-program one-on-ones with team members (if appropriate—likely if engagements are short, and not working with the team as a system)
- Deployment of an assessment

During the pre-program stage, coaches will want to meet with the team leader to discuss what he or she can expect from the team coaching process, and what is going to be required of him or her as the leader.

The coach will also want to find out from the leader what the team priorities are at the organizational and team level, the context in which the team operates, plus any other key insights about the team that will help the members work together. It will also be useful for the coach or coaches to get an understanding of the workflow, and any peaks or crunch times during the program.

The team leader's engagement and willingness to participate as one of the many voices of the process is critical to success in any team coaching engagement. If the leader is only paying lip service to welcoming change this can be a barrier to the effectiveness of coaching.

Once you have met with the leader and discussed the "high-level" or "macro" team coaching process, a welcome email or initial presentation should also be circulated to the team, including information such as:

- Team coaching overview: outline of the process
- What to expect
- Who you are as a coach
- Coaching process: what coaching is, what it is not, what it will look like
- The importance of confidentiality
- A focus on the team, rather than on the individual members (if team systems coaching) or a focus on the team and the individual (if team coaching taking a non-systems approach)

As we have discussed earlier, it is important for coaches to establish trust and a relationship with the team members as soon as possible. Pre-program one-on-ones may be held with the individual team members as well, if appropriate. This may be the case if the intervention is short, and the coach is not working with the team as a system. Coaches who are utilizing a systems approach may not undertake the pre-program one-on-ones, especially if they want to ensure transparency within the system (the entire team).

If coaches are not taking a systems approach to their work, pre-program calls with each member are *invaluable* in getting a high-level understanding. The conversations can allow the coach to understand the different roles and history within the team, the needs as seen from different perspectives, and the personal objectives and how they link to the larger teamwork. Holding these individual one-on-one meetings can provide high impact if you are only working with a team for a short time. It can allow for many of the key issues to percolate up, which are not often directly addressed in contracting. Use intuition and curiosity to pick up on threads that surface. With one team I worked with, it became apparent throughout the one-on-one conversations that the key issue at hand was navigating conflict. This allowed for the topic of conflict to have a much stronger focus. (Refer to Chapter 8 for team coaching one-on-one questions.)

Deployment of an Assessment

In working with teams, assessments can be very useful in providing the team with a snapshot of where they are at, in terms of strengths, or styles, or other measures. Deployed at the start and possibly the end of the coaching process, the dialogue stimulated by an assessment can form the foundation of what the team coaching will look like. An assessment will unearth the themes of importance to the team, as well as providing data and possibly a visual for the team to consider. Assessments provide teams with a snapshot of where the team is at any given time. The data often becomes the starting point for the team, as members determine what the data means to them and their work.

There is a range of assessments to choose from including the DiSC, Team Coaching International's Team Diagnostic and others. Coaches will want to consider the purpose of the assessment and how it is related to what the team is focusing on.

Deployment of an assessment takes some time, and requires some logistical coordination. Coaches will want to work backward with the team and the assessment company to see the last date responses are due from team members so that the reporting can be ready for the launch of the team coaching process. Coaches will need to consider how much time that gives team members, keeping in mind annual leave and other scheduled events. Not providing team members sufficient time to complete the assessment can start the process off on the wrong foot.

When bringing in assessments to coaching with teams, it is important to position the assessment with discussion/communication around:

What the Assessment Is

What will the assessment be exploring and measuring? How will the assessment be used? Is it foundational to the coaching process? Will it provide value to each individual? To the team? To both?

How Long It Will Take to Complete

How long will team members need to block off to complete the assessment? If a person needs to stop, how will they be able to save the work and return to it?

(Continued)

Technical Support

If team members have challenges technically, who should they reach out to?

How Data Will Be Presented and Used

For example, will comments show up verbatim (word for word), with attribution, or as a listing with no names? Team members should be aware of how their responses will be used so that there are no surprises when seeing them presented.

As coaches we also need to make sure that everyone has sufficient time to undertake their own assessment. Inquire about those who might be impacted by vacation and other meetings.

Stage 3: Offsite/Kick-Off

The kick-off meeting is ideally held outside of the regular team context for privacy and focus. It is optimal when a kick-off meeting is followed by a series of team conversations. The initial offsite or kick-off meeting will likely include key components such as:

- Ways of working (ground rules).
- Getting to know you: e.g., personal logos, personal histories (Lencioni), visual deck (refer to appendix).
- Team agreements: what are the key behaviors valued and accepted by the team? Team agreements may happen at two levels: first, agreements for behavior at the offsite, and second, a general team contract or agreements the team will integrate into their everyday work.
- Presentation of the assessment.
- Action planning.

The team should be leaving the offsite with:

- **A set of team agreements** or a **team contract** that outlines specific behavioral agreements. These are agreements created by the team in terms of how they will operate going forward. This is important when issues such as gossip (endemic to teams) crop up; in order to move forward the team may need to adopt a more transparent communication pattern. The team may have an agreement to not gossip, and may also create a gesture or "alert" if team members slip into old patterns.

- **Key focus areas and goals** going forward.
- **Key commitments** they will undertake collectively and individually.
- An **action plan** to work with (refer to Team Action Planning in Chapter 8).
- A **schedule** of future team coaching conversations.

The length of this offsite visit may vary from half a day to two days, depending on the budget available. Longer offsites can incorporate additional work around vision, values, roles and possibly some skill development areas such as changing toxic communication patterns or navigating conflict, as well as other areas identified on the outcome of the assessment.

Ways of Working

Ways of working are key agreements for the offsite, or how the team wants to operate during the offsite. What are the components that will make the process work for the team? Some key agreements for the process may include:

- Start and end on time.
- Confidentiality.
- Focus and being present: really participating and focusing on the team; keeping phones, emails and other things that might distract away during the course of your work.
- Finding the "two percent truth" in each person's statements. This suggested agreement comes from the organization and relationship systems coaching training from the Center for Right Relationship. This way of working really helps a team to find common ground. It simply asks team members to consider, "What is the two percent that you can relate with?"

My experience with highly dysfunctional teams is that the Two Percent Truth Rule supports team members by helping them see common ground with a person to whom they may feel diametrically opposed. Asking team members to find the small piece they can align with or agree to in someone else's comment can open up the door for working across differences. Finding the two percent truth does not mean that you have to agree with each statement 100 percent; rather, it is finding the common ground.

Identification of Success Measures

One of the greatest challenges mentioned by team coaches, as well as being one of the findings of the latest 2012 Global Coaching Survey from the International Coach Federation, is around measurement. An enhanced focus on measurement in the work we undertake with teams is critical.

It will be useful for team coaches to start the conversation early with a team or organization around what measures of success will be for the initiative. This may occur at the first point of contact in terms of identification of success measures and how the team can track the data. Most coaches may already ask about success measures that can be tracked by a team, but these may not necessarily link into other organizational or industry measurements. The digital chapter, Team Coaching in Action at www.groupcoachingessentials.com, spotlights a case study from health care from Team Coaching International that was able to leverage industry measurements.

Presentation of the Assessment

In presenting the assessment results to the team, the coach should give team members an opportunity to reflect on it as well as have dialogue around it. I continue to find that taking a "higher level" overview using the questions below can be much more beneficial at the start than zooming in on the micro-details. Note that as coaches we are not there as psychologists or assessors. Assessments used in coaching provide an opportunity for the team/individual to gain more self-awareness.

In working with assessments as a coach you will want to look at:

- Presentation of the data and report
- Allowing the team to identify with the results
  - What's the story behind this?
  - What's significant about what you see?
  - What are the themes you notice?
  - What stands out?
  - How does this show up in your everyday work?
  - What are the priority areas you want to take forward?

The data from the assessment can provide key insights into the topics that need attention. For example, low scores in conflict may indicate the team's lack of skill and confidence in navigating conflict. The results of the assessment should provide an indication of where the team needs to, and wants to, focus their conversations. It may also point to some skill development and training need.

Part of this stage may also involve some discussion as to whether the assessment will be redeployed down the road, for example, at the six-month mark.

Stage 4: Ongoing Team Conversations

Ongoing team conversations provide an opportunity for the team to:

- Work around key themes identified, deepening awareness, taking action
- Undertake iterative goal setting, check in on commitments
- Focus on action and accountability
- Enact capacity building/development: transfer of skills and processes

It is likely that team coaches will work with the team on an ongoing basis, whether it is a couple of additional coaching sessions or a more extended series over a period such as six months. It is these ongoing team conversations that provide an opportunity for the team members to notice their own evolution and the way they are applying their skills.

These ongoing touch points also provide an opportunity to team members to acquire or brush up on skills, such as providing feedback or having a difficult conversation. This is where team coaching really moves into some related grounds such as training and facilitation. If a team is having challenges with conflict, it is likely that some skill development around managing conflict, team toxins, or phrases to avoid in communication is needed in addition to work around conflict styles.

Throughout these calls, the team and coaches will work around the goals and commitments originally set, and like most coaching processes, evolve these over time. The coach will also want to put an emphasis on *capacity building and capacity development*. Ask the team what support it needs to internalize these new skills and processes into their everyday work context. Continuing to ask about the structures the team is finding useful and how members are internalizing the commitments can support the capacity building process, and transfer of skills and insights.

It is important for coaches to be aware of the frequency of these touch points. It may not be possible for the team itself to physically meet for each and every conversation. Consideration may be given to hosting virtual calls supplemented by a couple more in-person, longer sessions. Chapter 7 goes into possible virtual options for coaches.

Stage 5: Wrap-Up

As in the individual coaching process, every team coaching process will come to an end. Key activities during the wrap-up stage will include:

- Taking stock: creating an inventory of new skills, processes, awareness developed.
- Possible redeployment and sharing of results to support the team in seeing how far they have moved.
- Identification of future areas of focus from the redeployment or evaluations. Book future tune-ups.
- Evaluation of the process.
- Sustainability: How do you sustain this? How will you continue this work? What might lead to slippage? What might get in the way?

Evaluation

Team coaches will want to consider the benefits of evaluation in both the short term and long term. Coaches may wish to refer to Chapter 2 for the four levels of evaluation as a quick introductory framework.

If measures have been set at the start of the team coaching process, ensure that end point measurement is undertaken. While it is still "fresh" it will also be useful for teams to identify any other areas of focus. This can be integrated into future team meetings, retreats or even into future team tune-ups.

For coaches who are interested in more of the process behind team coaching, you may wish to refer to Peter Hawkins' CID-CLEAR model outlined in *Leadership Team Coaching*, or David Clutterbuck's description in *Coaching the Team at Work*.

Team Coaching Challenges

Team coaching can be challenging even for experienced coaches, who bring a clear framework and masterful skills. Consider these examples:

Situation 1

A new team leader starts a position and is in charge of a team that works mostly virtually. They are in a high-stress environment. The team coaches are brought in to improve communication and build trust within the team. The initial assessment identifies very low levels of trust and very low levels of confidence with the team leader. This is in addition to indicators that the team is not very agile in navigating conflict or working across differences. Comments in the assessment specifically address the new leader's inability to manage the team. The six-month team coaching engagement works on issues of trust, working across differences, and co-leadership. Two weeks before the end of the coaching engagement the team leader announces that she is moving on to another position.

Situation 2

You are brought in to work with an executive team on a strategic planning session. You have also been asked to create a "get to know you" for a team spread across the country as well as in Europe. As you undertake pre-program calls with each team member you find out that one person is ready to resign and will not be at the offsite. The day of the offsite you find out that one other team member has resigned overnight. The team leader announces this to the team at the start of the day.

Question to Consider

In Situations 1 and 2 what would you do as the team coach?

WHY TEAM COACHING CAN FAIL

In addition to not incorporating Ruth Wageman's team effectiveness framework, team coaching can fail or be weakened for seven reasons, namely:

1. **The leader is not engaged or ready to open up for the process:** Team coaching can be an extremely transformational process. It requires at times that team leaders be ready for and open to significant changes on their team. For some leaders this may be very threatening. The team leader often is undertaking growth as well, alongside the team.

2. **There is a lack of trust among team members:** If team members do not trust each other, the coaching work may only scratch the surface. It may

take several months for team members to trust each other enough to open up, especially if the team has had a history of conflict or trust being broken. As mentioned earlier in Chapter 3, this is a significant issue team coaches will find themselves working around.

3. **There is a lack of equal engagement:** Coaching is a process that goes to the depth individuals want to engage around. If team members are not equally engaged or do not see the value and importance of the process, the work will remain at the surface level.

4. **The elephant does not get surfaced:** As mentioned earlier, a common challenge is that the "real issue" (the elephant) does not get surfaced in time.

5. **It is not sustained or long enough:** Team coaching is a process that takes place over time. Some of the new behavioral practices team members may be adopting will take time to integrate and become new habits. For example, dysfunctional teams may have a history of very toxic communication. John Gottman describes the "Four Horsemen of the Apocalypse," which can show up in any type of communication system (team, intimate relationship, family relationship). These four horsemen are criticism, contempt, defensiveness and stonewalling.[13] (These horsemen are further described in Chapter 9.)

6. **The team does not internalize the skills and processes into everyday work:** Key to successful team coaching is linking the discussions and learning back to the environment the team operates within. For example, how can the team adopt a list of ways of working to make team status meetings more effective? How can the team use new skills in holding difficult conversations, so that the emotional charge of difficult conversations is minimized?

7. **There is a lack of tie-in/linkage to other contextual issues that may be at play:** Team coaching initiatives will also fail if there is a lack of tie-in or linkage to other contextual issues that are impacting the team. This can range from compensation issues, to reporting requirements, to hierarchical structure of the organization, to siloed culture. If the structure of the organization or reporting does not support a team approach, the sustainability of this work is difficult. Coaches can benefit from professional development and skill development in related fields such as performance improvement, human resource management and

---

[13] John M. Gottman and Nan Silver, *The Seven Principles for Making Marriage Work* (New York: Three Rivers Press, 1999).

organizational development to learn more about these topics. Coaches should also be getting team leaders and team members to connect all conversations with their contexts.

ADDITIONAL TRICKY ISSUES IN TEAM COACHING

In addition to the tricky issues mentioned in Chapter 2, some additional tricky issues in team coaching can arise in these areas:

- Coaching the team and coaching each member
- The various styles at play

Coaching the Team and Coaching Each Member

The stance of this work by the coach is critical in determining how we work with the team, as a system or as a collection of individuals. If a coach is coaching the team, he or she should be careful about the gray ethical areas that can emerge if they are also coaching different members (leader or other). To get around this, the coach may want to engage a second coach to co-facilitate, or keep it completely separate by bringing in additional coaches to work individually with key members. A very practical ethical gaffe can emerge when statements are made in a one-on-one coaching conversation about other team members. If an agreement exists around transparency, and the coach is coaching an individual in the team, the coach will need to divulge the sensitive issues to the team, or have that team member divulge it. In an instance like this, a team member will likely hold back in saying it in the first place if they know that the coach is working with the entire system. It is much clearer, and less complicated, if an additional coach is brought in to do the individual coaching.

Various Styles at Play

The team context is made even more challenging by the various styles at play and the styles at work. Phil Sandahl of Team Coaching International advocates that team coaches may wish to add individual styles work into their own Team Diagnostic assessment process, using MBTI, DiSC or other. The enhancement of skills and awareness of individual team members of the merging of styles is very supportive to a team's ongoing functioning.

Douglas Riddle succinctly lists three areas that can "derail" team coaching.[14] These are:

1. If the coaching team is not adequately prepared.
2. If a coach cannot simultaneously challenge and support the team and its members, then the trust built on creating a sufficiently safe environment won't be available.
3. A coach or coaches who aren't clear about their role and the limits of their expertise will disrupt the effective functioning of the client's leadership team.

Question to Consider

What tricky issues might emerge in the context of your work with a team?

Key Important Issues to Keep in Mind with Team Coaching

Powerful Team Coaching Engagements Are Additive

They link into the processes, structures and work that is already ongoing in the team. We leave space for the conversations had in an offsite or on a team call to link back to the team's everyday functioning. Ask regularly, "How can the team agreements be incorporated into the team meetings?" Some teams create a structure of the team agreements. It may be as simple as a plaque on everyone's desk that reminds the team of what's important, or it can be a trophy or a banner on display in the lunch room or entrance to the building.

Capacity Development Plays an Important Role in Team Coaching

This is different than in a group coaching context. Given that the team's lifespan will be sustained beyond the work with the coach, it is important for coaches to

---

[14] Riddle, *Senior Leadership Team Coaching*, 8.

place emphasis on the skill and capacity development as well. Capacity development is the topic of Chapter 9.

Task and Process Focus

As a team and group coach we will always want to maintain a healthy balance between "task" and "process" functions. The task focus for a team coach is on the "what." In this domain we are exploring the themes of relevance, working with the team or group to identify key themes, priorities and areas of focus. A process focus is just as important. The process focus includes a look to the structure and components of a team coaching engagement. Masterful team coaches provide a solid structure. What does the design look like? How do you ensure everyone's voice is being heard? What do you do (and what questions do you ask) to enable the team to deepen their awareness around issues, set better goals and take action on what's important? Accountability also falls under the process focus. A focus on the process, and creating a good structure that works, will help to mitigate some of the tricky issues mentioned in Chapter 2 and in this chapter.

Leverage the Relationships

The team comes to this process with relationships that exist, and a history behind them. Spend time focusing on these relationships and reminding the team that these relationships will endure beyond the coaching engagement.

Step Back and Let the Team Do the Work

In the team coaching context, it is all about the team. As coaches we need to fade back and let the group have the conversation among themselves. You may notice at the start that everyone is talking to you as the facilitator. Encourage the team members to speak directly to each other, rather than to you.

Remember That the Stakes Are Really High

Is there enough trust to create the open space needed for coaching? Given that this about people's livelihoods, and given the current economic climate, are team members really ready to engage in a coaching conversation—or is another, or hybrid, approach more appropriate?

The team conversation will continue beyond your interventions. Touch points may include inquiry about what members are using, what they are incorporating, what they are learning, and what is still getting in the way.

In closing, this chapter explored the following questions: *What is team coaching? What types of teams do we work with? What are essential ingredients for this work?*

This chapter also provided an in-depth overview of the team coaching process to provide further clarity on actual components of each stage. We also explored a couple of tricky issues that can emerge in team coaching, along with some key issues to keep in mind as you plan and implement this work.

Team Coaching in Action, a digital chapter at www.groupcoachingessentials. com, focuses on a number of case studies, bringing to life these team coaching processes. This digital chapter also includes various activities coaches may wish to integrate into their team coaching engagements.

End-of-Chapter Questions

What types of teams will you be working with? What considerations do you need to keep in mind?

Consider what you want your team coaching process to look like. What components will you incorporate at each stage?

What tricky issues do you want to be aware of throughout your work?

CHAPTER 7

VIRTUAL DESIGN AND DELIVERY

*Someday, in the distant future, our grandchildren's grandchildren will develop
a new equivalent of our classrooms. They will spend many hours in front of
boxes with fires glowing within. May they have the wisdom to know the
difference between light and knowledge.*
—Plato[1]

Technology continues to rapidly change the landscape in which team and group coaching is being rolled out. Coaches may find themselves working with a geographically dispersed group with members who connect from across the continent, or across the globe. Coaches working in organizations may find themselves connecting with both intact teams and virtual teams, for phone- and web-based programs. Virtual design and delivery is becoming the norm for many coaches.

This chapter will address:

- The role of the virtual facilitator
- Different ways coaches may be leading virtually
- The importance of creating connection and building trust in the virtual domain
- Key principles for successful virtual programs
- Voices from the Field: suggestions for virtual work
- Selecting technology that works for you and your group or team

---

[1] This quotation has been connected to Plato in a number of online instances. It's interesting to think he might be so ahead of his time. By the same token, if these really are not Plato's words, it is testament to how the Internet has the potential to create new truths.

This chapter will explore the different ways coaches and leaders may integrate virtual programming—whether it is group or team coaching conversations, webinars or teleseminars—and the skills required for virtual programming, as well as best practices, and technologies that enable sustaining the conversation over distance. The chapter also includes examples of how coaches are working in the virtual environment with groups and teams.

WHEN YOU HAVE DECIDED TO GO VIRTUAL

The role of the virtual facilitator is similar to facilitating an in-person group. In addition to core coaching skills, coaches who are looking to foray into the virtual realm will want to consider the following enhanced skills:

- Listening to what *is* being said and *not* being said, as well as to the energy, emotion and tone in each participant's voice. Given that body language often contributes up to 55 percent of the message in person, in the virtual environment we need to rely on vocal pace, pitch, tone and energy for the meaning of the message.
- Building trust at the start of the program (and even before the program starts).
- Creating connection among group members.
- Ensuring engagement and involvement of participants. Without the standard visual cues we rely on, it may be necessary to engage group members with questions, activities and discussion much more frequently.
- Evaluating and making ongoing changes by taking the pulse of the group regularly throughout the calls and getting feedback on takeaways and changes needed at the end of each call.
- Addressing call-management issues. There are a number of technical issues coaches will need to be comfortable in addressing. These include ensuring the call connection is clear, being able to mute as needed, knowing who is on the call, handling questions, handling recordings, etc.
- Handling group process issues. Even though a group may not be face to face, the group will move through similar phases of development. These are outlined in Chapter 8, on engagement. Of particular importance is keeping a finger on the pulse of the group, and normalizing issues (such as conflict) as they emerge.
- Dealing with "tricky issues." Refer to Chapter 2.

Questions to Consider

What is your current level of skill in these areas?

What is your current level of confidence in these areas?

What are your strengths that you can lean into?

What is the one real growth area for you? What specific action steps could you take to enhance your skill and/or confidence in this area?

Who can you tap into/rely on to support you in these areas?

Different Ways Coaches May Work Virtually

The variety of ways that coaches can choose to work with teams and groups continues to evolve quickly. Four separate approaches to working with participants or clients by phone include:

1. Group coaching by phone
2. Team coaching through virtual conversations
3. Teleclasses (or teleseminars)
4. Webinars

A summary of these is included in Table 7.1. Let's look at each one of these in turn.

Group Coaching by Phone

At certain times of the year, particularly the summer months, when I work remotely, the majority of my group coaching is completed by phone, usually bringing together participants from multiple time zones. The energy created for some group members in being part of a global connection can be infectious. I recently facilitated a group that met over a period of three months. Each participant indicated that one of the things they really liked about the program was its global focus.

For many group members the attraction of group coaching by phone is not only the convenience of not having to travel to participate, but also the anonymity created by connecting with others who live and work in different locations.

Table 7.1: The Different Virtual Approaches

Definition	Advantages	Disadvantages
Group Coaching		
"The application of coaching principles, skills and techniques in a small group context for the purposes of personal or professional development, the achievement of goals, or greater self-awareness, typically along thematic lines."[2]	• In person/by phone • Taps into the collective learning of the group, peer learning process • Focus on deepening awareness and taking action: accountability critical	• In virtual arena, can't "see" group members • May not go "as deep" on issues for individual clients • Focus on coaching, not content/training
Team Coaching		
Team coaching is a sustained series of conversations, leveraging core coaching skills. Focus is on goal setting, deepening awareness, supporting action and creating accountability for the team. The focus of the coaching may be on the team as a system and/or strengthening individuals within the team. Team coaching links back to business goals, focusing on results and relationships.	• Provides a pause and connection point for team members in their daily work • Sustains the conversation and focus without everyone having to travel • Virtual team coaching may be the only option for teams that are geographically dispersed	• Due to call length and numbers on team, may focus more on updates and accountability, rather than facilitating deep dialogue
Teleclass/Teleseminar		
"Teleseminars are used to provide information, [or] training, or to promote or sell products to groups of people interested in a particular topic. They are similar to traditional seminars in content and purpose, but they are given over a teleconference or bridge line rather than at a specific location."[3]	• No or low cost to host • Reduces travel • Enables connection across distance • Many traditional learning approaches can be adapted for this format	• Cannot see participants • No visual cues unless you integrate screen sharing

[2] Britton, *Effective Group Coaching*, 6.

[3] Wikipedia "Teleseminars," accessed May 6 2013, http://en.wikipedia.org/wiki/Teleseminars.

Webinar		
"Short for Web-based seminar, a presentation, lecture, workshop or seminar that is transmitted over the Web. A key feature of a Webinar is its interactive elements—the ability to give, receive and discuss information. Contrast with Webcast in which the data transmission is one way and does not allow interaction between the presenter and the audience."[4]	• Visual cues and anchor for people to follow • Able to interact with group (two-way)	• May create a number of new barriers for participants • Technology challenges • Typically a one-way passage of information; many webinars may mute all participants • Using chat function can be useful depending on numbers

Sometimes participants will open up more when they have the opportunity to connect with other group members who are hundreds of miles away. The fact that they are likely not connected face to face may allow group members to speak more freely about the setbacks, opportunities and frustrations they encounter over time.

There are some drawbacks to virtual group coaching programs, namely, the inability to see everyone in "the room." For some participants this may feel isolating or superficial in terms of meeting and connecting with others. Other group members may miss the intimacy created in a face-to-face environment. To address these concerns, it is important to keep virtual group coaching programs smaller in size rather than larger. As previously mentioned, an optimal size for virtual programs is around four to eight people.

Logistically, there are more details for the coach to manage. While most bridgeline services support large group conferencing you may need to utilize a paid service such as Maestro Conference to create smaller breakout groups.

Benefits of a virtual group coaching program can include:

- Not having to travel, connecting from a location that is more convenient.
- Anonymity: Participants may feel more open to sharing at a deeper level due to the fact that they may have no connection other than in the group. They may not live in a similar geographic area, or work in the same industry.
- The focus on the coaching process, not a training process. The focus on setting goals that are important, taking action on these and having a regular accountability structure.
- A peer learning process where individuals may learn and connect with other group members as much as with the leader/coach.

---

[4] Webopedia. "Webinar," accessed May 6, 2013, http://www.webopedia.com/TERM/w/Webinar.html.

Questions to Consider

When moving an in-person program to a virtual setting, ask yourself the following:[5]

- What are the components I can keep as is?
- What modifications do I need to make?
- How might I need to change my questions?
- Which exercises may be moved to an assignment that participants complete between calls?
- How do I need to change the materials I provide?
- How long will this program take in a virtual setting?

Team Coaching through Virtual Conversations

Team coaching undertaken by phone or web is likely to be incorporated with both virtual teams as well as intact teams. It is common for me to connect with teams located in the same geographic area, and even office, for virtual conversations in addition to in-person work. Refer to Chapter 6 for more on the different components of the team coaching process.

Many coaches opt to schedule some of the post-kick-off conversations by phone, interspersed with additional onsite work throughout the three to six months or more of working together.

The focus or structure of these calls may include a theme, or more of a check-in/accountability process.

The benefits of scheduling these regular coaching conversations include:

Keeping the momentum flowing: Scheduling team coaching calls every two to three weeks can be a good frequency. Team coaching is typically a sustained conversation. These regular touch points provide team members with the opportunity to build some momentum and to keep a focus on the goals and evolution of these.

Creating a touch point for all members to participate and connect: In today's business environment it may not be feasible for everyone to come together

---

[5] Britton, *Effective Group Coaching*, 127.

regularly. The team coaching conversations may provide the only touch points for some team members. Note with the teams that you work with the value of the conversation. Ask them about the value of the regular calls and how they might incorporate something similar going forward, beyond the coaching engagement.

Providing opportunities for pause, reflection, updates and change: As we know, change is a process that occurs over time. Different team members will be learning and changing in different ways. The team coaching calls can provide an opportunity to pause and reflect, to notice what's working well and what's not, and to determine what changes need to be made and what needs to be sustained.

Possible structure of these team coaching calls may include:

- An update from each team member or the team as an entity. Focus may be on:
  - Successes
  - Quick wins
  - Roadblocks
  - Burning issues
- How they are implementing things? What do team members notice?
- Focus on core skills
- How team agreements are being put into action. Are there any changes needed because of this? Do any new team agreements need to be added?
- Any changes needed to team agreements
- Focus areas going forward
- Individual and team commitments before next call/touch point

The call length should be determined by the team and the size. A minimum of one hour is usually recommended. Other considerations may be:

- **Time of calls:** When working with global teams, one time may not be convenient for all. How does the call time work for each team member? Is there need to rotate timing of the call to meet the needs of different members of the group?
- **Length of calls:** Many teams may only be available for one hour. What length will work for your team? Note the impact of the bookends. Consider how much time is spent at the start and end of the call, checking in and out. How much time will this leave for other pieces to be addressed? (For example, closure and feedback.)

- **Frequency:** Keeping the conversation going is key to the success and sustainability of the coaching process. A good rhythm can be created with meetings every two to three weeks. Beyond the three-week mark, team members may forget the focus of the month before, unless they are also incorporating it into their own meeting structures. Consider what is feasible and realistic with your groups and teams.

How do the calls link into what the team is already doing? As we will see in Part III, a key part of capacity development is to sustain the conversation and support the team in bringing the tools and structures into their everyday work environment.

Teleclasses/Teleseminars

Teleseminars and teleclasses may be another type of virtual offering coaches include in their programming. Teleseminar is a commonly used term for a seminar delivered by phone; it may be interactive or not. A teleclass or teleseminar will typically have a heavier emphasis on content and training than will a "pure" group or team coaching process, which is more conversationally focused. The level of interactivity also varies widely, with some teleclasses being small, and others having hundreds of people on the line.

For clients who are looking for more skill development, teleclasses and teleseminars provide the advantages of no or lower cost and reduced travel. Coaches may find using them an easy way to adapt their current training materials. Teleclasses and teleseminars can be supplemented with screen sharing so others can see your screen. This provides participants with both auditory and visual cues.

Teleclasses/Teleseminars: Five Tips

Here are five things to remember when leading a teleclass (and notice the similarity to group coaching):

1. Consider what's important for your learners. Focus on them, on their learning and on creating opportunities for them to connect their learning to real life.
2. Provide useful content, resource links and materials that members can sink their teeth into.

3. Provide an overview of the call. Provide an agenda or overview of the topic at the start of the call. Let people know where you are going. Recap regularly.

4. Provide visual anchors. I regularly speak with trainers, coaches and facilitators on the importance of these anchor points in the virtual domain. What will provide a visual focus for group members during the program? Will you create a handout? Have a slide deck? Integrate video?

5. Be familiar with the technology, and, most importantly, know how to mute callers. Test out your technology prior to the call, and know how to overcome the invariable echoes, dogs barking and other distractions by knowing how to use mutes, "raised hands" for questions, and other bridge line tools.

These are by no means comprehensive tips for teleclasses, but some of the ones you may not have considered yourself. What do you see as the key challenges for you in running a teleclass?

Webinars

Webinars are increasingly becoming a popular choice for professional development and learning. The added visual element can help to engage the group members. Later in the chapter we explore several different webinar options available for coaches to integrate into their work.

Traditionally, webinars have been viewed as a one-way passage of information. Coaches may wish to use webinars in this traditional format as a marketing vehicle for outreach and education. They may also wish to use the webinar technology or the platform's screen-sharing element to provide the added visual impact of PowerPoint slides. By opening up the lines and enabling conversation, coaches can bring together the best of visual impact and also conversation. The slides for a presentation such as this may be prompters for key parts of the coaching conversation. Your slide deck may consist of only a few slides including the "bookends" of the check-in and check-out, and a couple of slides around areas of key focus or themes.

Utilizing the webinar platform can also be useful if you are sharing models—for example, coaching models for providing feedback, or holding difficult conversations. If you have the model up on the screen while you coach one or more participants, the process can be made more visually explicit.

As with other presentation modalities, preparation and tailoring the presentation to your audience's need is critical. Webinars will often be supported by a number of persons beyond the facilitator. There may be a moderator whose role is to introduce the guest speaker, answer any questions, and watch the chat log, as well as a producer who may be more technically oriented, making sure recordings work, and addressing technical questions as they arise. Ensuring that you work together as a team requires preparation and collaboration. It may be useful to refer to some of the questions included in Chapter 11, on co-facilitation and partnering, in your team preparation meetings. As I have mentioned elsewhere, it is important to consider issues of confidentiality when bringing other players in as co-facilitators for any coaching work. Having a support who is not bound by the same ethical agreement may create some gray ethical zones.

Many coaches will use the web platform as a visual to supplement the coaching conversation. The addition of the visuals can be very useful and may be as simple as a couple of slides with key words on them. If you are using a webinar platform you may also encourage each participant to pick up their own pen and write on the whiteboard.

Some coaches will incorporate more "traditional" webinars or webcasts for larger audiences. If you are hosting a more traditional webinar, a key function is engagement.

If you are looking to incorporate more of an interactive experience, you may wish to incorporate a poll or dialogue every seven to ten minutes in addition to hearing from the different presenters. (Refer to Chapter 8 for additional engagement tips.)

WHAT IS REALLY IMPORTANT IN THE VIRTUAL ENVIRONMENT?

Regardless of which method you choose, a number of things are critical for success in the virtual environment:

- Building trust and intimacy in the virtual environment
- Personal touch points
- Breaking through the multitasking mindset
- Creating connections among group members
- Clarifying expectations
- Providing visual anchor points throughout the call

The following sections look at these core topics.

Building Trust and Intimacy in the Virtual Domain

As Francovich et al. write, "The increasing complexity of relationships at global and local levels requires deep, effective, and sustained collaboration built on a foundation of mutual trust."[6] Trust and intimacy are key requirements for successful group and team coaching in the virtual realm. What do you do as a facilitator to foster this? What do trust and intimacy look like? What does it mean for the group or team you are working with?

Personal Touch Points

As the coach you play a key role in creating the atmosphere of the call. Consider:

- How do you want to welcome people?
- What do you want to do if people call in early? Start a check-in? Have a question for people to think about?
- What pace is going to support the group?
- Keeping it small. "Small is beautiful" in my domain of virtual programming. What size of group do you want to work with?

Breaking through the Multitasking Mindset

A challenge for coaches working in the virtual domain may be to break through the multitasking mindset or culture some professionals have adopted on today's phone- and web-based calls. It is no longer "Death by PowerPoint" but "Death by Conference Call." For those professionals and teams operating at a national or international level, it may be common for groups to be plugged into a series of conference calls throughout the span of the day. Whether they are sitting in an office tower or home office in Toronto, Bridgetown or London, an individual's focus and connection may be primarily virtual throughout the day.

---

[6] Chris Francovich, Michelle Reina, Dennis Reina and Christopher Dilts, "Trust Building Online: Virtual Collaboration and the Building of Trust," in Michael Beyerlein, Jill Nemiro, Lori Bradley, Susan Beyerlein, eds, *The Handbook of High-Performance Virtual Teams* (San Francisco: Jossey Bass, 2008), 154.

A key presentation best practice we have used for years is around WIIFM (What's In It For Me?). Helping people connect early on, and throughout the conversation, with What's In It For Me quickly gets people thinking about the value and importance of the call for themselves. It helps to "prime" the learning process by shifting responsibility to the group or team member.

Coming up with group member agreements about being fully present and focused will also serve as a reminder, and help to set the tone for the group. At the same time, it is critical for coaches, as group facilitators, to ensure that there are ample opportunities for people to engage throughout a conversation. Some possible ideas to support this engagement include:

1. **Provide "face time" wherever possible:** Use FaceTime or Skype. Do this as much as is feasible and supportive of a confidential environment. When people know they are seen, it is much less easy to disconnect. Having a physical connection at some point in the coaching engagement (if feasible) may also help to foster the trust and intimacy with your group or team members.

2. **Adapt your pace regularly:** Consider what it's like to watch a "talking head" at the front of the room who goes on and on. Now imagine this in the virtual environment, where you cannot see anything. Changing your pace regularly is very important. I usually aim to switch pace every five to seven minutes to stimulate some new energy. This could include throwing out a question for individual reflection, something for people to take a note on, or have some discussion around. As you work with your groups and teams, keep an eye on what is the best frequency for the groups you work with. Ask groups or teams at the end of the call, "What worked well? What did you take away? What should we do differently?" These questions will usually surface feedback on pacing. If not, ask for feedback on the pace.

3. **Use questions:** Scaling questions are useful in getting immediate feedback on where the group is at. Ask, for example, "On a scale of 1 to 10, how engaged are you right now?" You may have people post their numbers up on a whiteboard or screen (a little more anonymous) or have people indicate their number (a lot more risk), or whether they fall, for example, in the 7 to 10 range, 4 to 5 range or 3 or below. Taking this "temperature" provides you, and others on the call, with information.

You may also wish to refer to Chapter 8 around other engagement techniques for teams and groups.

Creating Connections amongst Group Members

Some other ideas for creating connections within your groups (between group members) are:

- Inviting virtual participants to share a brief introduction and photograph with other group members
- Creating learning partners who meet or communicate in between the calls
- Encouraging communication between calls (whether you set up a private Facebook page, a private LinkedIn group, or a Pinterest board for people to openly share on)
- Incorporating more smaller group dialogue throughout the group coaching process itself and having smaller groups report some of their main discussion points
- Using a program such as JournalEngine (see appendix) where group members can opt to share their insights between touch points

Clarifying Expectations

As we have seen in other chapters, things can fall off the rails if expectations are not clear. This is even more true in the virtual domain, where people may already feel disconnected from others due to lack of proximity. Four areas you will want to clarify early on in the process are as follows:

1. What can participants expect from the program (before, during and after)?
2. How big will the group be? Preparing for a call with four other participants is very different from preparing for a call with forty others.
3. How much interaction and engagement will be expected? Set the tone and let people know that your webinar may not be like the traditional webinar.
4. What is the role of field work? Programming process is not just about the call time, so indicate the role of any field work—before or after the call.

Providing Visual Anchor Points throughout the Call

In designing your programs consider what people can refer to visually. Will there be a workbook, slides or something else to give participants a "visual anchor point" throughout the program? Will you incorporate a slide sharing component for some visuals?

As the facilitator, are you providing a roadmap of where the call is going? What's next? Providing recaps along the way offers an anchor point for participants. Note that in a virtual environment an even heavier emphasis on process is important.

Questions to Consider

What types of connections would you like to create in your next team or group coaching program? What will you need to establish or put in place to make this happen? What value do you think it will add for participants?

KEY BEST PRACTICES FOR SUCCESSFUL VIRTUAL PROGRAMS

Here are 10 best practices for successful virtual programs:

1. Less is more
2. Provide a clear overview of the process
3. Remember to engage
4. Reduce barriers to participation
5. Safety and connectivity
6. Utilize pre-program call
7. Don't be afraid to break it up (logistics)
8. Shared expectations
9. Pre-work between sessions
10. Small is beautiful

Less Is More

As with any team or group coaching process, the value of our work in the virtual domain is in the conversation. Avoid overwhelming participants. In the virtual environment, you may notice that you place a heavier emphasis on articulating process that you do in person: where you are, where you are going and what themes have emerged. In the virtual domain, it may take more time to hear from each other as well. *Even* less is more with your virtual groups.

Provide a Clear Overview of the Process

Provide participants with information and pointers around the agenda and what they can expect. As you move through the call, summarize what you have looked at already, and where you still have to go.

Remember to Engage

Frequent engagement in the virtual domain—every five to seven minutes—is key. It may be as simple as posing a question for group members to reflect on, or asking people to write down or share their insights. Pacing is key in the virtual domain.

Reduce Barriers to Participation

Supporting group members as they access the technology may take some of your time, but as they get comfortable it becomes much easier. You may want to consider providing group or team members with a Frequently Asked Questions (FAQ) or be available at a certain time to walk any members through technical challenges. Send out connection information early and ask people to try it out. You never know when a firewall issue may emerge. As part of the pre-program one-on-ones, talk about technology and ascertain client's levels of comfort.

Safety and Connectivity

Creating a sense of connection quickly with other group members is critical with group members. *What will help your grouping feel connected, and safe to engage and share?*

Utilize Pre-program Calls

Pre-program calls take on even greater significance in the virtual domain in terms of creating connection with each group member, and starting to build rapport.

Don't Be Afraid to Break It Up (Logistics)

Many coaches new to virtual facilitation struggle with how to engage the group in different ways. Depending on your call design and numbers you may wish to ensure that there are other touch points for people to engage. For example:

- A private Facebook page where they can sustain the conversation between calls.
- A paid service such as JournalEngine (refer to case study in the appendix).
- Introducing a learning partner in a group coaching context.
- Hosting small group breakouts for team and group coaching. If you are not using a service such as Maestro Conference, which automatically allows you break out small groups, you can send out instructions before the call with group members listed and the new bridge line. Ensure you give clear instructions on what the focus of the conversation will be, how long they will have to discuss, and what they should come back with to present to the rest of the group.

Shared Expectations

Creating shared expectations is even more critical in the virtual domain than when coaching in person. With no ability to "see" and measure reaction, it is important to facilitate conversation and invite feedback around how expectations are being met, as well as the pace and level of discussion. Having a hybrid mix of group and individual calls can be very useful in this process.

Pre-work between Sessions

To maximize the discussion time on each call, set some pre-work, so people have undertaken some of the work before the call. For example, if you are working with values, you may ask group members to complete some exercises around values identification before the call. During the call, to take the conversation to a deeper level, you may start with a laser coaching of one of the group members around a peak experience. This can be followed by some general group discussion, and possibly by follow-up field work/an assignment around looking at how they are honoring their values.

Small Is Beautiful

In the virtual realm especially, small is beautiful. I continue to find the optimum size anywhere in the three- to eight-person range. Managing expectations around group size and engagement is important.

Voices from the Field: Tips for Virtual Call Facilitation

Many of the coaches who contributed insights or case studies undertake virtual work with teams or groups. Here are their additional insights, tips and experiences around virtual calls.

Kevin Stebbings: Without the cues of body language and facial expressions, the group coach has to be particularly tuned into the energy level, emotions and needs of each member. It requires an added level of listening. Also, without the visual cues, group members are often unsure of when to speak up.

The group coach needs to be intentional about facilitating cross dialogue between members of a group. For example, when following up on action steps from the previous group session, I will model how to ask the questions with one member. For example, I might say, "Steve, what progress have you made on your action steps? What did you learn?" I will then invite that member to "pass it on" so that the members become used to asking the follow-up questions to each other in turn: "Steve, I would now like you to ask those same two questions to someone else in the group: 'What progress have you made on your action steps? What did you learn?' They will then ask someone else." We move through the group in this way until everyone has had an opportunity to report back on their progress.

I find this process in the beginning of the virtual group gets the participants used to talking with one another and not just to or through the group coach. In this way less dependence on the coach develops and the group learns to take ownership of the group conversation.

Renee Brotman: I did a little group coaching virtually. It was very challenging because the group never really felt accountable to each other in spite of having participated in a classroom experience together. People would come and go [attend] as they wanted. [In the future] I would ensure some better "hook" for accountability.

(Continued)

Shana Montesol: In virtual group coaching it is really important to have a contingency plan—a Plan B, Plan C, Plan D even. And be sure to test each of your contingency options, from the location where you will be holding your call.

Since I am based in a developing country myself (the Philippines) the Internet connection in my home office can be inconsistent. Power outages are also not unheard of. Prior to launching my group coaching program, using the Internet access option of a paid teleconferencing provider, I had developed options for what I would do in case I lost my Internet connection. I had purchased a calling card so that I could use my land line to affordably dial the U.S.-based phone number of the teleconferencing provider.

For one of my group coaching calls, I was unable to use my home office, so I hosted the call from an alternate location. When the Internet connection dropped for a few seconds, I was booted off the call. Although the Internet came back on, I was unable to reconnect. "No problem," I thought. "I'll just call from the land line." I confidently whipped out my calling card, only to find that I was unable to place the call from the phone in that particular office. For some reason, it was not enabled to use that type of calling card. Had I tested my Plan B at my new location, I would have known that. Luckily, I had a Plan C up my sleeve, and I ended up enabling a promotion on my prepaid smart phone that would allow me to call to the United States without breaking the bank.

There was even a silver lining to my tech troubles, related to the group process. I was actually off the call for a full 10 minutes. Later I went back and listened to the recording of the call (which thankfully kept recording even though I, as the call host, had dropped off). I was gratified to hear that the group members asked each other relevant questions, coached each other, and offered support. This was only the second out of six group coaching meetings, so the participants didn't know each other well yet. My 10-minute absence showed them stepping right up and taking ownership of the program—they even remarked at the end of the six sessions that that experience was an important time of bonding for them.

Catherine Carr: I work a lot with virtual teams. I recommend orienting team members to the use of the technology. Use virtual visual tools to keep participants engaged.

Michael Cullen: In virtual group coaching, be really well prepared and make sure to budget time for the participants to relate their insights resulting from the call. Guide the call in a professional manner from start to finish;

note the names of the callers and reach out to each of them by name at least twice per call.

Sharon Miller: Meet first if you can. If you can't, come up with some way of connecting to create relationship, understanding and camaraderie. This may include the sharing of bios, creating an (Intranet) team page where participants can connect, or videoconferencing. Design your alliance with the leader and the team around how you will work in the virtual environment. An example is, "I may be bold and ask an edgy question to stir up conversation." Decide as a coach whether you are okay working this way. Suggest some training around how to be effective as a virtual team leader and team member (How is it different? How is it the same?). There are some key differences that people won't spontaneously know just because they are now virtual.

Kim Ades: In virtual group coaching, use a private and secure online platform to allow the group to create a community of their own and interact in between calls or meetings. Provide homework assignments that are done online and shared. Invite the group to provide feedback to one another. Use content from this platform to drive your coaching calls/meetings (for example, quote people from the group, using their stories and content as learning modules.

Phil Sandahl: Virtual teams need to make a commitment to team sessions that is much different than the commitment to a teleconference call. There needs to be a redefinition of a virtual "team meeting" with new ground rules, a more personal interaction and deeper commitment.

Question

Based on these perspectives, what key insights do you want to incorporate or remember for your work?

Activity: Virtual Call Reflection Questions

As you prepare for or reflect on a recent virtual call you have hosted, think about the following components. As you prepare, what are key considerations or things you can do to support each area? If you are reflecting on a call you led, note what worked and what did not.

(Continued)

Table 7.2: Virtual Call Evaluation

Focus area	Comments
Welcome/kick-off	
Letting people know about flow of call/what to expect	
Helping people connect with the WIIFM (What's In It For Me?)	
Pace of the call	
Word choices	
Speech fillers ("umm," "ahh," "like" and other words commonly stated)	
Clarity of voice (too loud, too soft)	
Pace of speech (too fast, too slow)	
Engagement and involvement of all group members	
Check-in (amount of time, questions)	
Questions or activities used (amount of time, clarity of instructions)	
Sequencing (how one activity or idea flowed to another)	
Timing	
Check-out (amount of time, hearing from all)	
Feedback received	
Changes needed for next time	
Other	

MAKING VIRTUAL GROUP AND TEAM COACHING MORE EFFECTIVE

Facilitating and coaching in the virtual realm require some different skills, as well as structures. What are some practical things you can do to make your group coaching by phone or web more effective? Here are six suggestions.

1. Consider what you really want to use the call time for. With virtual programs my preference is usually to use the time in dialogue, discussion and coaching. This often requires that group members undertake some prep before the call, as pre- or post-work. *What do you want to use your call time for?*

2. Spend time before the program building relationships with group members. I have already discussed my insistence on holding short pre-program calls prior to public programs I host. This is an opportunity for me to learn more about each group member, their needs, goals and also preferences. *What focus do you want to have pre-program on getting to know your group members?*

3. Encourage relationships among group members. The peer component of group coaching learning is a key part of the group coaching process. The power is not only in the relationship between coach and client. Peer relationships and learning also play a vital role. *What do you want to include in between sessions to support group relationships and conversation? Who will organize this—you or members of the group?*

4. Consider spending time building relationships between sessions with and between individual group members. Especially with public programs, when groups will disband after the program, members appreciate more touch points with me as coach. Many of my programs over the years have had a hybrid one-on-one and group mix to address this issue. People usually love the opportunity to meet with me one-on-one, even if it is for a shorter call, to explore their topics/issues more deeply. *What touch points do you want to have between sessions—between you and the group, and among group or team members?*

5. Use visual supports. Technology is enabling us to incorporate visual media in many forms. What supports will the group members benefit from? A PDF workbook/worksheet? Slides that they can view as prompters? Streaming video? *What visual supports can your groups benefit from?*

6. Consider and address what barriers may exist to group members' participation. Many barriers can exist to virtual program participation for teams and groups. From lack of familiarity with the technology, to timezone issues, to low bandwidth issues, to lack of engagement, these factors can become barriers to participation and engagement. *What barriers might exist for your members and their participation?*

Adapted from Jennifer Britton, "Making Virtual Group Coaching More Effective—5 Tips," Group Coaching Ins and outs, October 26, 2011, http://groupcoaching.blogspot.com/2011/07/making-virtual-group-coaching-more.html.

USING TECHNOLOGY IN VIRTUAL PROGRAMS

Technology can make or break the experience for team and group members being coached.

In selecting a service that is going to work best for you, ask yourself these questions:

- What level of confidence and skill in navigating technology are my group/team members likely to bring?
- What accessibility challenges might be present (e.g., bandwidth, firewalls)
- What is the security and confidentiality of the platform?
- What features can I use to boost engagement? For example, if you are a coach who wants to incorporate smaller group discussions or breakout sessions you will want to explore technologies such as Maestro Conference.

Refer to Table 7.3 for a summary of some of these common technologies you may wish to check out to see how they can support your programs.

Table 7.3: Web and Video Options

Name	Description	Considerations
WebEx (webinar platform; at a cost)	WebEx is widely used across organizations. Callers have option to view online and call in to bridgeline. Note that high speed is often needed to download WebEx platform.	Bandwidth and location issues. If you bring on another person to moderate and look after technology consider making them a co-facilitator.
Go To Meeting (webinar platform; at a cost)	Similar to WebEx.	Bandwidth and location issues. If you bring on another person to moderate and look after technology consider making them a co-facilitator. Impact on confidentiality of the group.
Google+ (video streaming capabilities: up to 10 persons through Hangouts)	Refer to text.	Bandwidth issues. No way to secure the line so confidentiality may be an issue encountered.

Skype Video (add on to a regular account)	Ability have video calls among five people	Bandwidth and accessibility issues for every participant.
Maestro Conference (bridge line service at a cost)	Call facilitator has both a Web dashboard to see who is on the call, who has raised hands, etc. Also able to section group members into virtual breakout rooms with the click of a button (i.e., if you have a group of 8, you can put people into 2 groups of 4, and as facilitator you can drop in and have discussion).	Ensure that you are familiar with how to work the various Web portal functions, for example, breaking up the group into smaller virtual breakouts, dropping into the various groups to see if they have questions, recording, etc.
FreeConferenceCalling.com (free bridge line service)	Free recording, web portal so you can see who is on the call, mute, get participants to raise hands. Recordings can be listened to online, downloaded, and now tweeted and placed on Facebook.	International callers can call in by Skype, usually with no problem.
FreeConferenceCall.com (free bridge line service with local call-in numbers for many countries; also offers paid and free screensharing capability)	Is partnered with FreeScreen Sharing.com so callers can see slides at same time call is going on. This is an added benefit for those that have a preference for visual learning. You can also change presenters if one of the group members wanted to "take over and lead" the conversation with something visual.	Recording services are by phone by default only so people have to dial back to listen. Cannot capture recordings of screenshots with free screensharing at time of press. Ensure that each group/team member can get online (i.e., no firewall issues).

Selected Platforms

FreeConferenceCalling.com

I have used FreeConferenceCalling.com for most of my group coaching programs and teleseminars for years. The bridge line service is free to use, and also provides the option of recording. Recordings are created as MP3s, which you can make public for others to listen to online or download, or you can keep them private. The service also allows you to have multiple bridge lines available at any given time. This enables you to ensure that each class has a separate access code and place they can go to access their recordings.

FreeConferenceCall.com

Another free service, FreeConferenceCall.com has advantages including the fact that it now has local dial-in numbers for countries outside of North America. So, for example, if you have a caller dialing in from France or Brazil, they can dial a local or national bridgeline and join the group. I used to think that it was only possible to have group members listen by dial-in, however, you can access MP3 files through your account panel. Another advantage of using this service is that they have partnered with FreeScreenSharing.com, which allows you to have group members log in and see your screen during the presentation. It definitely ups the ante for those who want to multitask!

MaestroConference.com

Maestro Conference is a paid service that offers more innovative possibilities for coaches to use in their virtual programs. Of particular note is the ability for a facilitator or coach to break the larger group into smaller virtual groups. With the click of a mouse, using the web portal, group members can be paired off. The coach/facilitator can "drop in" and check on the smaller groups, and bring them back to the larger group with the click of a button. This provides the best of both worlds in terms of larger and smaller breakouts, without a lot of logistical challenges.

Google Hangouts

Google Hangouts are a good option for providing face-to-face contact time, and possibly for marketing. Google+ users can invite other Google+ members to hang out. Essentially, these are Web-based group calls. The advantages of a Google Hangout may be realized for marketing, promotion and relationship-building purposes. Once the threshold is hit in terms of numbers it is full. Hangouts at present can only support 10 individuals.[7] Hangouts on Air now

---

[7] Jeremy Vest, "Google+ Hangouts: Six Practical Uses for Online Education," *Learning Solutions Magazine*, October 19, 2011, http://www.learningsolutionsmag.com/articles/772/google-hangouts-six-practical-uses-for-online-education.

allow you to share your recordings with others. You can alert other members about the date and time of your Hangout. The disadvantage of a Hangout is that it is not secure enough to support confidentiality. Anyone can "drop in" during the hangout. However, Hangouts can be a great tool to support collaboration among group members.

As this technology is likely to continue to emerge, coaches are encouraged to check out the current "bells and whistles" of Google Hangouts.

Rebecca Bodrero, an instructor at Boise State University, leading online graduate programs, has used Google Hangouts in a program she leads on needs assessment.[8] She has found several advantages of incorporating Google Hangouts into the program. Students have identified the following benefits: being able to see both each other and their work products; integration with Google Docs, enabling them to work on the document simultaneously; screensharing; whiteboarding; and chatting within the Hangout window, which has been useful for posting links or other items relevant to the discussions.

Her blog post, "Google+ Hangouts in Online Education: Capable, Low-Cost Solutions," also identifies a number of technical challenges encountered in the process. These include things such as echoes, dropping off for no apparent reason, video freezing and challenges accessing it on mobile platforms.

Even over the course of writing this book, the capabilities of what can be done via Hangouts and how it can be used continue to expand exponentially and become more mainstream.

As with the integration of any technology (app, program or other), finding the common denominator for your group is very important. *What technologies can they access? Are they comfortable with? What learning curve and learning support may group or team members need to go through to understand and use the technology?*

Voice Thread

Voice Thread is a cloud-based application that allows for commenting via voice/ audio recording, video or text. Although I have not used it personally, I think it may be useful in providing more visuals material option sharing for participants. It also allows people to contribute to the conversation at a time that is convenient for them. This offers great possibilities for team coaching and team collaboration. There are currently monthly packages available for individuals, groups of five to fifteen, and for entire enterprises.

---

[8] Rebecca Bodrero, "Google+ Hangouts in Online Education: A Capable, Low-Cost Solution," *Learing Solutions Magazine*, July 23, 2012 http://www.learningsolutionsmag.com/articles/972/google-hangouts-in-online-education-a-capable-low-cost-solution.

Private Facebook Groups

At the time of writing, a number of coaches are exploring the use of private Facebook groups. The private or secret groups will not show up on individual members' timelines. Coaches can invite individual group members to participate in and sustain the conversation for the group between each weekly session. Note that Facebook privacy settings continue to change so coaches will want to confirm how secure and confidential these groups are before setting up their own Facebook group. Also consider if Facebook is a platform that all group members would use.

Webinar Platforms

Webinars are becoming standard practice in many contexts today, just as teleseminars were five or ten years ago. Coaches may also opt to incorporate a webinar element into their programs. Professionals may want to explore these options: Elluminate, WebEx, Go To Meeting and Go To Training. One of the major distinctions between Go To Meeting and Go To Training is that Go to Training has additional support for "testing" knowledge/uptake.

Question to Consider

There has recently been an explosion of new tablets on the market, several available for less than $150. This extra portability may enhance the allure and accessibility of mobile, virtual and portable learning experiences. How do you want to tap into the virtual domain?

The field of technology is changing the options available for coaches who want to deliver their programs virtually—and the change is happening very quickly. Remember that while the technology is changing rapidly, not everyone is an early adopter, and some client groups may experience challenges in accessing your programming, whether due to security settings (i.e., firewalls), the hardware they have available or bandwidth issues. As always, consider what your clients need, want and prefer.

This chapter took a look at facilitating programs in the virtual realm. In designing and delivering group and team coaching work it is likely that at some stage coaches will be incorporating a virtual component into their own programs and/or marketing.

Our next chapter looks at the themes of connection and engagement, critical for any group or team coaching initiative.

End-of-Chapter Questions

What approaches will work best for you and your clients?
What do organizational clients already have in place that you can tap into?
Where do your strengths lie in this domain? What is a learning edge for you?
What can you do to gain more experience in facilitating in the virtual realm?
What is a next step for you?

CHAPTER 8

CREATING CONNECTION AND FOSTERING ENGAGEMENT IN TEAM AND GROUP COACHING

Without involvement, there is no commitment. Mark it down, asterisk it, circle it, underline it.
—Stephen R. Covey[1]

This chapter explores:

- Engagement pre-program, during a program, post-program
- The context: a reminder of group and team processes (Bruce Tuckman's model)
- Strategies for boosting connection, in person and by phone
- Engagement in virtual programs
- The impact of learning styles and participant styles

Group and team coaching is grounded in the active participation of each group member. As discussed in earlier chapters on the core coaching

---

[1] http://www.goodreads.com/quotes/133327-without-involvement-there-is-no-commitment-mark-it-down-asterisk.

Figure 8.1: The Triangle of Coaching Relationships

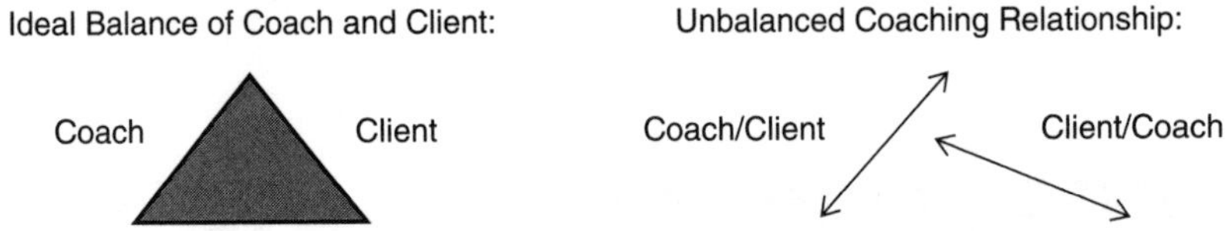

Ideal Balance of Coach and Client: Unbalanced Coaching Relationship:

Coach   Client   Coach/Client   Client/Coach

competencies (Chapter 3), coaching can be distinguished from other modalities such as training and counseling due to its focus on goal setting and accountability.[2]

Engaging learners has become a buzzword in today's talent management and learning lexicon. What does engagement mean in the context of group and team coaching?

Ultimately engagement is the foundation of any coaching interaction. For coaching to be successful, each individual group member must "lean into" the conversation, and be present.

Many of you will be familiar with the relationship triangle (depicted in Figure 8.1), which shows up in many coaching models such as the Co-Active Coaching model. In strong and effective relationships, the coach and client lean equally into the coaching relationship. If either coach or client leans more than the other, it is likely that the other will become unbalanced, overpowered, silenced or experience another unfavorable outcome.

In a group or team coaching engagement, it is important to consider the web of relationships that exists among all group members, coach included. In a team or group coaching process, the relationships created among and between the individual participants are just as important as the relationship between the coach and participants.

Spending time building connections among fosters the trust and intimacy of the group (recall ICF Core Coaching Competency #3), which is a critical part of engagement, connection and the coaching process. Without trust and intimacy, the coaching process cannot move forward. Unlike a training environment in which the trainer is the expert, and people can choose to participate, coaching requires the active participation of each individual, and commitment to bring themselves fully into the coaching process. If group or team members do not trust each other, or feel unsafe, they will not actively participate in the coaching process.

---

[2] International Coach Federation, First Global Coaching Survey, 2008.

Parts of the remainder of this chapter explore approaches and techniques that coaches can use to look at building and enhancing connection with and among team and group members before, during and after the coaching engagement, as well as techniques for the in-person and virtual environments. This chapter also provides a reminder of Bruce Tuckman's model for team development and strategies we can employ in our work to support groups and teams at each stage.

THE CONTEXT: RECOGNIZING NEEDS AT DIFFERENT STAGES OF THE TEAM AND GROUP DEVELOPMENT PROCESS

In *Effective Group Coaching* I provided an overview of Bruce Tuckman's model of team and group development. I've updated it in Table 8.1 to incorporate key issues we see in both the team and group environments. Throughout my years in working with groups and teams across cultures, I continue to see these stages showing up, and rolling through, any process we engage in.

Many of you may wonder, do these play out in the virtual environment? Absolutely! While the stages may not be as pronounced, the group and team still have similar needs at each stage. Likewise, the more intensive and connected the experience, the more pronounced the stages are. For example, the process may be more visible throughout several days of offsite work, versus in a group that meets one hour a week for six weeks. Note also that Tuckman indicates that groups can progress through these stages in a non-linear fashion. Also important to consider is that changes in the group or team composition (e.g., a new group member joins a call, or a new leader joins a team) will affect the stages that the team experiences.

Your level of support and focus areas will vary across the phases of your work with a team or group. As you will note, at the start, the group and team will need more support and direction from you. As the group gets to work more effectively on their own, it is important to "step back and fade out" and let the group or team engage by themselves, intervening when appropriate. This can be a stretch point for some coaches who are used to being "at the center."

A quick summary of the stages of team development follows (Table 8.2), which includes the needs of the group, the role of the coach and key issues that may emerge in group or team coaching. Note the similarities, as well as the differences.

Table 8.1: Group and Team Dynamics

Stage	Key Issues: Group Coaching	Key Issues: Team Coaching
Forming: *What?* **Needs** • Safety • Expectations • Clarity around what they can expect and where they are going • Connection **Role of Coach** • Create a safe environment • Build trust and intimacy with group members • Provide opportunities for connecting and getting to know each other • Providing information about expectations	• Designing the coaching alliance • What they can expect • Identification of key focus areas • "Ways of working"/ team agreements • Connections with other participants	• Establishing the coaching agreement • Identification of key focus areas • Team contract: behaviors they can go back to • Resistance • Elephant in the room
Storming: *What? So who are we? What's this all about?* **Needs** • Conflict • Figuring out roles and tasks needed • Fight or flight **Role of Coach** • Keep a focus on process • Normalize conflict • Shine light into what's going on (team context) • Scan for conflict that may not be explicit	• Watch engagement and participation levels • What about those more quiet? • Revisit ways of working	• Normalizing • Skills for conflict: navigation, difficult conversations • Noticing conflict patterns • Resistance • Addressing the elephant in the room
Norming: *What? So what?* **Needs** • Understanding roles **Role of Coach** • Focus on process and provide resources as necessary	• Planning to do the work • Explore and identify strengths that exist • Explore values: what's important to us? • Revisit and revise ways of working	• Roles • Perspectives • Preparation • What's needed • What are our strengths/biases? • Revisit and revise team contract

| Performing: *What's working? What's not? What will keep it going? What will take it to the next level?*

Needs
• Interdependence
• To be effective in different combinations

Role of Coach
• Support pause points for learning and adjustment
• Provide checkpoints for opportunities to look at learning, how goals need to shift, shifts needed for the group and team | • Allow the group to do the work
• Resources and time for getting things done
• Focus on action and accountability | • Systems and structures that will sustain this
• Keeping an eye on obstacles/ threats and opportunities |
| Adjourning: *Now What?*

Needs of Group
• Closure
• What now?

Role of Coach
• Celebration and acknowledgment | • Ample time for closure, thanks and acknowledgment
• What do you want to be thankful for?
• How do you want to stay connected? | • Celebration
• Sustainability
• Lessons learned and lessons that need to be transferred
• Scheduling "booster shots" |

CREATING CONNECTION THROUGHOUT THE COACHING PROCESS

> *"Group coaching is an intimate conversation space."*
> —Jennifer J. Britton (as quoted in *Choice Magazine*, 2011)

Throughout a group and team coaching process, participants go deeper into sensitive areas that they may not have divulged in a workshop, teleclass or other group process. As many coaches know, our work requires a deep dive around issues of importance and vulnerability, as well as an ability to share about important topics such as:

- Goals: What are my goals?
- Vision: Where do I want to go in my work and life?
- Values: What's really important to me?
- Strengths: What am I good at?
- Blind spots: Where do my blind spots lie?

The ability for a group or team to explore these issues requires a foundation of trust and connection among the people you are working and conversing with. For coaches, this has an impact on group size, length of engagement, connections between sessions, and/or philosophical stance.

As I discussed in *Effective Group Coaching*, the International Coach Federation's stance around when a group can be considered a group for the purposes of credentialing points to the fact that group coaching involves small groups. The maximum threshold is set at 15 by the ICF, and in the course of my research for *Effective Group Coaching*, I found the range was often much lower (four to eight in virtual environments, and a little higher in face-to-face environments).

In addition to overall program design of the topics or themes to be explored in each session, coaches will also want to consider varying approaches to use in building connection before the program even starts (pre-program), during the program and after the program.

Approaches for Building Connection with and among Group Members: Pre-program

Pre-program one-on-ones (see Table 8.2 for a related worksheet for pre-program one-on-one topics) for group and team coaching can support you as you get to know your clients (critical for the coaching process), identify themes you are going to work around, and start building rapport.

Have individual group members introduce themselves by email or other platform with a photo, and a brief paragraph about themselves—what has brought them to the program, and what they are looking forward to getting out of the coaching process.

Pre-program Group Coaching Calls

Pre-program calls are critical in setting the context of the work you are going to do together. It also provides an opportunity to clarify expectations: what the program will entail, what it won't. It will also provide an opportunity to explore expectations around coaching versus training, and key focus areas the participants want to explore.

For example, in pre-program calls for the 90-Day BizSuccess Group Coaching program for coaches and other business owners, I often get to learn more about each person's business, what focus they are bringing, and what they have done in terms of development around their business in the past. Pre-program calls play a key role in setting and discussing expectations and making sure that the program is a good fit. Pre-program calls also give participants a sense of what they can consider in terms of interactivity, commitments and accountability, as well as any field work that will be expected from week to week. This expectation setting is foundational to success.

Key questions I like to ask at this stage include:

- What brought you to this program? What led you to enroll?
- What are you looking forward to from this process? Note if specific themes come up.
- What should I know about how you learn best?
- What are your primary needs and interest areas around this topic?
- What will success look like at the end of the engagement for you? (This is an important link to planning and goal setting.)

In earlier chapters we have talked about systems for our work. Creating a worksheet to capture information about your group or team members can be very useful. Table 8.2 provides prompts around many potential discussion areas in a pre-program one-on-one call. Feel free to adapt it for your own groups.

Table 8.2: Pre-program One-on-One Worksheet for Group and Team Coaching

Participants	
Who are they?	
What are they looking forward to?	
What do they want to get out of their participation?	
What should I know about how they learn best or other support needs?	
Other:	
Myself as Facilitator	
My own background	
Background to the program	
Other	

(Continued)

Table 8.2: (*Continued*)

The Program	
Where?	
When? (dates and times)	
Start and end time	
When materials will be sent out (also to check bulk and spam filters)	
What to Expect from the Program: • Approaches • Themes/focus areas • Number of participants	
Confirm: • Email address • Phone contact • Any payment/installments • When participants can expect to receive materials from you	

Pre-program Team Coaching Meetings

Just as with groups, it may be appropriate to hold pre-program team coaching meetings, particularly if your time with a team is limited. These pre-program meetings can help you get the lay of the land very quickly, seeing the multiple perspectives at play. They allow you to "hit the ground running" and start the conversation quickly with new teams. For example, in the last couple of months I have started working with two new teams. With one team I only have eight hours of contact over four two-hour sessions. The pre-program meetings with each team member have been invaluable in getting to know the context of the organization, the different personalities and priorities on the teams as well as what priority interest areas are. It allowed for us to start the conversation at a much deeper level from our first session.

An Exception to the Rule

Where pre-program meetings with each individual member may not be appropriate is in team systems coaching. In team systems coaching, the coach is there to support the entire web of relationships. In team systems coaching the coach or coaches are wanting to create and maintain a transparent communication channel with the entire team.

The value of pre-program team coaching meetings can include:

- Discovering what the key issues are for these team members—as a group and individually. Sometimes issues that are "hot buttons" may not surface in a larger context, but may be shared individually with the coach. These topics, themes and ideas can be integrated into the coaching work before it officially begins.
- Flagging any issues that are outstanding or not being covered already in the program.
- Building the trust and rapport with individual group members before you get in the room. These calls may serve to reduce some of the tricky issues that may emerge.

Team Coaching Pre-Questions for Discussion with Each Member

- Tell me about your role. (How long in role, in company, what do you do?)
- What are key priorities for your work?
- How does your work relate with others in the team?
- What do you see as key priorities for the team?
- What are you looking forward to from the team coaching process? (Explore expectations.)
- What resources and support do you need to enhance your team and individual performance?
- What will success look like for the team?

Approaches for Building Connection with and Among Group Members: During the Program

Designing the coaching agreement is a fundamental part of the coaching process, as outlined in Chapter 1. Part of this foundation includes a discussion around what group and team members can expect from the coaching process (welcome kit, questionnaires), and identification of areas or topics they want coaching around.

Connection and engagement are key issues throughout any group or team coaching process. Seven activities you may wish to incorporate in a first or second conversation are the following:

1. **Personal Logos:** This kick-off activity is excellent in having group and team members share their responses to the question, "What do you bring that is unique to this coaching process/the team or the group?" (Refer to the appendix of *Effective Group Coaching* for further detail on this topic.)

2. **Hopes, Fears and Fantasies:** This activity explores what people are looking forward to in the process (hopes), what people are concerned about happening in terms of the process (fears—e.g., that it's going to be "the same old, same old,") and fantasies (i.e., the most amazing thing that could happen!). This is a fun way to get at both aspirations and practicalities. Have group members discuss these in small groups. (Refer to the appendix of *Effective Group Coaching* for further detail on this topic.)

3. **Email and Photo Introduction among the Group/Virtual Team:** See Pre-program one-on-one suggestions above.

4. **Questionnaire and Survey:** What are key goals the individual is looking for from the coaching process? Starting with the person's key goals is an important foundation for the coaching process. Just as we create questionnaires for "an intake pack" or a "discovery" session, it is important to get people thinking about what are they looking forward to. Even if the team is being coached on an issue such as "enhanced communication," it is likely that each team member will have their own unique goals for the process as well. It is important to not assume that the group or team is homogeneous or similar in its goals without checking this out.

5. **Virtual Table Map:** Get participants to draw a table map of who is on the call. This table map can be a useful reminder of who is who on the call, as well as a place to take notes around items such as coaching commitments, successes, challenges, and themes emerging in the group. Refer to the description of the Virtual Table Map later in this chapter.

6. **Ways of Working/Ground Rules:** Ground rules or "ways of working" create a "safety net" by defining what types of behaviors are acceptable within a group or team coaching context. You may find that you spend more time working with a team around the process of coming up with their team contract than around their "ways of working." Some key components you will want to include, and have discussion around, are:
    *   Confidentiality: What does this mean to the group/team? What is acceptable/not acceptable to share? Why is it important?
    *   Starting and ending on time.

- Respect for differences and different opinions/insights/perspectives.
- Being 100 percent present (focusing on the conversation 100 percent).
- Being prepared for the calls/sessions (doing the pre-work).
- No cell phones, PDAs or other distractions.

7. **Using Colored Dots and Post-it Notes:** As we described earlier, using colored dots and Post-it Notes is a wonderful way to ensure all group and team members' "voices" are being heard and visually seeing interest areas when designing with a team or group what topic or theme areas are going to be explored. Depending on the number of sessions you have, it may become a clear-cut choice or you may wish to facilitate a short discussion around the topics that surfaced to come to final agreement. Some coaches may also prefer to take the data away and return with some suggestions the next week if there is great variance. Some themes may be able to be compressed or collapsed, or covered during field work.

For Teams

Engagement and connection within teams is an interesting topic area. There are always relationships and roles that exist before and after the coaching process. A coach may be working with a team for very short and intensive bursts of time. Given that they have connection points every day, many of the opportunities for practicing new approaches (such as having difficult conversations), and taking action on the action plans, occur outside of the coaching conversation. Team coaches can enhance the impact of their coaching processes by asking team members how they can bring the tools and concepts they are working around into their own systems, such as team meetings. For example, if you are working with roles that exist in the team during one of your coaching sessions, part of their fieldwork may entail noticing in meetings what roles are showing up.

As coach, it is important to always keep an eye on the team dynamics that exist. The coaching process is an opportunity for people to connect with others they may not otherwise know too well. Team coaches should be aware of the dynamics that occur naturally within the team.

In the Virtual Environment

Engagement in the virtual environment is even more important when visual cues are not present. Today's "death by meeting" syndrome has desensitized many professionals to communicating by phone and through web-based contexts, making it easy for virtual participants to think that it is okay to multitask, answer emails and surf the web during a virtual call. As coaches it is important to set expectations about what is acceptable around participation and focus in the virtual domain. Groups and teams may also come up with an agreement on "being fully present"—which means focusing on the call, not on your phone, email or other distractions.

Practically speaking, in a virtual (phone- or Web-based environment) you should be engaging your group members every seven to ten minutes at minimum.[3] Recently I participated in a webinar on webinar best practices which indicated that it is best practice to engage your web audiences every one to two slides. As we explored in Chapter 7, there are many ways to roll out your work in the virtual sphere.

In addition to the suggestions already posed in the chapter, approaches and strategies for engaging and focusing your audiences over the phone or web include:

Hybrid Calls

Staggering a group coaching call with a one-on-one call in between is a popular option for clients who want to have the opportunity to be coached at a deep level around issues of importance, while still being able to go broad or wide with comments and insights from their peers on group calls. The deeper the connection between group members, the more apt they will be to really listen and participate in the group calls.

Visual Cues

Visual anchor points (e.g., handouts) are another important component to consider. Worksheets can be designed for a group coaching process in a fluid enough way to ensure that they remain useful if you are "coaching in the moment" or are more structured around anchoring themes. You may wish to consider including the following in your worksheets. Space for:

- Check-in
  Questions may include:
  - What have you accomplished since the last call?
  - What do you want to focus on today?
  - What would you like to celebrate?
- Space to explore the weekly theme/focus area (Refer to the digital chapter Group Coaching in Action for different approaches. This can be downloaded at www.groupcoachingessentials.com.)
- Check-out

---

[3] Britton, *Effective Group Coaching*, 127.

Questions may include:

- What became really clear for you during the call?
- What are you committed to doing before the next session? Why? When? How will the group know?
- What focus do you want to hold this week?

- Field work—other individual or group assignments (refer to Chapter 1 for more on field work)

Bridge Lines

Breakout groups of pairs/dyads and triads are another wonderful way to engage group members during a call. If you are using a conference service like Maestro Conference you will automatically be able to break your groups into smaller breakout groups with the touch of a button on your Web portal. If you are not using a bridgeline service that supports this you will want to:

1. Set up a selection of bridge lines.
2. Prior to the call, email group members with instructions about what is going to happen on the call. For example, the call will start off in the larger grouping at the main bridge line. Part of the call will involve paired work. List the pairings, as well as the bridge line number those people should call when instructed. From experience, the more "pre-warning" you can give as to the process, and numbers, the better. Note that not everyone may read the instructions, or have access to them, if you send them out just prior to the call.

Learning Partners

You may also wish to consider pairing group members throughout the length of a program as learning partners. This can be more of a structured process where learning partners meet in between group calls, or it can be less structured. Whatever process you decide upon should be clearly communicated and agreed upon in the design of your coaching agreement during the first session.

You may opt to have learning partners do the following:

- Share accountabilities and become accountability partners
- Explore powerful questions more deeply
- Have deeper discussion around field work

How could learning partners be an asset to your program?

Virtual Table Map

Another approach that generates positive feedback from group and team members is a virtual table map. A sample is seen within Figure 8.2. Encourage each participant to draw a table on a piece of paper in their office. As people check in during the call you will want to invite them to "seat" themselves at the table around you. As each person checks in I write their name or initials along with any significant notes. This enables me to visually (and quickly) remember who is on the call. It can also allow me to call on people in order, then reverse the order for a bit of a change. I encourage group members to draw their own table maps each week. I often receive comments from group members; some like knowing that they will be called on as it "keeps them on their toes," whereas others find that it reminds them too much of "school." Adjust your approach accordingly.

Figure 8.2 is a shot of the typical layout of notes I take when leading a group or team coaching conversation. The check-in form in Figure 8.2 may be a useful

Figure 8.2: Virtual Team and Group Coaching Session Notes Page

Check-In Form

You may wish to use this as a template for your phone-based coaching work with groups and teams:

Date: _____

Session: _____

Focus/Theme Areas: _____

Names of Participants:

Virtual Table

template for you to adapt for your team and group coaching work. You will note spaces for you to take notes around date, session number, focus or theme areas, along with the table. The space on the right hand side can be used for taking notes, noting themes and identifying questions for follow-up or individual coaching conversations.

THE IMPACT OF STYLES ON THE TEAM AND GROUP COACHING PROCESS

Team and group coaching processes will bring together multiple personalities, and you will likely be working with many different styles. Over the last few years I have become increasingly aware of the impact of styles on the coaching process, particularly as I have tended to undertake work in highly specialized industries. It has been in these contexts where the approaches and language used have deviated from my more traditional coaching approaches. These experiences have highlighted for me the value of bringing into early coaching discussions the concept of styles, as well as exploration of the synergies and diversity that exist within a team or group.

Styles can vary according to:

- Learning styles (auditory, visual, kinesthetic)
- Generational differences
- Cultural differences
- Personalities (MBTI, Personal Style Inventory)

Learning Styles

A lot has been written on different learning styles, ranging from Howard Gardner's "multiple intelligences" to Kolb's "learning styles." I personally like to keep things simple and recognize that many of my learners will bring a preference for visual, auditory or kinesthetic learning. Table 8.3 is a reminder of key preferences and approaches you may wish to incorporate to meet the different learning needs within the group.

I continue to see that learning styles have a profound effect on how we see and engage with the world in which we operate. In the group and team coaching environments it can be very useful to ask group members about their learning styles early on and adapt your approaches accordingly. Some groups may be more kinesthetically inclined and may prefer to explore the "Wheel of Life" using a wheel

Table 8.3: Coaching Approaches for Different Learning Styles

Learning Style	Enjoys/Key Question	Approaches to Incorporate
Visual	• Prefers things that they can see • "What does it look like?"	• Worksheets, workbooks, readings they can review before a session • In person: flipcharts • Virtual: visual anchor points, Web-based slides
Auditory	• Learns by hearing • "What does it sound like?"	• Phone/in person: auditory touch points • Communication that is voice related, not just written • Podcasts and other audio files
Kinesthetic	• Learns by doing • "What does it feel like?"	• Geography/body-centered coaching • Activity on phone/Web programs • Have people draw a line, take notes

taped on the floor, whereas other groups may want to individually reflect on this visually in a worksheet and then enter into dialogue around it.

In the individual coaching context we have been taught to ask only one question at a time. In the team or group coaching context we may be even more effective by asking a similar question in different ways. For example, consider how these three questions will have different resonance for people with varied learning styles: "What does it look like?" versus "What does it sound like?" versus "What does it feel like?"

Coaches can benefit from asking for feedback about the different approaches being used and how they are meeting learning style preferences individually and collectively. On a related note, it can also be useful to receive feedback on the pace of the conversations (too fast, too slow, just right) throughout the coaching process. Each group and team will have its own rhythm.

Generational Differences

Generational differences continue to be a hot discussion topic in business today. We now have four generations in the workplace, ranging from the Silent Veterans who may be mentoring or consulting to the younger generation, to the Baby Boomers, many of whom have delayed retirement, to Gen Xers, still squeezed in the "middle," and Gen Yers or Millennials. Key to understanding these differences in the group and team coaching context is that we have been socialized and educated in different ways. Different social and world events have also shaped what we value and how we prefer to work.

Members of different generations are likely to be present in team and group coaching contexts. Of particular note for coaches is to be sensitive to the various differences that may exist within a group, as well as to be aware of any assumptions that may be at play. Even though individuals are part of a certain generation, we want to avoid any stereotyping and look at what individual values and experiences are shaping and driving each group or team member.

Table 8.4 outlines the characteristics and values different generations tend to hold. Coaches will want to pay attention to the column on coaching and learning

Table 8.4: Coaching and Learning Support Needs for Different Generations[4]

Generation	Focus Areas	Coaching and Learning Support Needs
Silent Veteran/ Traditionalist		
Born before 1946 **Key Influences:** WWII, Depression **Key Characteristics:** Loyal, experienced, respectful, dedicated, values hard work	Many are now retired but may be back in workforce on special projects or in mentor role	Support for the changes in lifestyle Pacing may be slower Support for them to transfer their skills and insights Technology may pose some barriers/challenges
Baby Boomer		
Born 1946–1964 **Key Influences:** 60s and 70s, gender equality **Key Characteristics:** Team player, loves meetings, loyal, experienced, may not be comfortable with technology	Team focus, support for technology, personal touch: communication and community	Work/life and transition to retirement likely key issues "Lives to work"

(Continued)

---

[4] An amalgamation of many sources including Bea Fields et al., "Generation Y: Everything You Ever Wanted to know about the Millennials," Millennial Leaders, accessed May 6, 2013, http://millennial leaders.com/Gen_Y_Brownson.pdf and presentations done by Cam Marston of www.generational insights.com.

Table 8.4: (*Continued*)

Generation	Focus Areas	Coaching and Learning Support Needs
Gen Xer		
Born 1965–1981 **Key Influences:** 1980s MTV and pop culture 1990s recession and downsizing **Key Characteristics:** Risk taking Individualistic Walk the talk: cynical Work life very important More individualistic Entrepreneurial	Often motivated by "why?" Comfortable with technology Support for sandwich generation: children and aging parents	Support for work/life issues and multiple "roles": parent, caretaker Focus on individuality Balance is key Appreciates feedback and coaching on the spot
Gen Yer		
Born 1982 to present **Key Influences:** Computers/technology Connectivity **Key Characteristics:** Values peer support Work/life "balance/ harmony" is key Collaboration and teamwork critical Does not value meetings Technology is part of the everyday Values the "now" and "just in time": quick communication, feedback, advancement	Enjoys peer learning and collaborative learning experiences Most comfortable with technical applications and virtual environment Moved by visuals Real-time learning and communication: texting may be as important if not more than face-to-face communication Community is key: technologically supported Welcomes coaching and mentoring	Just in time Fast pace May benefit from combination of coaching and mentoring (skills focus, culture) Integrate technology into coaching: apps, etc. "Works to live"

support needs. Regardless of what type of programming you are offering (coaching, teleclass, webinar), the right column provides issues and topics to consider around program implementation and focus.

As Judy Feld states in her article "Bridging the Gap: Group Coaching Across Generations," "The coach must park any generational bias and ensure maximum inclusion of all generations."[5] Given that generational labels have often become a topic that gets thrown around, almost a new stereotype, with individuals being labeled because of their age, as coaches we need to be careful to approach individual team and group members as individuals.

Judy suggests that group coaches can do a number of things to make group coaching meaningful for all generations. Coaches can vary the venue, clarify the agenda and outcomes, establish the group coaching structure, and ensure that all get a chance to be coached, and close with commitments and feedback.

Many articles have pointed to the fact that younger generations in the workforce value coaching and mentoring. This may be an emerging area for future coaching opportunity. Jane Buckingham and Marcus Buckingham state that three of the values Gen Y hold are: everything is customized; change must be embraced; and constant, immediate feedback.[6] With these in mind it is encouraging to think about how Gen Y will embrace group and peer coaching processes.

Cultural Differences

I spent the first 13 years of my career in the international development sector, working for the United Nations and British and Canadian NGOs in international cooperation. As a leader it was typical that my teams were made up of staff members from multiple cultural backgrounds. With the advent of virtual teams, today it is commonplace for teams to be more culturally diverse than they were five years ago. What has been fascinating for me to see is how group coaching work has rippled out around the world in many different ways. Take note of the work of Shana Montesol, a coach based in the Philippines who works across cultures, and Kevin Stebbings, who is based in and works primarily in Asia.

---

[5] Judy Feld, "Bridging the Gap: Group Coaching Across Generations," *Choice: The Magazine of Professional Coaches* 9, no. 1 (March 2011): 36–40.
[6] Jane Buckingham and Marcus Buckingham, "Note to Gen Y Workers: Performance on the Job Actually Matters," *Time*, September 28, 2012. http://business.time.com/2012/09/28/note-to-gen-y-workers-performance-on-the-job-actually-matters.

A great resource for coaches who are involved in intercultural coaching is the work of Philippe Rosinski, author of *Coaching Across Cultures.*[7] Several books could be dedicated to this topic. What is certain is that in today's global business environment, coaches are likely to be working with group and team members who come from varied cultural backgrounds. Consideration should be given to structuring your program to take into consideration differences based on language, culture, etc.

When working with groups or teams that have diverse group members, be aware of the following:

- **Role of language:** The language you use may vary depending on the different groups and teams you work with. For example, my language when working within the safety industry is different from the language I use when working with educators. Within each group there may be varied language needs, which may require that you pose questions and use activities that meet the varied needs of the group. Note that these link to the core ICF coaching competencies of Direct Communication and Creating Awareness; these competencies mean that the coach is able to express insights in ways that are useful and meaningful to the client. Using meaningful language is key to engagement.
- **Differing needs for pacing and processing:** It is likely that different group members will process in different ways (some slow, some fast, some through speaking, others through writing). As such, it is important to provide a variety of approaches and techniques to meet the different processing needs, offering individual reflection activities for those who prefer to process on their own, as well as pre-work and post-work (or field work) for those who need more time to process and like to take a deeper dive around issues.
- **Preferences for communication in different channels:** Some people prefer to communicate orally (by spoken word) whereas others prefer written communication. This may be an issue if multiple languages are at play within the group or team. As the coach, be aware and inquire about people's preferences. Depending on the group or team needs you may opt to vary your approaches. If members have a preference for written communication, for example, encourage more email communication or sharing of materials participants have worked on as field work.

---

[7] Phillipe Rosinski, *Coaching Across Cultures: New Tools for Leveraging National, Corporate and Professional Differences* (Boston: Nicholas Brealey Publishing, 2003).

Personality Styles

Other differences may show up in a team or group coaching process due to the personalities involved. Many coaches may find themselves working with assessments such as Myers-Briggs Type Indicator (MBTI) or the Personal Style Inventory (PSI). The PSI is available from HRD Press. These assessments can be very useful in supporting individual team and group members to become more aware of their preferences. In terms of their membership in a group or team, the sharing of these styles can be very insightful and lead to a lot of "Aha! moments."

In most groups you may have a mix of styles and different personality types. However, if you are undertaking work in specific industries you may find that certain styles are more represented than others. For example, one industry I work with has overwhelmingly had a similar style emerge in almost 95 percent of participants over four major groupings. Being aware of preferences is important in terms of adapting your structure, activity and language. I have learned over time (from their feedback and my observation) that for that 95 percent of participants they enjoy more kinesthetic learning approaches (physical movement), and conversations in pairs or smaller groups rather than in the larger group. This has significantly impacted the design of our work together.

Coaches may opt to bring in a new assessment for the work they do, or they may piggy-back off assessments that have been done previously in the organization. This is a useful area for discussion with a sponsor to find out what has been used, and what is planned to be used in an organization.

APPROACHES FOR ENGAGEMENT AND CONNECTION AT THE END OF THE COACHING PROCESS

Coaching processes have start and end points. We often place a lot of emphasis on the start, but not as much attention on the end. As we wrap up this chapter, I want to turn our attention to the end of the coaching process.

As coaching begins to wind down, it is important to consider and build in with your group and team coaching clients how they will sustain the momentum and commitment around the goals they have been working on after the coaching process ends.

Questions that are key at this stage are:

- Who do they want to be accountable to going forward?
- What will support them in continuing to make momentum?
- What will they do to build in "pause" points along the way of their work/ life to check in and see where they are, set new goals, celebrate?

At the end of a group or team coaching process you may wish to include some or all of the following activities:

- **Organize a post-program group or team call four to six weeks after the process ends:** Ask participants what they have been using, what they have been noticing, what is getting in the way of roll-out, and what additional supports and conversations they need to have.
- **Plan for post-program one-on-one calls:** You may also opt to meet with each participant individually after the coaching process is done. It can be important for the individual to use this as an opportunity to refocus on the commitments they have made, look at what they have achieved so far, and define their focus going forward. In general, post-program calls are very important from an evaluation standpoint to see the more medium-term impact of the program, and changes that may need to be made, as well as other coaching or programming supports needed going forward.
- **Communities, centers of practice or alumni groups:** As a coach or leader you may opt over time to start creating a community or alumni group for the group and team members (as appropriate) you have worked with. The focus of these communities may be around sharing of experience, skills and resources, as well as key issues of interest. In my work over the years I have developed a community made up of group coaching alumni as well as a business leaders community. The alumni group meets by phone four times a year. Each call has a different educational focus, and also provides an opportunity to share best practices.

    Different group members may find varying value out of the communities, centers of practice or alumni groups. Ask your alumni what they want in terms of support. Vehicles can be as simple as a regular call, or may incorporate some of the social media vehicles such as Facebook to sustain the conversation and bring different cohorts together.

Throughout this chapter we have explored different ways to ensure your group engagement. From considering group and team development to looking at what you can do to boost interaction and connection in the virtual domain to suggestions on closure, there are many opportunities for coaches to be present and listen for what the people they are working with want.

End-of-Program Reminders

Logistically, at the end of the program, you will want to make sure that:

- Final evaluations have been sent and received
- Final one-on-one calls are scheduled
- Certificates of completion are sent
- Any logs updated (ICF coaching log)
- Any client communication patterns are updated (e.g., contact emails included in email management process, if approval given by client)

Part III expands our view of coaching many. The first two chapters of Part III will connect us to the bigger-picture level of program design for leadership and capacity building within organizations. These are two areas in which team and group coaches may find themselves connecting their programs to wider corporate initiatives. The final two chapters of the book look at the important topic of co-facilitation and collaboration in coaching, as well as trends in team and group coaching.

End-of-Chapter Questions

For Coaches

- What issues do you want to keep an eye on as a coach throughout the coaching process?
- What techniques do you want to employ as a coach to support the connections with and among group and team members—before, during and after the coaching process?
- What special considerations or adaptations do you want to make with your virtual programs?
- What coaching activities do you already have to strengthen connection? Which ones do you want to add to your toolkit?

For Leaders

- In your context, what will be the biggest barriers to engagement?
- What one to two approaches will support better engagement? For in-person discussions? For virtual programs?

EXPANDING OUR VIEW OF COACHING MANY

Part III expands our view of what "coaching many" means. So far in this book, coaching many has focused on an expansion of coaching skills from the individual coaching context to the team and group coaching context. Coaching does not take place in a vacuum. The sustainability of the outcomes of many of our initiatives is connected to other initiatives that go on in an organization, such as mentoring and supervision. For example, in working with a team of mid-level managers, the coaching engagement plays one part in enhancing performance. In the larger picture, there will be additional supports from their bosses, peers and mentors to boost managerial abilities. This part of the book expands the lens to incorporate a view of these related players, their typical roles and how programming can best be positioned.

The next three chapters take a look at specific issues coaches may encounter when undertaking team and group coaching work in the organizational context, and expanding their coaching to many.

Chapter 9 looks at the topic of capacity development, the opportunity to strengthen the organizations we work with. The chapter explores our connection with our work as team and group coaching to other learning initiatives that may be ongoing, including mentoring, leader as coach and peer coaching. Team and group coaches may be called upon to develop train-the-trainer programs for leaders as coaches, as well as peer coaches.

Chapter 10 looks at the specialized coaching area of leadership development. Voices from the Field explores an example in which group coaching was introduced, in the words of Ursula Lesic, as "a vehicle to bring cohesiveness to an organization while building communication skills." For those involved in the design or implementation of leadership development programming, we also look at the sticky factor, or transfer and application of learning through the positioning of group coaching, mentoring and specific supervisory support. Other common coaching areas in leadership development, such as emotional intelligence, are also explored.

Chapter 11 looks at the topics of collaboration and partnering. In many corporate engagements, working as a coach with larger groups, teams or entire organizations, a coach may partner with a co-facilitator, someone who is another coach or possibly an internal resource. The first part of Chapter 11 looks at ingredients for successful partnering and co-facilitation. Related to partnering is the topic of collaboration. Team and group coaching are increasingly viewed as approaches to boost collaboration. So, what should we consider and know as coaches about collaboration? The last half of Chapter 11 explores the topic of collaboration in general.

Chapter 12 looks at trends that have emerged in our work in coaching teams and groups.

The appendix includes a selection of activities and exercises that practitioners may want to incorporate into their work.

CHAPTER 9

CAPACITY DEVELOPMENT: MENTORING, COACHING, SUPERVISION, LEADER AS COACH AND PEER COACHING

*What's really driving the boom in coaching is this: as we move from
30 miles an hour to 70 to 120 to 180 . . . as we go from driving straight down
the road to making right turns and left turns to abandoning cars and
getting motorcycles . . . the whole game changes, and a lot of people are
trying to keep up, learn how not to fall off.*
—John Kotter, Professor of Leadership, Harvard Business School[1]

Themes including the ever increasing pace of change, doing more with less, globalization, virtualization and external shocks such as natural disasters are having
a tremendous impact on today's business environment. These issues shape the
development context for teams and individuals in today's workforce. *How are our
approaches as coaches, and supporters of enhanced performance, shifting to meet
these real-time issues?*

---

[1] "Why Good Coaching is Critical Now," BlessingWhite e-news 2, no. 8 (August 2002). http://www
.blessingwhite.com/Content/Articles/enews/August2002.asp?pid=2.

This chapter discusses the need for coaches working with organizations to synergize with the myriad of different types of learning and development initiatives that exist in an organization, whether mentoring, coaching skills training for leaders or other initiatives. These endeavors are supporting top-level performance as well as sustainable change within organizations.

Key in this process of enhancing productivity and performance is *building organizational capacity* or capacity development. Capacity development can be defined as the "process of developing and strengthening the skills, abilities, processes and resources that organizations . . . need to survive, adapt and thrive in the fast-changing world."[2]

Capacity building is all about building internal capability, as well as building a series of skill sets, processes and resources that will strengthen the organization. Supervisors, leaders as coaches, mentors and team and group coaches can all play key roles in capacity building, ensuring greater support to employees and impact on organizations. As coaches it is important for us to understand the different roles of these players and how they relate to one another.

As stated earlier, coaching does not happen in a vacuum. At any given time there may be a multitude of ongoing initiatives in an organization, strengthening teams, leaders and the organization itself. As coaches we may also be asked by HR or senior leaders about how our work can be positioned for even greater impact. Coaching has a discrete start and end point. To maximize the impact of our work, it can be useful to consider the linkages and connection points with other corporate initiatives. For example, coaching a group of new managers may be one part of a larger talent management initiative to grow the succession pipeline. These new managers may also have internal supports, such as mentoring, and onboarding support and regular feedback from their supervisor.

This chapter looks at:

- The context of capacity development and engagement in today's organizations
- Players in capacity development: the roles of mentor, coach, and supervisor
- Mentoring: what it is, and developing a mentor training program
- Developing your internal cadre of coaches: peer coach and manager as coach—skills, models and the coaching arc
- Coaching many and the impact on culture

---

[2] Ann Philbin, Capacity Building in Social Justice Organizations, Ford Foundation, 1996, accessed May 13, 2013, http://www.pactworld.org/galleries/resource-center/Intro.

MY OWN STORY

As much as many of the themes I mention at the start of the chapter appear to be taken from today's headlines—*the ever-increasing pace of change, doing more with less, globalization, virtualization and external shocks such as natural disasters*—in fact, they have been a part of the fabric of my work since the early 1990s. My passion for work in the realm of capacity development started early in my career. As a newly minted Master's graduate, I entered a work environment spanning four continents, connected only by a fax machine. In this "real office job" after my grad work, I stepped into a role as an acting international programs director (IPD), with an organization that had had 80 percent of its funding base cut only months before. As the IPD I had responsibilities for field support and field staff training in two locations in Central and South America—thousands of miles away from my desk in Toronto.

After months of ups and downs with the organization's operations, a new board in place, and a renewed commitment to field programming, the new executive director approached me on the second day of her job. She asked me, as someone who already had several years of experience within the organization at the field and headquarters level, what would give the organization the greatest impact in our context of "doing more with less." I didn't hesitate to say, "Better training for our field staff." Up to that point, trainers had been flown in to deliver an intensive three-week training program for national and international staff who were tasked not only with leading teams in remote conditions, but were also responsible for the development and implementation of essential medical, environmental and health projects in Central and South America.

"Right, then," she told me. "You've got forty-eight hours to pull together a proposal." Forty-five hours later the courier picked up the proposal for funding a new capacity building initiative in which national trainers would be identified and by the next year would assume the training role for field staff in the project locations. Over the span of the next six months, together with a new team of incredibly talented partners from Guyana and Costa Rica, we pulled off what a year before would have been impossible—especially given the fact that the doors might have been closed for the entire organization.

I was sure that building the capability of the in-country orientation programs was going to transform the field staff training. I also felt that it would move the organizational programming for our national partners forward significantly—and it did. Early the next spring as I participated in the national training in Costa Rica, I could see how transformed the training had become. We also learned *together* as a global team that the one-off was not enough. I was fortunate after this six-month period to return to Guyana for another 18 months, ultimately leading the field operations and seeing firsthand how the training process had been nationalized as well as infused with more local-level practicalities over time. My Guyanese counterpart, the national director, played a key role in strengthening her organization. Just as we will see through this chapter and the rest of the book, success came from great training and empowering supervisors, supported by coaching and mentoring. Success of this initiative also came from ongoing conversation, evaluation and tweaking.

Keep in mind the year was 1995 and coaching as a modality was still very new. It had not been heard of where I was based in Guyana. As a program director, I could see the critical importance of ongoing virtual support to my team members, those field professionals tasked with youth and community development projects. After they left headquarters, our only connection for three months (other than one visit mid-stream) was often a piece of mail or three times a day "sit-reps" on a high-frequency radio.

This experience led me to almost another decade of work at the field level, building onto this initiative with other organizations and local non-governmental and governmental partners in the realm of capacity building. Creating new generations of leaders was often the focus area, as was enhancing team performance with teams who were geographically dispersed. Teams I worked with were sometimes located across the same country, where travel could take up to a week, and sometimes they were across sub-regions, as was the case in my last role where my staff team was spread across 10 countries.

These experiences have led me to become a real advocate for boosting internal capability through the intersection of the role of the supervisor with mentoring and also coaching (peer coaching, internal coaching or external coaching). Leadership in a complex, ever-changing environment requires that we build the capabilities of those around us, enabling them to do their best work possible.

These early experiences for me as a leader created much of the "DNA" I continue to operate from. Supervisors, mentors and coaches play a critical role in supporting teams to do more with less, adapt to unknown and ongoing change to create world-class organizations.

THE CONTEXT OF BUSINESS TODAY

Look at the business headlines, pick up any business conference brochure, or read any of the business feeds online: *engagement, toxicity and ongoing change are all key themes in today's business context.* Capacity development is an opportunity for building internal capability and strength. Let's look at each one of these and the connection with coaching.

Engagement

Disengagement costs the U.S. economy $350 billion per year.[3] Disengagement translates to absenteeism, as well as highly dysfunctional behavior. Organizations may look to bring in coaches to work with teams that face engagement issues. As we know, engaged employees are those employees who show up every day excited and motivated to do work. Engaged employees comprise about 29 percent of the North American workforce today. Many organizations take a proactive approach and may pair these engaged employees with coaches to help them excel. As these individuals move into leadership roles it creates a more enabling environment for team and group coaching.

Disengaged employees make up approximately 52 percent of today's business environment, and actively disengaged employees make up 19 percent.[4] Actively disengaged employees are not only unmotivated to do good work, they are workers who sabotage or undermine the corporation's objectives and goals.

Engagement Is Essential

"High employee engagement is strongly correlated with a range of productivity-related measures such as revenue per employee, absenteeism, and turnover," says Neil Crawford. "Highly engaged employees have slightly more than one-half of the absenteeism of disengaged employees. This translates into an average difference of about six days per employee per year. If the total annual employee cost is $40,000, the productivity savings for high engagement could be as high as $1,000 per employee, per year from absenteeism alone."[5]

Control, Opportunity and Leadership: A Canadian Study of Employee Engagement in the Canadian Workplace from Psychometrics in 2010 looked at the impact of engagement (and disengagement) in the Canadian workforce. HR respondents indicated that for engaged employees, "common results are a willingness to do more than expected (39 percent), higher productivity (27 percent), better working relationships (13 percent) and more satisfied

---

[3] Curt Coffman, interview by Barb Sanford, "The High Cost of Disengaged Employees," *Gallup Business Journal*, April 15, 2002, http://businessjournal.gallup.com/content/247/the-high-cost-of-disengaged-employees.aspx.

[4] 2011 Gallup Employee Engagement Index.

[5] Aon Hewitt, "Aon Hewitt's Top 50 Best Employers in Canada Study Shows Slight Increase in Employee Engagement," *Canada Newswire*, October 18, 2012, http://www.newswire.ca/en/story/1055247/aon-hewitt-s-top-50-best-employers-in-canada-study-shows-slight-increase-in-employee-engagement.

customers (10 percent)." For disengaged workers the "most common results of disengagement were dysfunctional work relationships (29 percent), lower productivity (25 percent) and an unwillingness to go beyond the job description (17 percent)."[6]

So what's the connection with coaching? Notice how the results above focus on productivity and relationships. These are areas that can have significant impact from coaching at the team and group level. Sometimes coaches are brought in to support engagement initiatives, directly or indirectly. We may also be called in to work with those high-flying, high-performing teams; the teams that have new leaders; or sometimes the teams that are in desperate need of support.

Questions to Consider

How is engagement important to the teams and organizations you work with?
What do they measure around engagement (e.g., Hewitt Survey)?
What is the connection for your partners between coaching and engagement?

Working with Toxicity

Coaches are often called in to address the dysfunctional work relationships mentioned above. Historically this has typically been a one-on-one approach, but more coaches may find themselves coaching these dysfunctional systems, whether they are pairs or entire teams. As conversations start, it becomes apparent that the dysfunctional working relationships are poisoning or impacting others.

Research by Elizabeth Holloway and Mitchell Kusy found that 94 percent of leaders have worked with someone toxic or chronically unproductive and 27 percent experience direct mistreatment by them at least once.[7] In a related study of nurses, 91 percent had experienced verbal abuse, in which they felt devalued or humiliated, and more than 50 percent did not feel competent to respond![8]

---

[6] Psychometrics, *Control, Opportunity and Leadership: A Study of Employee Engagement in the Canadian Workplace*, 2011, 4. http://www.psychometrics.com/docs/engagement_study.pdf.
[7] Mitchell Kusy and Elizabeth Holloway, *Toxic Workplace! Managing Toxic Personalities and Their Systems of Power* (San Francisco: Jossey-Bass, 2009), quoted in Elizabeth Holloway and Mitchell Kusy, "Disruptive and Toxic Behaviors in Healthcare: Zero Tolerance, the Bottom Line, and What to Do About It," *Medical Practice Management* (May/June 2010), 335.
[8] Kusy and Holloway, *Toxic Workplace!*, 5.

The impact of this toxicity is significant from a business perspective. Christine Porath and Christine Pearson found that for those working in a toxic environment:[9]

- 48 percent decreased their work effort
- 47 percent decreased time at work
- 38 percent decreased work quality
- 68 percent said their performance declined
- 80 percent said they lost time worrying about it
- 63 percent lost time avoiding the person
- 78 percent said their commitment to the organization declined

These results have impact and implications at the three levels we have discussed: individual, team and organization.

In working with teams that are toxic, coaches may find themselves working to rebuild trust and respect. Enabling team members to become aware of the toxic nature of their behaviors is an important part of the coaching process. Many teams feel that the toxic behavior is "just the way it is." With its significant business impacts, toxic behavior is neither sustainable nor acceptable.

Teams may benefit from becoming more aware of how toxic behaviors undermine relationships of every kind—teams, partnerships and even intimate relationships. Psychologist John Gottman has developed a useful framework of the most dangerous toxic behaviors, a framework that he calls the "Four Horsemen of the Apocalypse."[10] The four horsemen are:

Criticism

Criticism is different from a complaint. A complaint is a comment that addresses a specific action. Criticism is more global and throws blame on the other. Criticism involves attacking someone's personality or character rather than the behavior, usually with the intent of making someone right and someone wrong. Those who are criticizing may use language like "You always" or "You never . . ." Criticism may morph into other "horsemen."

---

[9] Christine Porath and Christine Pearson, quoted in Holloway and Kusy, "Disruptive and Toxic Behaviors in Healthcare," 338, 339.

[10] Gottman and Silver, *The Seven Principles for Making Marriage Work.*

Defensiveness

This escalates the conflict, pointing the finger at someone else or saying, "It's not me." In defensiveness, team members see themselves as victims, warding off perceived attacks or challenges to how they seem themselves. Defensiveness is often seen in the "us versus them" approach.

Stonewalling

This involves withdrawing from the relationship as a way to avoid conflict. Imagine a stonewall that "goes up" with no way around it. Stonewallers act as if they don't care what the other party is saying, even if they hear it. With stonewallers there is little, if any acknowledgement, of what is being said.

Contempt

This is one of the most toxic of all behaviors. Contempt has physiological impact over time. Contempt is attacking another with the intention to insult or psychologically abuse the other. Common contempt signals can include rolling of the eyes, and sayings like "there she goes again."

Some of these behaviors may be so ingrained that team members do not recognize the four horsemen when they do emerge. In working with highly dysfunctional teams it can be very useful to introduce this framework and get the team to self-identify when these behaviors are present. Given that many of these toxic behaviors become second nature, the enhanced self-awareness can be very useful.

One team I worked with found the framework to be an important way to compartmentalize the different behaviors they were experiencing. Gossip, eye-rolling, and shutting down during meetings were all endemic to the team when we started our work together. One of their lowest ratings in the Team Diagnostic assessment was trust.

As we started our work together, and they saw the map of their strengths and weaknesses, the team recognized that these behaviors were eroding their performance as well as making their workdays miserable. The shared framework of the four horsemen, and the invitation to name the toxins that were present, became a way for team members to begin developing positive new habits and ways of communication. Over the next six months, toxic behavior was minimized, with slippages being reduced over time. Commitment to adopting new types of behaviors, supported by the team contract, kept this issue front and center for the team.

Ongoing Change

From the rapid pace of information and knowledge where the body of knowledge is doubling every one to two years,[11] to the globally connected business environment we operate within, it is likely that coaches will be working with teams and organizations around change issues.

It can be important to remind team members of the process of change—the ups and downs, as well as the time required to undertake change. Within any change process, different team members will adjust at different paces. As Everett Rogers identified, approximately 2.5 percent of people will be Innovators, welcoming change with open arms. Behind them come the Early Adopters (13.5 percent), those who are excited to try something new with encouragement. The Early Majority are slower to change, and often rely on "seeing" or "hearing" from the Innovators and Early Adopters that things really will work. The Early Majority is about one-third (34 percent) of any work force percent. The Late Majority make up another 34 percent and are more resistant to change. Finally, the Laggards (14 percent) are those who resist change, often digging in their heels. Introducing this framework to team members can help to normalize the change process for each individual and help individuals identify where they are. Collectively teams can also map out their team composition and what their change preferences are.

Dorothy Nesbit writes, "In times of significant change, team coaching can help whole teams make plans and co-ordinate effective action, while supporting individual team members in navigating the personal implications of change."[12]

Some teams may reach a point of "change fatigue," especially if they have been in the throes of downsizing, new leadership and change for a while. Coaches can support the conversation about what impact change fatigue has had on productivity and results, as well as what is needed for renewal.

Within change there is challenge as well as opportunity. As Elaine Biech writes, "In the Chinese language the word 'crisis' is comprised of two characters. One represents danger and the other represents opportunity. Change, which is sometimes crisis-driven, has the same positive/negative relationship. There is danger in change, but there is also huge opportunity."[13]

---

[11] Elaine Biech, *Thriving Through Change: A Leader's Practical Guide to Change Mastery* (Virginia: ASTD Press, 2007), 4.

[12] Nesbit, "Coaching in Hard Times," 66.

[13] Biech, *Thriving Through Change*, 7.

THE PLAYERS IN CAPACITY DEVELOPMENT

Whether we are working on talent management initiatives, boosting emotional intelligence in a team, or looking to develop a new generation of leaders, learning and sustainable change requires support from many different players: mentors, coaches and supervisors. Each player has the opportunity to play a distinct role. Figure 9.1 identifies the diffident focus areas of each of these players.

The Role of the Coach

Coaches in today's business context may be external or internal coaches. Increasingly organizations are also developing a network of peer coaches and leaders as coaches. The role of a coach is to provide support to the coaching client on enhanced goal setting and deepening awareness around issues faced at work, and to support action toward individual and organizational goals. Keeping in mind that "coaching is a conversation with intent," coaching:

- Supports the application of KSAs (knowledge, skills and abilities)
- Taps into the knowledge base of the employee (employee as expert)
- Leads with powerful questions
- Focuses on goal setting and enhanced awareness, action and accountability around key goals (self, team and organization)

Figure 9.1: Coaching, Mentoring and Supervision

Coaching
- KSAs
- Tapping into knowledge base of employee
- Powerful questions
- Goal setting
- Awareness, Action and Accountability

Mentoring
- Not direct line management
- KSAs
- Experience
- Internal workings
- Practical past experience

Supervision
- Supervision
- KSAs
- KPIs
- Feedback—constructive and positive
- Disciplinary context

The Role of Supervisors/Managers

Supervisors provide guidance, feedback and direction regarding individual and organizational performance. Management historically has been focused on four key activities: planning, organizing, leading and controlling. This concept was made popular by Henri Fayol in the late 1800s. More recently, managers and supervisors have been encouraged to add people to the equation.

Supervisors:

- Provide day-to-day supervision
- Focus on the day-to-day development of knowledge, skills and abilities of their team
- Focus on support for key performance indicators (KPIs), team-based goals and/or organizational objectives
- Provide feedback: positive and constructive
- Operate within the disciplinary context

The Role of Mentors

Mentoring is believed to have started back in ancient Greece, when Mentor took Telemachus, the son of Odysseus, under his wing and passed on all the wisdom he could. From those early roots, mentoring has played a key role in building organizational capacity. Mentoring today can play a key role in supporting the development of a more engaged, skilled and productive workforce. Mentors play a key role in translating into action "what's important" and "how to get the job done" in an organization.

Mentors:

- Are typically not direct-line management
- Focus on transferring their knowledge, skills and abilities through stories and sharing of their own practical KSA application
- Provide insight around the internal workings of an organization, departments and processes and industries
- Bring practical experience of how things work, and how to get things done

The Glasgow Mentoring Network provides this comprehensive definition of mentoring:

Mentoring is a goal oriented process that seeks to complement and add value to other sources of learning, development and support. Mentoring is a form of learning; a process in which a (usually) more experienced person (the mentor) passes on know how to someone less experienced. Mentoring sets out to capture the informal learning, knowledge, experience, networks and skills that exist . . . making it an exceptionally effective developmental tool for companies, communities, groups/teams and individuals.[14]

Many organizations struggle to understand the differences between coaching and mentoring. Having worked to deliver mentor training for mentors and protégés in a range of industries, including financial services and global services, I continue to make the distinctions between coaching and mentoring depicted in Table 9.1.

Table 9.1: Distinctions between Coaching and Mentoring

Coaching	Mentoring
More focused on specific (performance) needs of the person being coached	Broader in scope: increasing contacts, knowledge about the culture
May be provided by coach, leader or other	Role of a formal or informal mentor
Taps into what the employee "knows" or is learning	Mentor "shares" knowledge
Coach asks questions, provides guidance when asked/required (particularly leader as coach)	May bring in coaching skills such as listening and questioning
	Focused on issues specific to the organization (networks, culture, processes)
Issues may be professional and also personal	Meetings may be infrequent
More regular interaction with stronger accountability	Confidentiality important
	Focus on "how things are done"
Confidentiality is paramount	Goal setting, accountability and feedback are optional
Focus on goal setting and accountability	

---

[14] Glasgow Mentoring Network, quoted in Alan Hatton-Yeo and Scott Telfer, *Generations Working Together: A Guide to Mentoring Across Generations* (The Scottish Center for Intergenerational Practice, 2008), 7, http://www.volunteermoray.org.uk/resources/mentoring_across_generations.pdf.

Given the similar affinity, coaches may be called upon to work with HR to develop some of these talent initiatives. Coaches should keep in mind the distinctions and overlap with organizational mentoring. Some of the benefits and value of organizational mentoring are:

- A "bird's eye view" of how to get things done
- A practical scoop on the "real" role that people occupy, for example, "what it's really like to be". . . a financial analyst, or a safety inspector, or a community-based health care professional
- A perspective and stories of how one person's career path or leadership has emerged and played out
- A deeper understanding of the nuances, politics and culture of an organization

Mentors:

- Help junior staff see/understand the unwritten rules, culture and politics of an organization or industry
- Act as a sounding board/confidante
- Provide perspectives based on their experience
- Provide insights about networks, resources and processes available in an organization or industry
- Connect mentees with activities and people

Interestingly enough, successful mentoring processes undertake paths that are similar to coaching. Key success factors in mentoring include developing a mentoring partnership, setting goals, regular meetings/conversations (often less frequent than coaching), and adjustment to the areas of focus (which may include career, work/life issues, technical questions). Like coaching, mentoring processes usually have a defined start and end, and are evaluated.

As Susan Murphy and Ellen Ensher state, "Research supports the wisdom that mentors and protégés who communicate more frequently are happier and more productive than those who communicate sporadically."[15]

Mentoring can fall off the rails when:

- Roles and responsibilities are not clear
- Expectations are not clear (including focus areas, what each person expects from the mentoring relationship, roles and lack of matching expectations in terms of commitment)

---

[15] Ellen Ensher and Susan Murphy, "Establish a Great Mentoring Relationship," *T+D Magazine* (July 2006): 27.

- Trust is not present
- Communication is infrequent

Key skills for successful mentoring are very similar to coaching: asking good questions, listening, providing feedback and encouragement, and working around goal setting. Key to exceptional mentoring relationships is developing a relationship built on trust and rapport. Susan Murphy and Ellen Ensher continue, "For a mentor relationship to be effective, both parties must commit the time and energy to work with each other."[16]

Just as in coaching, mentoring can benefit from adopting a strengths-based approach. Some suggestions for using a strengths-based approach with teams are included in the Team Coaching in Action digital chapter at www.groupcoaching essentials.com and the appendix.

Field Journal: Designing a Mentoring Program

In looking at leader or team development in totality, mentoring along with coaching may be a consideration. Mentoring has the advantage of providing real/life insights into a job or industry. Mentoring can support the development of new strategies and technical skills for an employee. Mentoring also plays a key role in helping employees understand and navigate the culture of the organization or industry.

Over the past few decades I have been involved in developing several mentoring programs for organizations that I worked in, and in recent years with organizations that I partner with. Often mentoring is identified as a necessary strategy by the human resources department, or sometimes by new leaders themselves. Mentoring can be an effective vehicle for building organizational capacity in the era of budget constraint.

Just as in developing a coaching program or engagement, we will go through a series of stages in program development for mentoring. These stages include needs assessment, design, implementation, evaluation and maintenance or sustainability of the program. Figure 9.2 outlines the five stages in program development and some considerations at each stage. Consider how they may also be applicable to any coaching program development.

---

[16] Ibid.

Figure 9.2: Program Development Stages and Considerations

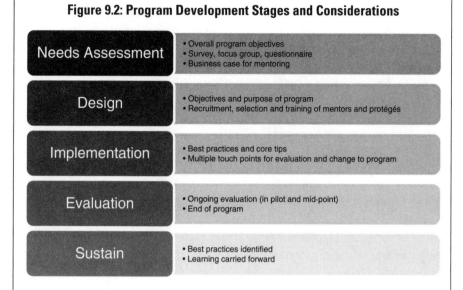

Needs Assessment	• Overall program objectives • Survey, focus group, questionnaire • Business case for mentoring
Design	• Objectives and purpose of program • Recruitment, selection and training of mentors and protégés
Implementation	• Best practices and core tips • Multiple touch points for evaluation and change to program
Evaluation	• Ongoing evaluation (in pilot and mid-point) • End of program
Sustain	• Best practices identified • Learning carried forward

Needs assessment is often the first step of any program development process. Depending on where a request has come from, you may wish to set up a series of interviews, or even focus groups relevant to stakeholders. For example, imagine that the organization is looking to develop a program for new leaders. Coaching is going to be one part of the process, as is mentoring. You will likely want to set up focus group meetings with those who are currently in the role (new and experienced), those who may be moving into the role, supervisors of those new leaders and HR. Some of the questions you may want to incorporate are:

What's the overarching purpose of this program? Is it to:

- Build capacity internally/externally?
- Transfer skills, knowledge and experience?
- Increase employee engagement?
- Support succession planning?
- Develop a talent pool?
- Enhance networks?
- Increase employees' understanding of different points of view?

(Continued)

Who is involved?

- Protégés:
    - Is it just for high-performers?
    - An integral part of your employee lifecycle?
- Mentors:
    - Seasoned?
    - Specific expertise?
- What type of issues do they want mentoring around?
- What support will they need?
- How much time will it take?[17]

One of the key success factors for mentoring programs is that the mentors have the necessary support and time to undertake the conversations. It may be very useful to hold a mentor training session, covering some, or all, of the topics listed below. Likewise, a separate initial training for the protégés is also useful, ensuring that both parties have access to the same tools, resources and support. Training of both mentors and protégés can be useful in setting expectations as well as providing key skills and frameworks and building relationships.

Depending on the scope of your program, you may have an hour or even half a day to work with mentors. One professional association I have worked with for the last five years offers a series of separate mentor and protégé training sessions over the lunch hour. I have delivered this one-hour session, multiple times, with similar content for both mentors and protégés. This is the start of a series of special events for mentors and protégés with subsequent events throughout the year being organized by an internal manager and involving industry specialists.

Another organization I have delivered mentor training to originally started off with a two-hour session for new mentors, which we did face to face. As new cohorts required training, some of the experienced mentors opted to take on a second or third mentee/protégé. This meant that the training numbers dropped to the point where the training is now done by phone, supplemented by a comprehensive mentor kit. The mentor kit includes support resources for the mentor, including an overview of the leadership development program they are supporting, with support questions. Regular group phone calls are also facilitated throughout the program with mentors and protégés to check in and see how the mentoring process is coming.

[17] Jennifer Britton, "Mentoring: An Essential Ingredient for Any Talent Management Strategy," presented at HRPA Conference 2010, Toronto.

Core Training Topics for New Mentors and Protégés

- Purpose of the mentoring program
- What is mentoring?
- Expectations:
  - Of the program regarding mentors and protégés
  - Between mentors and protégés
  - Different roles and responsibilities of the mentor and protégé
- Developing a powerful mentor-protégé relationship
- Setting boundaries
- Best practices for your mentoring sessions
- Suggested mentoring topics
- Mentoring dos and don'ts
- Mentoring pitfalls[18]

Another best practice around mentoring from experience is to create regular touch points for mentors to connect and share best practices they are evolving, and share resources; likewise, groups of protégés or mentees can connect to discuss their experiences. This can be very useful from an evaluation perspective as well.

Question

Taking a look at the program development stages, how can this be useful to you in creating programs for your clients (in mentoring or coaching skills or other areas)?

THE ROLE IN CAPACITY BUILDING OF OTHER COACHES: PEER COACHES AND MANAGERS AS COACHES

In addition to internal and external coaches, organizations may be working to create a cadre of peer coaches, or supporting their leaders to develop coaching skills. The following two sections address tips for creating your own peer coaching network or managers as coaches.

---

[18] Ibid.

Building a Peer Coaching Environment

Boosting the internal muscle of all team and group members is an important strategy in building a sustainable culture. Core coaching skills such as "enhanced listening," and the art of "better questioning" can have a profound ripple effect in internal communications and connections, as well as with customers and stakeholders.

As the Ohio Resource Center Network, Peer Coaching for ABLE Professionals states,

> A peer coach:
>
> - Supports another towards their goals
> - Helps develop planning, reflecting, problem-solving, decision-making, listening & speaking skills
> - Uses a non-judgmental stance
> - Focuses on assumptions, perceptions, thinking & decision making process of the other person to mediate resources, clarify intentions & identify options[19]

Robert Maitland identifies the different benefits provided by peer coaches versus mentors in his research undertaken in South Africa. His research found that peer coaches were a useful support to leadership development, succession planning and "accelerated development" processes.[20]

Table 9.2: Comparative Relational Outputs as Identified by Maitland

Peer Coaching	Mentoring Relationships
• Leadership skills Broad range of psycho-social skills: • Academic development • Diversity awareness • Decision-making skills • Assertiveness skills • Systemic thinking (pragmatic)	• Technical skills • Skills transfer • Decision-making skills • Self-awareness skills

---

[19] Ohio Resource Center Network, Peer Coaching for ABLE Professionals, "What Is Peer Coaching?", May 23, 2009, http://literacy.kent.edu/coaching/information/background.html.

[20] Robert Maitland, "Peer Coaching: Enabling Skills Development and Diversity Awareness in Corporate South Africa," Lifelab, accessed November 30, 2012, http://www.i-coachacademy.com/media/research/Peer%20Coaching%20Enabling%20Skills%20Development%20and%20Diversity%20Awareness%20in%20Corporate%20South%20Africa.pdf.

Maitland's research found the impact of peer coaching and mentoring relationships in different areas, as listed in Table 9.2. Notice how peer coaches and mentors can serve to support this new awareness and skill development in the different areas. Consider how the role of mentors and coaches could support your talent management or leadership initiatives.

Developing Your Cadre of Peer Coaches

Building capacity in teams and organizations continues to be a key challenge and opportunity today. As we have seen throughout the book, there is great opportunity for enhanced peer coaching, to make the coaching conversation part of the everyday culture.

Some of the key skills that peer coaches will want to develop include:

- **Temperature check:** asking the team/group to identify what's going on. What's the temperature in the room/environment right now?
- **Mirroring:** reflecting back (verbatim) what you have heard.
- **Listening:** listening at several different levels. What do you notice about the pace and pitch of the speaker? What is being said and what is not being said?
- **Questioning.**
- **Direct communication.**
- **Working around vision:** looking at where you want to go.
- **Working around values:** looking at what's important.
- **Support for priorities:** working with others around identifying priorities. Many different models exist for this, including Stephen Covey's Matrix, or our colored dot process.
- **Powerful questions.**
- **Curiosity.**
- **Assumption busting and perspective shifting.**
- **Support for goal setting and achievement.**
- **Creating accountability supports.**

Question to Consider

As you consider your work, how might a peer coaching approach be useful?

COACHING SKILLS TRAINING FOR LEADERS

"The growth and development of people is the highest calling of leadership"
—Henry S. Firestone

A final approach to building capacity in organization's today may include coaching skills training for leaders.

Leaders as coaches in today's world will benefit greatly from adopting a "Just in Time" approach to their coaching skills. In the coaching context *Just in Time* means that it can be utilized right now. Coaching skills such as powerful questioning and more focused listening are highly portable and can be integrated into any conversation. As I've reinforced throughout this book, "Coaching is a conversation with intent." Coaching has the possibility to enable team leaders and their staff to have greater clarity and quicker results. Leslie Bendaly states, "Coaching is one of the most powerful tools a leader can use to tap the best of their team members and to propel the team forward."[21]

Skill development for leaders as coaches can be in the areas of:

- Listening
- Asking good questions
- Emotional intelligence for self as leader and working around this with those you coach
- Building trust, respect and influence
- Developing core skills within your organization, in your managers and/or peers is key to building a coaching culture

Core components of any coaching skills training for leaders may include:

- Designing the coaching agreement: what coaching is, what coaching is not, confidentiality
- The change process
- Coaching within our organization: how coaching fits into the culture and how it has evolved
- Understanding the coaching arc
- Core skills for coaching
- Communication: questioning, listening
- Goal setting
- Gap analysis

---

[21] Bendaly and Bendaly, *Improving Healthcare Team Performance*, 172.

- Support for expanded awareness and action
- Accountability: creating accountability and working with your staff member to check in around their progress toward their goals
- Field work, coaching requests, challenges, inquiries
- Self-management, feedback and acknowledgement
- Connection with mentoring and/or learning
- Practice, practice and more practice (with feedback from peers and the coach trainer)

It is also useful for managers to get a sense of the arc of the coaching conversation (Figure 9.3), whether they will be working with individuals, teams or groups. Table 9.3 outlines the phases and focus areas of any coaching conversation.

Some organizations may have the opportunity to invest in one-day training or one week of training for their staff. Group coaching can be a great way to sustain

Table 9.3: Phases and Focus Areas of the Coaching Conversation

Phase of the Coaching Conversation	Focus
Establishing the coaching relationship	Focus and frequency of meetings, what coaching is and is not.
Building trust and rapport	As needed, especially if the leader is not coaching one of his or her own staff.
Identifying focus areas for the work and/or conversation	Identifying "What is the focus in our conversation today?"
Creating goals	The goals will form the backbone of each coaching conversation. Goals will shift. SMART-E. Link goals to corporate objectives/goals, team or department objectives.
Support for awareness and action	The coaching conversation will explore both domains of coaching: action and awareness. As coaches we want to create the opportunity to expedite results. If a person is naturally inclined to "get things done," what value can be had by deepening awareness around an issue?
Identifying commitments	What is the employee going to commit to do? By when? How will you know?
Check-in and review	Each coaching conversation will likely start with a check-in on commitments. The conversation will cycle back to identifying a topic or goal area for the conversation. Conversation focuses on deepening awareness and support of action.

Figure 9.3: The Arc of the Coaching Conversation

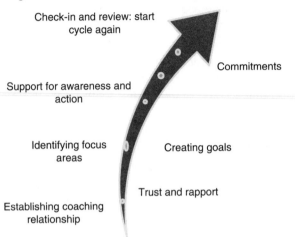

the learning and skill transfer process. You will want to refer to my Field Journal entry in the digital Group Coaching in Action chapter at www.groupcoaching essentials.com, The Coaching and Mentoring Skills Training Program. This is an example of the development of a customized coaching and mentoring skills training program with six months of follow-on group coaching support for the transfer of skills back to the workplace.

LEADER AS COACH COACHING MODELS

For several years I have worked with leaders and teams to develop their coaching skills. One of the models which I find works really well in today's Just-in-Time coaching environment, providing an easily remembered structure, is the GROW model from John Whitmore. One other coaching model leaders may find useful is Myles Downey's Big Three for teams.

The GROW model is Sir John Whitmore's foundational coaching model as first published in his book *Coaching for Performance*.[22] This framework is widely adopted and appreciated by professionals in all industries for its simplicity and ease of remembering. The GROW model is grounded in using questions to take the person being coached through a series of questions:

---

[22] John Whitmore, *Coaching for Performance* (Boston: Nicholas Brealey Publishing, 2002).

G - Goals: What are the goals of this coaching conversation? What do you want to explore?

R - Reality: What is the current state of this situation? What currently exists, happens at this stage?

O - Options: What options does the person have available to them to address the issue? What can you do to move from A to B?

W - Wrap up: This is the accountability piece. What will you do? By when? How will I know?

In leading many of these coaching skills workshops, I continue to hear how managers find this framework easy to remember, malleable, and also adaptable for different conversations.

Keeping in mind that coaching is a conversation with intent, the GROW model can support managers and also peers in holding a conversation that is more focused, and geared to develop awareness and support of meaningful, grounded action.

As always, questions are the backbone of the conversation. Table 9.4 shows some possible questions that team leaders or peer coaches may want to use in their conversations.

Table 9.4: Questions and the GROW Model

Goals	What is the goal of this meeting (conversation or discussion)?
	What are the goals for the short term? Long term?
	By when do you want to achieve it?
	What makes your goal:
	Specific?
	Measurable?
	Achievable?
	Realistic?
	Timely?
	Exciting (and challenging)?
	What does success look like?
	What are the milestones?
Reality	What's the current situation? What is taking up your time?
	Where are you noticing your time being spent?
	Who do you need support from?
	How much time are you spending on that task?

Table 9.4: (*Continued*)

Options	What options do you have?
	What else could you do?
	What if . . .?
	What are the costs and benefits of each of the options/alternatives?
	What's going to have the most impact?
	What's going to be easiest?
	Would you like another suggestion?
Wrap-Up	What are you going to do?
	By when?
	Will this action meet your goal?
	How will I know?/How will your accountability partner know?
	What follow-up is needed?
	What other obstacles may you face along the way?
	Who needs to know?
	On a scale of 1 to 10, how certainly will you undertake these actions?
	What will ensure that it is a 10?

In his book *Effective Coaching*, Myles Downey talks about the importance of exploring The Big Three with teams, or the "Who, What and How:"[23]

Who: Each team member needs to understand who each other team member is, what they are responsible for and how they are going to achieve it. The Who in team coaching explores the team's values and goals.

What: What do we want to create? This is about creating a common vision.

How: The How is our "ways of working." How are we as a team going to operate together? These are acceptable behaviors and norms agreed upon by everyone in the team. The How becomes our modus operandi.

The Who, What and How is a simple but effective framework for leaders to keep in mind as a foundation for team coaching work, or in undertaking any type of coaching conversation with their teams.

---

[23] Myles Downey, *Effective Coaching: Lessons from the Coach's Coach* (Cheshire, UK: Texere, 2003).

COACHING MANY AND THE IMPACT ON CULTURE

As we have seen, building organizational capacity takes more than one person. In the organizational context of doing more with less and ongoing change, coaches can play a key role around the support of individuals, leaders and teams as they address key business issues today. Coaches may be undertaking coaching work themselves or they may be working at the strategic level to build internal capability.

The role of coach in the team and group processes becomes intimately connected with culture change. Group coaching initiatives that bring together members from different parts of the organization have a significant impact on building new relationships. These new relationships often transcend across the silos that exist.

As coaching becomes more integrated throughout different parts of the organization, a coaching culture is developed. Years ago, the external coach was often "parachuted in" to work with executives. Today, "shadow coaches" may shadow teams and leaders as they go about their work, providing real-time opportunities to pause, reflect and reorient their skills and approaches. Several of the case studies included here, including Sharon Miller's case study in the digital chapter Team Coaching in Action, show how coaches can evolve their work. (The digital chapter can be viewed at www.groupcoachingessentials.com.) As we saw in Sharon's case study, the initial individual coaching work expanded into coaching initiatives with much greater scope for change across the organization—through work with separate teams and also the entire national operation.

Coaches were asked, "In building a coaching culture, what is important for organizations to consider? How can group and team coaching be positioned to do this?" Here are some of the reflections from coaches about building a coaching culture.

Voices from the Field: Building a Coaching Culture

Jacqueline Peters and Catherine Carr: Big question! Definitely team coaching can support a coaching culture. Training people in coaching skills is important so that there is more peer coaching going on informally in the system. A coaching culture isn't about hiring lots of outside coaches; it's about developing a way of being as leaders and colleagues that supports a coaching approach to discussions, meetings, problem solving, and even informal conversations. Gossip—in a culture that values coaching and self-accountability—has a chance to be turned into a coach opportunity. This requires training and clear

(Continued)

agreements that set up the skills, permission, and safety for team members to coach each other more informally, which ultimately supports a coaching culture. Team coaches can strategically implement and model this and teach leaders/individuals how to coach each other better.

Peter Hawkins just wrote a great book called *Creating a Coaching Culture*.[24] He suggests that coaches work with teams and the spaces in between teams to effect change throughout the system. To be successful, there needs to be executive and key decision maker support. The key is to work top down, bottom up, and side to side to really affect the culture.

Kevin Stebbings: In creating a coaching culture it is important for the organization to consider how it can help shift the perspective of coaching from being viewed as remedial to one of reward. A senior executive of a global banking corporation shared with me that executives and senior managers in her organization see coaching as something that is offered to those who need help. This creates the perspective that coaching is for individuals who somehow need fixing. This remedial viewpoint then limits the opportunity for the development of coaching and a culture of coaching. Offering coaching to executives who have excelled so that they can thrive and take things to "the next level" speaks of the powerful value of coaching. This creates a shift in perspective to a reward and places a higher value on the role of coaching within an organization. Promoting team and group coaching as a "greenhouse" where ideas, talents and opportunities are birthed and grown also communicates the value that group coaching offers. An added bonus of the group coaching process is that it reduces the isolation that people often feel in their organizations. Experiencing and seeing that others also want to develop and grow their skills together can be a very powerful motivator and leverages the inspiration that is often left untapped within organizations.

Michael Cullen: With the erosion of the all-important middle manager position and buffer between upper management and front line workers, many HR personnel have been given training in coaching in order to help mitigate performance issues. Not only is this untenable, but rarely sustainable. By engaging certified group and/or team coaches, organizations will benefit enormously from the non-judgmental, ethical and professional coaching results that have typically had a seven-times ROI on the fees paid—and employees will benefit from the increased ability for themselves to adequately handle new challenges while successfully addressing the very important issue of having a healthy life/work balance (resulting in less absenteeism and fewer stress-related illnesses).

---

[24] Peter Hawkins, *Creating a Corporate Culture* (Maidenhead, UK: Open University Press, 2012).

Kim Ades: Are the leaders getting coached? Are the leaders taking responsibility for their part in the current culture? Do the leaders have the level of awareness they require in order to build a coaching culture that truly fuels personal responsibility and excellence or is it just rhetoric? Leaders are crucial to the process and they must have 100-percent buy-in—both philosophically and practically. Leaders must be willing to "go first" through the coaching process and turn it into a way of life and not just a short-term experience.

Ray Rigoglioso: In my training work as a consultant, I have introduced coaching to organizations. While I have not offered coaching groups within organizations, I will say this: exploration of values is so important. I have participants identify the values of their organization, then their personal values. I ask them to identify where the two sets of values overlap. It produces immense insight and can lay a very strong foundation for a coaching culture.

Sharon Miller: Several key components to building a coaching culture include:

- Create and position the business case.
- Make sure this is seen as a core competency for leaders and why. Some reasons include: it is a key strategy for developing talent, aligning around business strategy, building effective relationships, leverage capability, etc.
- Link the coaching work to key business outcomes.
- Build engagement of key stakeholders. Have the coaching culture begin with the top. Ensure their visibility: attend training, work with seasoned coaches, etc.
- Develop a model and build training to support it.
- Integrate coaching into other people management processes (rewards and recognition as examples).

By visibly using group and team coaching as solutions, it embeds the belief that coaching is a key business strategy and part of the culture—a reminder that "Training plus coaching yields greater productivity improvements than training alone." *Public Personnel Management* found that training alone increased productivity in the workplace by 22.4 percent, while training plus coaching increased productivity by 88 percent.[25]

(Continued)

---

[25] Gerald Olivero; K. Denise Bane; Richard E. Kopelman, "Executive Coaching as a Transfer of Training Tool: Effects on Productivity in a Public Agency," *Public Personnel Management* 26, no. 4 (Winter 1997): 461.

> Group coaching is an action learning intervention. It solves real business problems and at same time focuses on what learning about change is and the process of working with others throughout the change process.
>
> **Phil Sandahl:** In my view, organizations have begun to shift from a focus on individual performance to team performance. The pressure is on doing more with less in order to compete successfully. Collaborative work teams can accomplish results that individuals, acting alone, simply can't. The future source for productivity improvement is with the team.

I believe that as the coaching profession continues to evolve, an increasing number of coaches will become involved, if they are not involved already, in working with their partners around capacity development issues. Throughout the chapter we have explored what capacity development is, as well as described the critical role of peer coaches, leaders as coaches, mentors and supervisors—related players in building stronger organizations.

Our next chapter takes a look at the topic of leadership development and developing a new cohort of leaders. Coaches working in the realm of coaching many may find themselves working in this domain.

End-of-Chapter Questions

What conversations can you have with organizations about how coaching fits into the larger context?

What is the role that mentors, coaches and supervisors can play in capacity development and culture change?

What would you incorporate into a training program for peer coaches or leaders as coaches?

What would you incorporate into a program for new mentors and protégés?

CHAPTER 10

DEVELOPING A NEW COHORT OF LEADERS

In times of change, learners inherit the Earth, while the learned find themselves beautifully equipped to deal with a world that no longer exists.
—Eric Hoffer[1]

One specialized area in which team and group coaches may find themselves working is the realm of leadership development, succession planning or developing a new cohort of leaders. There is ample room for coaches to work within the organizational context—whether working at the traditional executive coaching level of the C-suite, working with executive level teams, or working with mid-level management and supervisors.

Coaches can play a key role in creating space and focus for conversations across organizations, working with groups and teams to boost capacity and create a culture of collaboration. These topics are central to our last two chapters on building capacity, and co-facilitation, partnering and collaboration.

This chapter looks at team and group coaching in the sphere of leadership development. We will explore several areas team and group coaches will find themselves working, including emotional intelligence and styles. Several examples of how group coaches are working to support leadership development are also included in the chapter.

---

[1] http://www.brainyquote.com/quotes/quotes/e/erichoffer109153.html.

THE CONTEXT OF LEADERSHIP DEVELOPMENT

The context and players of the workplace are changing. Many of the "old school" leaders are retiring, ushering in new values and approaches for leadership. As I move across organizations it is common for me to hear comments such as, "Our new CEO is really different from the last—he actually remembers people's names," and "There is a difference happening in terms of leadership."

Many Gen Xers are now assuming senior leadership roles and, as we saw in Chapter 8, they bring different values than those held by the Boomers. The newest entrants to the workforce today are Gen Y, who value collaboration. As Bill Patterson writes:

> Generation-Y, or as some generationalists define—workers born from 1976-1991, represent a new class of employee: one shaped with a deep appreciation of technology combined with a desire to work collaboratively as teams versus seeking advancement solely on the basis of individual contribution. Interestingly, studies have shown that this new generation of employee not only thrives in highly collaborative workplaces, but is now making this a key requirement in *selecting* where to work. And it is in this area—becoming a highly collaborative workplace—which many organizations have their work cut out for them."[2]

Coaches play a key role in creating the spaces for conversation that are critical in a collaborative workplace.

LEADERSHIP DEVELOPMENT AND TEAM AND GROUP COACHING

Leadership development coaching contributed to more than 50 percent of the focus of executive coaching, according to the Seventh Annual Executive Coaching Survey from Sherpa Coaching. The survey also found that "in 2012, the majority of coaching [was] designed for leadership development, with the balance of coaching split pretty much equally between transition and problem solving. That applie[d] equally to companies of every size. Over seven years'

---

[2] Bill Patterson, "Gen Y and the Collaborative Workplace," *Forbes*, May 29, 2012, http://www.forbes .com/sites/microsoftdynamics/2012/05/29/gen-y-and-the-collaborative-workplace.

time, the amount of coaching used to solve a specific behavioral problem [had] dropped from 40 percent to near 25 percent."[3]

Peter Hawkins writes in his book *Leadership Team Coaching*:

> In a series of research projects into best practice in leadership development, we found that it was best when it was:
>
> - Real time—based on the real challenges that were current for the leaders and which they had a hunger to resolve
> - Behaviourally transformative—not just leading new insights and good intentions, but new actions and relating, live in the workshop, coaching session, etc.
> - Relational—leaders learning together with colleagues, where attention is given not only to the individuals changing but also changing the relationships between them
> - Including real stakeholder perspectives—including the challenges from employees, customers, partners, commissioners and regulators in live interaction
> - Including unlearning—addressing limiting assumptions, mindsets, habitual patterns that have been successful in the past and previous roles but need to be unlearnt for leadership to progress.

Hawkins continues, "Coaching has been the fastest growing component of leadership development in the last 10 years. However, if we judge it against the aspects of the most effective leadership development quoted above, we find a lot of leadership coaching does not match up. Nearly all coaching is of individuals, focusing on the personal development of the leader."[4]

There is great opportunity for team and group coaching to provide tremendous value in the leadership development realm.

Throughout the book we have seen several examples of team and group coaching for leadership, including Sharon Miller's Voices from the Field included in Team Coaching in Action at www.groupcoachingessentials.com.

In this chapter, the Voices from the Field from coach Ursula Lesic describes a group coaching initiative for managers in her organization. A key outcome of the group coaching engagement was to "improve the managers' communication with one another as a whole, within departments (operations/maintenance), with the

---

[3] Sherpa Coaching, 2012 Executive Coaching Survey, http://www.sherpacoaching.com/pdf%20files/Survey-Executive-Coaching-2012.pdf.
[4] Hawkins, *Leadership Team Coaching*, 17.

union workforce and with the customer." Her case study at the end of this chapter illustrates the value of bringing together managers from different parts of an organization, in a geographically dispersed organization.

If we return to Hawkins' best practices for leadership development, group leadership coaching is:

Real time: Group coaching encourages individuals to bring their "real work issues" into the conversation with others. The focus is usually around "what's working and what's not," with an emphasis on how they can make a change. An action planning component and accountability around commitments made provide leaders with an opportunity to do something about these key issues.

Behaviorally transformative: Group coaching is supportive of behavior change, beyond the immediate conversation and back in the workforce over a longer period of time. We know that change takes time. The ability for individuals, teams and groups to create and maintain the changes also takes time. Later in this chapter, in Ursula Lesic's Voices from the Field, we will see how enhanced communication in a managerial grouping has been supported.

Relational and stakeholder-based: A group coaching approach creates the opportunity for group members to build relationships across a wider web, including individuals who may actually be stakeholders. Ursula's case study is a great example, incorporating the focus on relationships, as well as being able to strengthen the conversation among multiple stakeholder groups.

Team coaching is:

Real time: In the work that I undertake with new leaders as coach, and in training group coaches, I often use the terms *it depends* and *be flexible* and *it may change*. These phrases point to the fact that coaching work is really undertaken in real time. A key priority in the first week may no longer be a priority for the team in month 2, having been taken over by a new, competing and pressing focus. As such, team coaches are adept at "dancing" with their team clients to place focus on what is important in the moment.

To keep this work grounded, it is important for the coach and team to keep an eye on the 30,000-foot view of the engagement, and the related success measures for the engagement. The 30,000-foot view usually provides the anchor point for the engagement over time. For example, a team initially identifies that the engagement will be successful based on an increase in clients served, and better communication among team members. Coaches will want to keep pointing the team back to these areas, asking them to identify and report on progress made around these success measures. These key focus areas provide the anchor point for the coaching engagement, longer term, even if some of the focus areas do change. It is easy for coaches and the teams to get pulled "into the weeds," focusing too myopically on issues that may not really have an impact. Taking the 30,000-foot view provides a wider lens, allowing for a view of the key issues in the larger, longer-term, context.

Behaviorally transformative: The sustained series of conversations in the team coaching engagement, underpinned by the team agreements, lead to behavior changes on the part of the leader and the team back in the workplace. We have seen how coaches can emphasize and inquire about how the team itself will be taking its learning, insights and skills back to the workplace.

Relational: A main focus in team coaching is around deepening awareness of who the team are, what they bring and the relationships among team members. These relationships are the vehicle through which business results are achieved. Team coaches will focus on connecting the conversations to the three levels of self, team and organization.

Involves unlearning: Teams develop habitual patterns, many of which they are not aware of. Gossip or "talk around the water cooler" is a common symptom that shows up in toxic teams. Becoming aware of these patterns around gossip is the first way to start addressing the issues, and using team agreements to support new positive behaviors.

Voices from the Field: Group Coaching for Leadership Development: Ursula Lesic, ACC

Our organization is in an exciting time of change. Due to retirements, a number of opportunities to bring outside talent into the organization and provide promotional opportunities to those within the organization have existed this past year. Communication with one another, the union work-force, and the customer is critical to the success of the organization.

I looked at group coaching as the vehicle to bring cohesiveness to the organization while building communication skills. To allow for face-to-face interaction, groups have been broken down by state, which is how they operate. Several weekly 30- to 45-minute in-person group coaching sessions over eight weeks are offered at various times per week to accommodate the 24/7 schedule our managers work. This format provides the opportunity for the managers to work in smaller groups with a variety of fellow managers and accommodate their various work schedules.

(Continued)

The key outcome of the group coaching engagement was to improve the managers' communication with one another as a whole, within departments (operations/maintenance), with the union workforce and with the customer. With improved communication, the organization would be stronger in serving our customer, aid us in dissolving the us/them climate and enable us to provide a supportive learning/growing environment.

A number of benefits have been noted by participants. An increased level of awareness in what is going right and what is going wrong in their conversations is fuelling improved communications. Providing a safe environment to openly discuss communication struggles and successes has been supportive. Learning the challenges of others and other departments is allowing room for additional conversations. To date, this has been measured by feedback from the managers. Over the next year, I will look to customer surveys and 360-degree feedback for additional feedback.

The engagement is successful as it is a group coaching program. Through group coaching, we have been able to co-create a depth of learning, work through the challenges the managers are faced with on a day-to-day basis with communication, and enhance relationships through communications skills.

The challenges in working with this group is that it operates 24/7, is geographically dispersed, and is a male-dominated industry. Providing a safe environment to share their struggles has been vital for this group; it is a venue that they had not had until group coaching.

As a coach, many lessons have been learned. Let the client do the work. In a corporate environment, it is easy to take on the role of trainer rather than coach. Designing the alliance and ground roles is sacred to the group coaching relationship, especially if you are operating in dual roles. Creating and holding the space for the group requires much patience and energy; it is important to hold participants and yourself accountable.

MAKING IT STICK: POSITIONING GROUP COACHING AS A FOLLOW-ON TO LEADERSHIP DEVELOPMENT TRAINING

Group coaching conversations can also be positioned after formal training initiatives if a leadership curriculum has been established. Many organizations now have developed internal training programs for new leaders, "high potentials" or those in the succession pipelines. Training is not the only way to build capacity. The new leaders, or those in the succession pipeline, can be supported by mentors, in addition to the group coaching conversation.

Figure 10.1 provides an overview of how coaching, along with supervisory support and mentoring, can really boost the impact and "stickiness" of a leadership development initiative. It is common today for many organizations to have developed their own internal leadership development programs. Whether the program runs for three months or two years, it is likely that new leaders and those in the succession pipeline will come together for a couple of days at a time for each workshop module and then return to the workplace. As program designers, what can we do to sustain the focus and transfer of learning from these workshop modules?

As we saw in the last chapter, supervisors, mentors and coaches can all play a key role in supporting the cohort members between the module sessions. In designing a leadership development program with enhanced emphasis on transfer of learning and integration, program developers will want to consider how to create and encourage more formalized support by supervisors, mentors and/or coaches. One possibility as outlined in Figure 10.1 is to have *each module* supported by a series of conversations and structured supports from coaching, mentoring and supervision. Practically speaking, after each module *specific activities* can be developed for the coach, mentor and supervisor. It is likely that the new leader will find learning from one area will merge into another.

Supervisors can reinforce KSAs acquired by members of their team, and provide feedback on performance measures and insights around daily tasks. Consider what supports the supervisors will need themselves for supporting their new leaders. What information do they need about what is being learned in the

Figure 10.1: Making It Stick—Leadership Development Module Follow-On

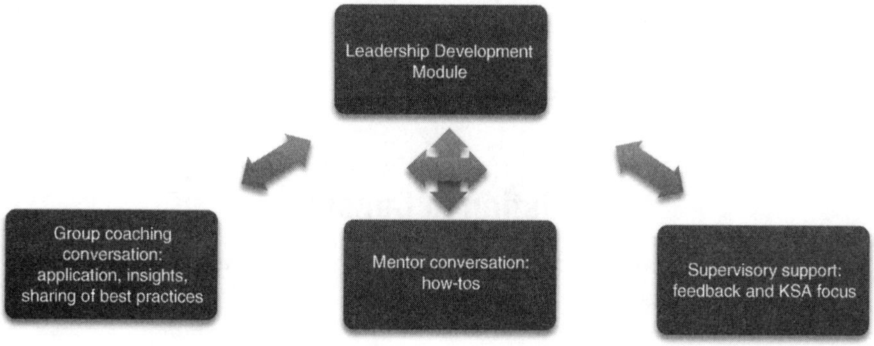

classroom? What additional resources or skill building can the supervisory team benefit from?

Mentors can support their cohort members by sharing practical insights around "getting the job done," shortcuts and who to go to. It can be useful to provide formalized resources for the mentors in terms of overview of what the modules are and where their protégé is, along with prompting questions for discussion.

Group coaches can provide space for cohort members to reflect on what they are learning, applying as well as facilitating a conversation among peers to develop a series of shared practices. These coaching calls may also serve to keep the "learning alive" in between module deliveries.

The group coaching conversation may focus on:

- What skills and insights have you been applying since our workshop? What do you need more of?
- What are you noticing about the impact you are having?
- What are the strengths that you are leading from?
- What do you want to make a commitment around? *Or* take action on? *Or* deepen your awareness about?

As we know, the first step into leadership, moving into the front line supervisory role, can often be the most challenging for many individuals. It is in this context that I have seen new leaders and leaders in the succession pipeline really benefit from the "sustained conversation with intent" that coaching offers. The peer learning and sharing of best practices that can occur in the group coaching conversation are critical for the first 90 days and beyond, what most business leaders point to as a critical phase. The need for team coaching may grow out of these conversations, as team leaders become aware of the value of focus and dialogue for their own teams.

At the same time, supervisors also play a key role in the development of their team members, and mentors bring invaluable insights around the way things are really done.

Question to Consider

What can you incorporate into the leadership development work you are currently undertaking?

Challenges for New Leaders

Common challenges in stepping into the leadership role are:

- Understanding the business context and developing the language of business and leadership
- Acquiring interpersonal skills in areas such as conflict management, communication and influence, while building onto the baseline of technical skills
- Learning how to lead and manage others
- Moving from what is often referred to as "buddy to boss." Many leaders move from a peer to boss relationship, making this a tricky issue.

Jean Hurd indicates that for technical and scientific professionals the following areas can be most challenging in navigating the leadership role:

1. Managing others
2. Collaborating cross-functionally [addressed in our next chapter]
3. Having the business conversation.[5] [Having the business conversation refers to the ability of a staff member to understand the business priorities and context and use the relevant language.]

FOCUS AREAS IN LEADERSHIP DEVELOPMENT

The focus areas in which coaches may find themselves working are vast. Just as we looked at capacity development in the last chapter, in this context we need to consider "leadership capacity" as defined by David Weiss and Vince Molinaro: "the extent to which organizations can optimize their current and future leadership to drive business results and successfully meet the challenges and opportunities of an ever-changing business environment."[6]

Over the last several years I have worked with a number of organizations to develop learning strategies for their front line leaders. The main question driving

---

[5] Jean Hurd, "Development Coaching: Helping Scientific and Technical Professionals Make the Leap into Leadership," *Global Business and Organizational Excellence* (July–August 2009), 41.
[6] David S. Weiss and Vince Molinaro, *The Leadership Gap: Building Leadership Capacity for Competitive Advantage* (Toronto: John Wiley & Sons, 2005), 5.

this work was, "What makes an exceptional leader at your organization?" The main goal of these learning strategies was to identify the key competencies as well as attributes required for successful leaders (front line managers or supervisors) at their organizations. These activities may in fact not be things that are currently being done, but rather things that, in order to succeed, really do need to be done. As part of the learning strategy, in addition to identifying what the competencies are, we also want to explore the question, "What are the best approaches to equip these new leaders?" This may include training (in person, online, off the shelf, customized), coaching, mentoring, or job aids.

Inherent to developing a learning strategy is tapping into the wisdom of those who do the work, and are connected with those in the position. It is typical to hold a series of focus groups, interviews and conversations with a range of stakeholders. Different stakeholders include those that currently occupy the role (new and experienced), junior staff as well as HR and senior leaders in the organization.

Regardless of whether the position was in safety or transportation, financial services or health care, it has been common to see similar topics emerge across industries for new leaders. It is likely that coaches working in this terrain will find themselves working around these critical areas for leaders today:

- Emotional intelligence
- Communication: styles, difficult conversations, providing feedback
- Myself as leader: styles, strengths, influence
- Coaching skills
- Developing trust and respect
- Team leadership issues
- Relationship management issues
- Conflict resolution
- Managing up and managing down
- Leadership styles and strengths (Renee Brotman's Voices from the Field in this chapter provides an illustration)
- Navigating change

In today's move to more team-based contexts, coaches may find themselves working with individuals, groups or entire teams in the organizational realm around these topics. Depending on the strategy of the organization, coaches may find themselves working extensively at the executive or C-level (with the chief executive officer, chief financial officer and chief operating officer), or may find themselves working to equip those in the succession pipeline much further down the organizational levels. The focus of the areas listed above may shift with C-level leaders placing more emphasis on topics such as strategy, change and influence, with front line supervisors looking at topics such as managing up and managing down, and team leadership issues.

In developing group or team leadership coaching for leadership development, coaches will often find themselves weaving tougher varying approaches, including mini-teach pieces, followed by discussion and accountability, or assessments followed by dialogue.

Leadership coaching conversations, whether individual, team or group, will widen the discussion and focus not only on the individual as an entity, but also their impact on their team and the organization.

Jean Hurd offers these four questions for leaders to consider:[7]

1. How will my work group and the broader organization benefit?
2. Where will I personally gain by achieving this goal and by participating in the process?
3. What will I have to give up?
4. What obstacles might I encounter, and how might I manage them?

In her book *Teaming*, Amy Edmondson distinguishes "Large-L" and "small-l" leadership. She writes, "Large-L leadership generally includes high-level executive and involves decision and activities that influence everyone in the organization. The role is critical to effective teaming and usually includes developing organizational culture, direction setting and the creation of goals."[8]

She continues, "But much of the time, what's needed is what I call leadership with a small l. This type of leadership is exercised by people throughout the organization, not just at the top, and especially by those at the front lines where crucial work affecting customer experiences is carried out. This kind of leadership is about developing other skills and shaping effective processes. In small-l leadership, those in the thick of collaborative activity help ensure that teaming occurs effectively."[9]

In the coming years, it is likely that coaches will be engaging with leaders, groups and teams across organizations around these key leadership topics. One area where coaches may be called in to support groups is in the area of leadership styles. Renee Brotman has provided this Voice from the Field around working with leadership styles using the Visual Explorer tool.

---

[7] Hurd, "Development Coaching," 46.

[8] Amy Edmondson, *Teaming: How Organizations Learn, Innovate, and Compete in the Knowledge Economy* (Hoboken, NJ: John Wiley & Sons, 2012), 4.

[9] Ibid, 5.

Voices from the Field: Group Coaching Case Study: Working with Leadership Styles by Renee Brotman

A picture can tell the real story. In group coaching many different experiential tools can be used to aid in the group learning. One of my favorite tools is the Visual Explorer, which is a collection of beautiful photographs.[10] Visual Explorer comes with directions for many ways to use the pictures; however, I like to invent my own ways of integrating the photographs into my work.

Specifically, I have used the Visual Explorer with leadership group coaching. At the concluding session, I will spread out the photographs and ask participants to pick out one that represents the current leadership style of their organization and one that represents their hopes and dreams for future leadership. The pictures seem to give words to unarticulated thoughts. They seem to give participants license to speak more freely.

Participants enjoy rummaging through all the beautiful photographs. They freely select what evokes thought and action for them. Each person has his or her own story to tell. The conversation that follows, in which everyone explains their individual selections, is a powerful, value-added dialogue. Based on previously established group ground rules, everyone's point of view can be heard and agreement is not necessary. Newer people to an organization are enlightened by the response of individuals who have been with the organization a long time and vice versa. This exercise builds to each person developing their own individual development plan for continuing their personal learning journey.

The question(s) the coach poses to the group using the Visual Explorer are endless. Other ideas include:

- Checking the individual mood of participants
- Pre- and post-learning over the course of a group coaching cohort
- Explanation of unique topic (i.e., How would you describe your personal view of the world?)

Summary

- Tool: Visual Explorer.
- Key outcomes: Increases ability to articulate both thoughts and feelings.

---

[10] Charles J. Palus and David M. Horth, *Visual Explorer Facilitator's Letter-Size Set*, Center for Creative Leadership Press, accessed May 6, 2013, http://solutions.ccl.org/Visual_Explorer_Facilitator's_Letter-size_Set.

- Benefits: Enhanced ability for everyone to contribute to the conversation.
- Successes: Everyone wants to show their photograph selections; it gets them talking and contributing.
- Challenges: Sometimes can be overwhelming for participants when presented with too many options; sometimes difficult to get back the pictures for future use.
- Lessons learned: Be clear on what the question/task is. Be specific on the amount of time; some people will take up all the time and others will be done in a moment.
- Illustrates: Group participation, integration of thought and emotion, active listening.

EMOTIONAL INTELLIGENCE

"In hard times, the soft stuff often goes away. But emotional intelligence, it turns out, isn't so soft. If emotional obliviousness jeopardizes your ability to perform, fend off aggressors, or be compassionate in a crisis, no amount of attention to the bottom line will protect your career. Emotional intelligence isn't a luxury you can dispense with in tough times. It's a basic tool that, deployed with finesse, is the key to professional success."

—Harvard Business Review[11]

One of the key areas team and group coaches may find themselves working around is emotional intelligence (EI). Emotional intelligence focuses on supporting individuals to enhance their self-awareness, awareness of others (social awareness), as well as develop capacity in self-management and relationship management.[12]

Daniel Goleman defines emotional intelligence as, "The capacity for recognizing our own feelings, and those of others, for motivating ourselves, for managing emotions well in ourselves and our relationships."[13]

---

[11] "The 2003 HBR List: Breakthrough Ideas for Tomorrow's Business Agenda," *Harvard Business Review* 81, no. 4 (April 2003): 92-98.

[12] To learn more on this topic, see Daniel Goleman, *Working with Emotional Intelligence* (New York: Bantam, 1998), and Daniel Goleman, Richard Boyatzis and Annie McKee, *Primal Leadership: Learning to Lead with Emotional Intelligence* (Boston: Harvard Business Press, 2002). Another useful resource is Reldan S. Nadler, *Leading with Emotional Intelligence: Hands-on Strategies for Building Confident and Collaborative Star Performers* (New York: McGraw-Hill, 2011).

[13] Daniel Goleman, *Working with Emotional Intelligence* (New York: Bantam, 1998), 317.

"So what?" you may ask. What is important about this? Did you know:

- "The research shows that for jobs of all kinds, emotional intelligence is twice as important an ingredient of outstanding performance as ability and technical skill combined. The higher you go in the organization, the more important these qualities are for success. When it comes to leadership, they are almost everything."[14]
- Emotional intelligence is a key skill set as we learn to build relationships across silos and across geographic distance. The more we know ourselves (self-awareness), the more we can be sensitive to what our impact is, in building relationship across differences.

Team and group coaching are two vehicles that help to expand awareness of self and others, as well as relationship management. A core part of building EI is in navigating relationships. Team and group coaching give us "real time" opportunities to try, apply, adjust and retry new skills and connections.

Why is emotional intelligence so important for groups? As Vanessa Urch Druskat and Steven B. Wolff write:

Many executives realize that EQ (emotional quotient) is as critical as IQ to an individual's effectiveness. But groups' emotional intelligence may be even more important, since most work gets done in teams.

A group's EI isn't simply the sum of its members'. Instead, it comes from norms that support awareness and regulation of emotions within and outside the team. These norms build trust, group identity, and a sense of group efficacy. Members feel that they work better together than individually.

Group EI norms build the foundation for true collaboration and cooperation—helping otherwise skilled teams fulfill their highest potential.[15]

In order for groups to operate like this, Druskat and Wolff indicate that "trust, identity and efficacy" need to be present. Group members need to trust each other. They need to feel part of a "group," and they also need to believe in the team's abilities and that they can get more done in the group than alone.[16]

---

[14] Daniel Goleman quoted in Jeff Feldman and Karl Mulle, *Put Emotional Intelligence to Work* (Virginia: ASTD Press, 2008), 3.
[15] Vanessa Urch Druskat and Steven B. Wolff, "Building the Emotional Intelligence of Groups," *BusinessWeek*, September 30, 2007, http://www.businessweek.com/stories/2007-09-30/building-the-emotional-intelligence-of-groupsbusinessweek-business-news-stock-market-and-financial-advice.
[16] Ibid.

Another area coaches may want to consider is exploring team emotional and social intelligence (TESI). This comes from the work of Marcia Hughes and James Terrell, authors of *The Emotionally Intelligent Team: Understanding and Developing the Behaviors of Success.*[17]

Emotional and social intelligence (ESI) can be defined this way: "ESI is a set of emotional and social skills that influence the way we perceive and express ourselves, develop and maintain social relationships, cope with challenges, and use emotional information in an effective and meaningful way."[18]

The TESI assessment allows teams to "measure their effectiveness in the competencies of Team Identity, Motivation, Emotional Awareness, Communication, Conflict Resolution, Stress Tolerance, and Positive Mood."[19]

Team coaches may find it useful to support the skill development and conversation in these areas. Coaches interested in exploring this may also wish to tap into the exercises Hughes and Miller have put together in their 2010 book, *Developing Emotional and Social Intelligence: Exercises for Leaders, Individuals, and Teams.* Exercises in the book support team development in the seven competency areas of the ESI.[20]

Other ways coaches may work with emotional intelligence:

- Integrate discussion with teams and groups on what emotional intelligence is.
- Facilitate conversations around the importance of emotional intelligence in the work that each person undertakes.
- Support/coach on the different levels: boosting individual capacity, boosting team capacity, looking at the context the team operates within.
- Support team and group members to explore on relationship management issues: see the appendix for several different activities, particularly the "Traffic Light List: Red, Green, Yellow" relationship mapping exercise.
- Deepen awareness of styles and strengths for the team and how they mesh and do not mesh.
- Focus on the development of EI skills individually and collectively.

---

[17] Marcia Hughes and James Terrell, *The Emotionally Intelligent Team: Understanding and Developing the Behaviors of Success* (Hoboken, NJ: Jossey-Boss, 2007).

[18] Marcia Hughes, Donna Dennis and James Terrell, "Can Virtual Teams Exhibit Emotional and Social Intelligence?", accessed December 5, 2012, http://www.leadership-solutions.info/can_virtual_teams.pdf.

[19] Marcia Hughes and James Terrell, *TESI Short: Frequently Asked Questions* (San Francisco: John Wiley & Sons, 2009), 2, http://media.wiley.com/product_data/excerpt/94/04702590/0470259094-1.pdf.

[20] Marcia Hughes and Amy Miller, *Developing Emotional and Social Intelligence: Exercises for Leaders, Individuals, and Teams* (San Francisco: Pfeiffer, 2010).

- Review the 20-plus competencies that underscore the four areas of EI. How does each team member rate themselves on each one of the competencies. Where do the team or group's strengths lie? What gaps exist?
- Develop shared behavior practices within the team

Coaches may also want to undertake further skill development by becoming trained and certified in EQ assessments such as EQ-i 2.0.

Field Journal: Using DiSC to Expand Individual, Team and Departmental Self-Awareness

Enhanced self-awareness is critical to team success. Those who work in teams are aware of what they bring to the team and what potential impact they have as an individual and professional. Understanding different styles that exist and how these mesh and also potentially conflict is also important. Personal level assessments such as the DiSC are useful for enhancing awareness as an individual, and as a member of a team. Creating a common framework for dialogue within a team or organization can be very useful as organizations incorporate working with DiSC at the organizational level.

I recently co-facilitated a session in which we used DiSC for an organizational division. It was part of a larger strategic team learning meeting. Prework for the half-day session involved all individuals completing the DiSC. Even before we met, the group members for the offsite had already started having discussions with those they worked with.

We designed a two-hour process to provide the opportunity for the team to explore the results of the DiSC. It consisted of several rounds of discussions in different groupings around the room (tables of 10).

The first round had people of similar styles explore the strengths and preferences of their styles. The second round, also in similar style groups, encouraged discussion about blind spots their styles created, and what adaptations would be useful in working with others. The final round of discussion had teams reconvene and share their styles.

The two hours we spent on this DiSC activity with the division was very important in starting to deepen awareness around styles and how they impact the work, relationships and results of the organization. The teams have identified individual action plans to take this work forward.

Throughout this chapter we explored a number of ways team and group coaching can support current or future leadership development initiatives in an organization. We explored a case study of how group coaching has been positive in bringing cohesiveness to an organization while building communication skills. We explored how group coaching can be positioned after leadership development modules, along with mentoring and supervision to really make the learning stick. I highlighted emotional intelligence as one area team and group coaches will likely find themselves working within. Coaches will likely find this a rich area to explore.

Next we are going to turn our attention to the topic of co-facilitation and collaboration. Coaches working in the realm of team and group coaching will often find their work linked to building collaborative cultures. At the same time, we often find ourselves partnering with others in program design and delivery. Sometimes we are called on to work with subject matter experts. Other times we may be co-facilitating with other coaches, particularly if we are working with teams or a larger organizational entity. In addition to exploring the topic of collaboration in general, we also explore tips for making co-facilitation work.

End-of-Chapter Questions

What opportunities do you have to be working in the area of leadership development?

What are the biggest needs around leadership for your clients right now?

What ideas can you take forward from this chapter?

CHAPTER 11

CO-FACILITATION, PARTNERING AND COLLABORATION: WHO HAS YOUR BACK?

Relationships are all there is. Everything in the universe only exists because it is in relationship to everything else. Nothing exists in isolation. We have to stop pretending we are individuals that can go it alone.
—Margaret Wheatley[1]

Collaboration is one of the hottest business topics at present. Changes globally in the economy are pressuring organizations, businesses, teams and individuals to approach things differently. Complex problems, and often diminished resources, are pressuring businesses, teams and individuals to span across silos and work together. In today's business context, teams and leaders are continually being called on to collaborate and reach across silos to address the complex challenges and ever-changing environment of business.

Collaboration is also at the core of team and group coaching processes. Group coaching as a modality creates an opportunity to open up the conversation among individuals—in communities, organizations, teams and businesses. Team coaching is all about the conversation among peers and leaders.

The topic of partnering and collaboration is critical for group and team coaches on two levels. First, partnering and collaboration is critical in approaching

[1] http://www.wisdomquotes.com/authors/margaret-j-wheatley.

current business challenges in a new light. Team and group coaching as modalities invite collaboration. Collaboration across silos and functions is imperative.

Second, as coaches, partnering through co-facilitation is a key activity, providing more eyes and voices for the groups and teams that we are working with. In 2012, 47 percent of coaches indicated that the economic downturn led to increasing collaboration with other coaches.[2]

This chapter explores the important topic of collaboration and partnering. It focuses on two main areas, the first being co-facilitation, which is developing strong partnerships with other practitioners in service of enhanced team and group coaching. The first part of this chapter can also be implemented by team members who find themselves co-facilitating team meetings.

The second part of the chapter focuses on fostering a more collaborative workplace. Chances are that coaches may be involved as part of the culture change process, in shifting to a more collaborative workplace. The second half of the chapter provides useful considerations as you move with a team or organization through this process—tools as well as questions to consider. As coaches we can approach the conversation around these topic areas on two levels: first, for our own knowledge; and second, for the clients we work with.

THE ART OF CO-FACILITATION

As I wrote in the digital accompaniment to *Effective Group Coaching,* "Co-facilitation enhances the possibilities and outcomes of group programs, ensuring that the facilitation experience comes from a place where the "sum is greater than its parts."[3] Co-facilitation offers us the advantages of:

- Additional eyes to notice process, what is happening in the room, what is being said, and *not* being said.
- Additional perspectives, and voices, to bring to the clients we work with.
- Support for more technologically complex environments like program delivery using webinar platforms. Unlike using a "producer" to support the more technical elements of a webinar, in a group or team coaching context we will want to ensure that the person looking after logistics maintains confidentiality and is part of the structure we develop.

---

[2] 2012 Global Coaching Survey, accessed May 13, 2013, http://icf.files.cms-plus.com/includes/media/docs/2012ICFGlobalCoachingStudy-ExecutiveSummary.pdf
[3] Britton, *Effective Group Coaching,* digital accompaniment, 1.

- An opportunity to bring a fuller range of skills, and supports. As we will see, complementary skill sets can support enhanced co-facilitation.
- Coaches may find that in working with teams or larger groups, co-facilitation is a "must-do." Holding the space, observing process and keeping a program running for larger teams and organizations usually requires more than one set of eyes.

Coaches may also find themselves working with subject matter experts, trainers or HR professionals. In this context, developing a solid partnership as co-facilitators, allows you to "dance" together in service to the group or team you are working with. The principles and recommendations included here can be applied to these partnerships as well. As Dr. Catherine Carr and Dr. Jacqueline Peters state, "Co-facilitation is useful in tracking different elements. There are benefits to having two sets of eyes and two different coaching styles."

Over the years I have partnered with a range of co-facilitators. It is common for me to work with a co-facilitator in a majority of my team coaching engagements. Team clients have noted that they really enjoy having two different approaches and styles available to them. It is also common to have comments from teams and leaders about the modeling that a co-facilitator and I go through in terms of "working on our feet" and making adjustments, as well as co-leading.

Many coaches will feel comfortable facilitating smaller team and group sessions on their own. When challenges may exist due to a really dysfunctional team or high levels of toxicity, it is worth bringing in a co-facilitator. Likewise, for larger organizational engagements (25 people or more), a second pair of hands and an alternative approach and perspective can be useful.

Key to making co-facilitation really work is laying the foundation with your collaborator.

It is also likely that coaches working in organizations will need to partner with internal members such as subject matter experts, and possibly HR specialists, if their work moves into the realm of capacity development (refer to Chapter 9) or as a follow-on to training, such as in a leadership development program (refer to Chapter 10). Setting the foundation and creating a powerful partnership is key with these individuals as well. Consider how you may use the tips and ideas from this chapter to support you in creating a mutually supportive collaboration.

Drawbacks to co-facilitation can include:

- Pieces falling through the cracks because you think the other person has done it
- Not pulling together or at an equal weight: lack of alignment
- Egos not being "checked at the door"

Figure 11.1: The Co-facilitation Arc

At the Start	During Design	During Implementation	Post-program
• What are our strengths? • How are we complementary? • Where do gaps exist? • What blind spots do we have? • What is important in our work? What values drive our work? • What business philosophies are important to us? • Share samples of work	• Who will take a lead on what? Design and facilitation • Accordion points: what can be expanded and can be contracted, if needed? • What is our common stake for this program? • What do we want to ensure happens, no matter what?	• Review leads for each section • Observations with group—energy, impact, engagement • Add additional questions • Accordion • Touch base throughout regarding changes needed	• Review of program: what worked well? • Successes • Roles, flow and fit • Lessons learned • Changes for next co-facilitation

When co-facilitation does not work, it *really* may not work, and has the potential to impact the team's or group's experience.

Masterful co-facilitation also requires a sustained conversation throughout the program process: from the pre-design phase as you start to explore the possibilities of working together, through to the design phase, through implementation and into evaluation and post-programming. This is illustrated in Figure 11.1: The Co-facilitation Arc.

At the Start: Exploring Synergies

A core project management adage is that "10 minutes of planning can save one hour of unfocused effort." This is so true in the world of partnering and co-facilitation.

Initial discussions to explore fit, values and vision about you and your business are critical in laying a foundation of success in co-facilitation. Questions potential co-facilitators and partners will want to explore at this phase are:

- What are our strengths? Individually? Collectively?
- How are we complementary?

- Where do gaps exist?
- What blind spots do we have?
- What is important in our work? What values drive our work?
- What business philosophies are important to us?

Share samples of work. Nothing speaks like our past experience. Share past program designs, facilitator guides or workbooks. Notice what's different about your styles, and what is possible if you combine the best of both of your approaches.

Sometimes collaboration fails because of too much similarity and the massive blind spots that can be created through too much complementarity. Spending time to look at what skills you bring and how they are complementary can pay off in the long run. As you discuss, consider what gaps exist and blind spots are created through your partnership.

Another core area to explore together is your values and stance around your work. What is really important for you as a coach/leader? As a business? What is important in terms of the value you bring to clients, and the quality of your work? How do your values align? Dig deeper around your values and define what *excellence* or *world class* may mean.

One activity we often undertake with our clients to explore values is the Values Word String. This can be a great example in bringing to life how similar values held by co-facilitators may mean two completely different things. For example, Steve and Sally are partnering together. They both hold the values of "quality," "excellence" and "impact." When asked to define these values, here's what they reply:

Quality

Steve: detailed, visual, interactive
Sally: punctual, complete, value added for the client

Excellence

Steve: world class, thorough, stands on its own
Sally: best in the industry, consistent, client centered

Impact

Steve: business results, team results, applicability
Sally: usability, application, team focused

Notice the similarities and differences that show up here. What do you see as important for Steve? What is important for Sally? If you were their coach, what questions would you ask them?

The Values Word String can be a useful exercise in uncovering the unique values we hold, as well as where some of what we think is common or shared is actually different. One of the main reasons co-facilitation may not work is when values are not aligned. Spending time really looking at the compatibility and meaning of our values is very useful in setting the foundation for successful co-facilitation.

Field Journal: Critical Co-facilitation Questions

Over the past three years I have heard from coaches who have used some of the practical questions I developed for co-facilitators. These were originally included in *Effective Group Coaching*'s additional commentary. I have used these when working with both coaches and subject matter experts as co-facilitators.

Some practical questions to ask (individually and together) when you are starting a new co-facilitation include:

About ourselves as a partnership

- Who are we as individuals? As a pair? As a co-facilitation team?
- What are our values as individuals? What are our values as a team?
- What are our goals for a partnership? What do we hope to accomplish?
- What unique skills, abilities or characteristics do we bring to the partnership?
- What are you looking for in a partner? To enhance your weaker areas? To expand you into new markets?
- What particular skills are we looking for in a partner?
- What particular characteristics are we looking for in a partner?
- What are our expectations from the partnership?

About the program itself

- What do we want to model in our work together for the group?
- What are the "must-haves" for our work together?

- What's the stake we have in this work?
- How will we measure success?

Creating the context for our work

- What is the atmosphere we want to create?
- To create safety and trust in our group, we will . . . ?
- What is my stake as an individual? What is our stake as a team?
- What is our stake for this program—what are we committed to creating together?
- How and when will we check in with one another?
- What is our shared vision for this program?
- What is our philosophy as a co-facilitation team?
- What can we do to keep on target?
- What will we do if we get off target?
- What will I be responsible for?

Practical questions

- Who will take the lead on each section?
- What roles and responsibilities will each person have along the way?
- Make a list of all the things that need to happen and who will do them—i.e., developing the evaluation form, marketing materials, etc.
- What will I do while the other is facilitating in the front of the room?
- How will I deal with differences that arise in front of the group?
- How will I check my ego at the door?
- What changes will I make to elongate the program as needed? (accordion out)?
- What changes will I make to shorten the program as needed (accordion in)?
- Discuss how each person would like to be supported by their partner. Remember that one person's idea of support is not the same as another person's.
- How will we make the changes mid-stream during the program?
- What are the "must-haves"? (Musthaves are those topics that really have to be included in the program.)
- What will each one of us do to spread the word about the program?

Co-facilitation During the Design Phase

There are a number of activities co-facilitators can undertake during the design phase. Some of these practical tips include:

Start with a Draft

It can be very useful to draft the program together and/or to bounce it back and forth. This can be very useful in creating a shared program.

Walk through the Draft

A walk-through allows you as a co-facilitation team to look at the program in its entirety. Identify together your accordion points. What is a "must-cover" and what can be condensed if there is not enough time? Identify any areas that you think can be elongated or condensed

Also identify what needs to happen in terms of logistical setup. Perhaps you are moving from a conversational component into a session that needs some setup, such as a wheel taped to the floor. Make note of when things are needed, when, and who will do it.

Meet Regularly

Meeting regularly (with focus) in lead-up to the event can be very useful in terms of keeping the project front and center and making sure that key milestones are met. As a team, together, notice where you each get your energy and what excites you about the work. Leverage this where possible.

Co-facilitation During Implementation

The subtitle of this chapter is "Who Has Your Back?" Part of masterful co-facilitation is ensuring that you each have the other's back, covering any blind spots. During the actual program itself, it is key to keep the communication open between you. Changes "on the fly" are quite likely. Throughout the program you will want to:

- Review leads for each section.
- Touch base regularly to share your observations with the group: What do you notice about the energy of the group? What impact are the activities having? Where does the team light up? What do you notice about engagement—in general, and with specifics?
- Add more questions. Just because someone is taking the lead on a section does not mean that the other coach should stop listening. In fact, the addition of another voice or type of question may stimulate the group or team in different ways.
- Accordion. The accordion is a metaphor to remind us of identifying those sections that can be expanded if things are moving quickly, or contracted if moving too slowly.
- Touch base throughout regarding changes needed in terms of the order or approach of things. Are there any changes needed on the fly?
- Surface additional issues or observations. One of the greatest gifts of co-facilitation is the additional set of eyes. While partner one is leading the process, partner two can be reading the room: noticing body language, patterns, energy and nuances.
- Model "dancing" or collaboration in the moment. It can be a powerful process to observe real-time shared leadership and how you make changes in the moment.

Post-program

The program does not end at the event. It can be very useful to hold a post-program conversation to debrief the experience and capture learning. As co-facilitators you will want to explore at the end of the program these areas:

- Review of the program: What worked well? What didn't? What would you do next time?
- Successes to note for future programs or work with the team.
- Key issues to keep an eye on with this team.
- Roles, flow and fit: How did your roles work? What was the flow like? What was the fit between you?
- Lessons learned regarding your co-facilitation, the process, needs for the team and group, etc.
- Changes for next co-facilitation with this group or others.

ROLES WITHIN THE CO-FACILITATION TEAM: CHECKLIST

A successful program requires the management of many different details. When working with another partner it can be easy to fall into the trap of thinking someone else has it covered. The checklist in Table 11.1 can be useful in identifying some of the core activities that need to be undertaken at different stages of the program process.

Table 11.1: Co-facilitation Checklist

Role/Task	Person Responsible/Notes
Initial Meetings	
Explore complementarities and synergies: What's important in our work? Where are we similar? Where are we different? How do our skills complement? What blind spots exist?	
Pre-program and Design Phase	
Liaising with client	
Creating worksheets/binder for group/team	
Evaluation form	
Design of activities	
Lead for each activity	
Accordion points	
Walk-through of the program	
During the Sessions	
For each section of your program you will want to consider who will take a lead on: • Flipcharting • Setting up new exercises • Probing • Timekeeper • Facilitator • Observations with group: energy, impact, engagement • Accordion points	

Managing logistics: liaising with facility, temperature/ lights, meals, etc.	
Post-program Follow-Up	
Follow up with group or team members regarding field work or course	
Material distribution	
Posting materials online	
Evaluation summary	
Summary of materials produced and/or reporting (if required)	
Capturing lessons learned and/or any changes needed for materials	

BUILDING A COLLABORATIVE CULTURE: PARTNERING AND COLLABORATION

"Collaboration . . . is a work ethic that recognizes that work gets done through people."

—Edward Marshall

As I mentioned at the start of this chapter, partnering and collaboration are key considerations in today's business context. As organizations and teams are being encouraged to do more with less, and work across different functions, departments and teams, collaboration is key. As coaches and leaders, we may be trying to foster collaboration, and may be involved in the culture change process. Team and group coaching are modalities that are grounded in collaboration. As such, it is useful to have a better understanding of what collaboration is and how we can work with clients to better support it.

The last part of this chapter takes a look at key considerations for starting to engage in the conversation about building collaborative cultures. Increasingly organizations are looking to explore different ways they can build more collaborative cultures. As we saw earlier, more Gen Y employees will also be looking for more collaborative approaches to learning and work. As such, it is useful for coaches to understand what collaboration really is and what makes it work, as well as the larger performance context of building a collaborative culture. The last part of the chapter explores these topic areas.

As Michael Beyerlein, Jill Nemiro and Susan Beyerlein state, "Collaboration occurs when individuals work together toward a shared goal, completing the work is dependent on relationships with a purpose, and individuals working together in purposeful ways toward a shared goal are committed to one another's success."[4]

This definition is aligned with what we have explored about team coaching this far. In collaboration, like coaching, *goals, relationships with purpose,* and *commitment* are key.

KNOWING WHEN AND WHEN NOT TO COLLABORATE

At the same time, there is some danger in thinking collaboration is always the best way to go. In his book *Collaboration*, Morten Hansen shares the concept of "disciplined collaboration," which he defines as, "The leadership practice of properly assessing when to collaborate (and when not to) and instilling in people both the willingness and ability to collaborate when required."[5]

Disciplined collaboration is critically thinking about when it is best to collaborate. Knowing when it is best to do so, and when it is not best to collaborate, is a rich area for coaching, as it may be the roots of some tensions or even conflict within, and between, teams today.

In building a skill set for collaborative work within the workforce, coaches may find themselves positioning coaching skills training as a capacity builder for the workforce. At the same time there are also several areas we work around as coaches that are related to becoming more effective in a collaborative culture. To be effective in a collaborative environment, all employees can benefit from more skills, strengths and awareness in the following areas:

- Communication
- Questioning
- Listening
- Decision making

---

[4] Michael Beyerlein, Jill Nemiro and Susan Beyerlein, "A Framework for Working Across Boundaries," Jill Nemiro et al., eds., *The Handbook of High-Performance Virtual Teams* (San Francisco: Jossey-Bass, 2008), 32.

[5] Morten T. Hansen, *Collaboration: How Leaders Avoid the Traps, Build Common Ground and Reap Big Results* (Boston: Harvard Business Press, 2009), 15.

- Relationship building
- Influence
- Emotional intelligence (particularly in the areas of self-management and relationship management)

As we explored in Chapter 9, it is likely that coaches will be working to support teams and groups around these topic areas. Individual coaches may already be undertaking a bulk of their work in these areas. What is important for the teams and groups you work with around these topics?

Training is not the only solution for good performance. Learning of these collaborative behaviors can be supported by:

- Sharing by leaders their own collaborative partnerships, successes and activities
- Focus on collaboration through the orientation program
- Mentoring program
- Coaching by manager
- Job supports: learning journal/checklists
- Cross-training with other departments and teams

Each one of these activities provides the employee or team member with a larger view of the organizational context.

WORKING WITH TEAMS TO EXPLORE COLLABORATION

"90% of team failures are caused by support system problems."
—Susan Albers Mohrman, Susan G. Cohen and Allan M. Mohrman, Jr.[6]

When working with teams and groups who are shifting to a collaborative culture, it may be very useful to explore with them how the systems they operate within and their processes support collaboration. Sometimes collaboration does

---

[6] Susan Albers Mohrman, Susan G. Cohen, and Allan M. Mohrman, Jr., *Designing Team-based Organizations: New Forms of Knowledge Work* (San Francisco: Jossey-Bass, 1995), as quoted by Beyerlein, Nemiro and Beyerlein, *The Handbook of High-Performance Virtual Teams*, 31.

not occur, because the system or environment does not support it. For example, a team may be moving to mutual accountability across the team with each team member taking on more responsibility; however, individual team members may be rewarded for individual contributions. Likewise, positive and constructive feedback is necessary for enhanced team performance. An organization's culture may be such that constructive feedback is seen as something that could be documented for a disciplinary process. This might lead to team members withholding real feedback or information on what is really happening within the team.

Exploration of the following can unearth some important areas for exploration and action. Do the following support or hinder collaboration within your team or organization?

- Performance management systems
- Compensation
- Incentives
- Rewards
- Feedback
- Job design
- Values
- Trust and respect

Table 11.2 provides you with an opportunity to reflect on the enablers and blockers to a collaborative culture.

Table 11.2: Collaboration in Your Team/Organization

Item	Enable or Block?	Change Needed
Performance management systems		
Compensation		
Incentives		
Rewards		
Feedback		
Job design		
Values		
Trust and respect		

SUPPORTING THE DEVELOPMENT OF A COLLABORATIVE LEADERSHIP STYLE

One of the key themes of the book has been building the leadership capacity within organizations. Another area coaches may find themselves working with individual leaders, or collectively with groups and teams in an organization, is in supporting the development of a more collaborative leadership style.

As Morten Hansen asserts, collaborative leadership style focuses on:[7]

- **Redefining success:** defining success as a bigger goal, rather than narrow agendas
- **Involving others:** being open to input, different viewpoints, debate and working with others in the decision making process
- **Being accountable:** members seeing themselves as responsible for reaching goals and accountable for decisions made and holding others accountable

As a coach or leader, how are the coaching conversations addressing this? Note that Hansen has created a Collaborative Leadership Style Inventory, which could be used as part of a 360-degree process, or a coaching conversation. Daniel Rasmus indicates that in order for employees to make collaboration work, employees will need skills in:[8]

- Facilitation
- Team building
- Conflict resolution and negotiative
- Brainstorming
- Technology
- Ethics

What is the current state of skills and abilities of your team in these areas?

As we have explored, in order to really support teams, groups and organizations through sustainable change, coaches need to be able to partner with other service providers and also to tailor their offerings.

As Phil Sandahl of Team Coaching International indicates, "The most successful team coaches have a portfolio of things they can offer to teams. It may include strategic planning, succession planning or expertise in decision making tools."

---

[7] Morten Hansen, *Collaboration*, 165.

[8] Daniel Rasmus, *Best Practices: How to Make Collaboration Work* (White Paper), Giga Information Group, Inc., 2003, 8, http://www.slideshare.net/guestb10b8c/best-practices-how-to-make-collaboration-work.

Question to Consider

As a coach or leader, how can you support the development of these skills with team members?

This chapter took a look at two variations on the theme of collaboration. The first part of the chapter explored the topic of partnering and co-facilitation. At some point it is likely that coaches working in the realm of coaching many will be involved in co-facilitation, whether they are co-facilitating with another coach, or perhaps bringing in a coaching approach and partnering with a subject matter expert. It is hoped that coaches will find the questions posed early in the chapter useful in stimulating conversation between you and your partner.

The second part of the chapter explored building a collaborative culture. Our team and group coaching work is often linked into building awareness of, and capacity for, the need for collaboration. Several areas have been spotlighted for coaches to consider exploring with their teams and groups as they explore the terrain of building collaborative cultures.

End-of-Chapter Questions

Where would co-facilitation benefit your work?

Who do you want to collaborate with?

What conversations do you need to have to create *exceptional* co-facilitation?

How is collaboration important for your clients—the teams and groups you work with?

How can you foster the development of these skills in yourself, and others?

What organizational systems act as enablers and barriers in fostering collaboration?

Consider how your team and/or group coaching processes can facilitate conversation around these areas.

CHAPTER 12

TRENDS IN TEAM AND GROUP COACHING

The future will be determined in part by happenings
that it is impossible to foresee; it will also be influenced
by trends that are now existent and observable.
—Emily Greene Balch[1]

So, what's next? Where do we go from here?

The 2012 ICF Global Coaching Survey indicated that key issues facing the coaching profession in general are:

- tackling *obstacles* such as untrained individuals who call themselves coaches;
- availing of opportunities to increase awareness of coaching benefits; and
- answering the question of whether coaching should be regulated.

The top two *opportunities* identified in the ICF Global Coaching Survey are:

- increased awareness of the benefits of coaching (36 percent); and
- credible data on the return on investment (ROI)/return on expectations (ROE) from coaching (28 percent).[2]

---

[1] http://www.quotesarchive.com/authors/b/emily-greene-balch/quotes/the-future-will-be-determined-in-part/page-24.
[2] International Coach Federation, 2012 Global Coaching Survey, 12.

Specific to team coaching, the Annual Executive Coaching surveys from Sherpa Coaching have been tracking for a few years. Team coaching was initially raised as a trend in the 6th Annual Executive Coaching Survey. The 2012 report poses the questions, "Will facilitators use a published process? Will standards of practice emerge, or will team coaching and coaching skills be a 'hit or miss' proposition for many organizations?"[3] The 2013 Annual Executive Coaching survey notes that "37% of coaches offer established team coaching programs [and] just 24% of HR and training professionals do."[4] The survey found that there was little change in terms of the numbers of firms offering team coaching between their 2012 and 2013 reports. It also notes that "External coaches offered team coaching programs earlier, and have more established programs than their internal counterparts. Internal coaches are on the move, with far more [team coaching] programs in design or start-up mode."

As I researched this book, and spoke with coaches undertaking their work with teams and groups, I was very interested in finding out what they saw as trends emerging in their work and within our field. Their thoughts are included at the end of the chapter.

In my own work and in discussions with clients, I continue to see opportunities arise in the areas of:

- Teaming
- Virtual teams
- Virtual learning
- Making technology work for you and your clients
- Support to execution and silo softening (role of accountability)
- Longer-term impact of doing more with less

Teaming

Amy Edmondson, in her book *Teaming*, states:

> Fast-moving work environments need people who know how to team, people who have the skills and the flexibility to act in moments of potential collaboration when and where they appear.

---

[3] Sherpa Coaching, 2012 Executive Coaching Survey, http://www.sherpacoaching.com/pdf%20files/Survey-Executive-Coaching-2012.pdf.
[4] Sherpa Coaching, 2013 Executive Coaching Survey, http://www.sherpacoaching.com/pdf%20files/2013-Executive-Coaching-Survey.pdf.

They must have the ability to move on, ready for the next such moments. Teaming still relies on old-fashioned teamwork skills such as recognizing and clarifying independence, establishing trust and figuring out how to collaborate. . . . Instead, people need to develop and use new capabilities of sharing crucial knowledge quickly. They must learn to ask questions clearly and frequently. They must make the small adjustments through which different skills and knowledge are woven together in timely products and services.[5]

It is likely that the business context will continue to be characterized as a fast, ever-changing context. The ability of teams to be flexible and nimble will continue to be an important skill set. As coaches we can support teams and individual group members in asking better questions as well as building deep connection with others quickly. As we explored in Chapter 11, in collaborative workspaces, many of the skill sets we can support our clients around will be invaluable.

Question to Consider

What is the role you want to play in supporting groups and/or teams in the ever-evolving context in which we operate?

Virtual Teams

As a former virtual team leader myself, I have always been sensitive to what is required in connecting and harnessing the various talents of virtual teams. As virtual teams become more prevalent in organizations, I see this as an area for focus, as building connection in the virtual environment is still seen as foreign for many professionals and leaders.

With many virtual teams being spread across vast geographic distance, often straddling cultures, coaches may find themselves needing to become more versed in working with multicultural global teams. What is the bias you bring as a coach—or, to use and adapt the meaning of a term coined by Peggy McIntosh several decades ago, what is your "invisible knapsack"? My former work in the

---

[5] Edmondson, *Teaming*, 14.

international sector from the early 1990s into 2004 had me based outside of Canada. Many times I was the only Canadian, and even Westerner, on a team. This made me very aware of the culture lenses I wear. A great resource to start dipping your toe into this important area is Philippe Rosinski's *Coaching Across Cultures*. Coaching approaches such as Organization and Relationship Systems Coaching (ORSC) also contain tools to start exploring the topics of rank and status.

The challenge for virtual teams in building connection is likely to continue. Supporting teams to understand one another's skills and preferences, while leveraging the diversity that exists, is often the key for high performing teams.

Questions to Consider

What are the key skill and focus areas needed for the virtual teams you work with?

What are the skills you want to develop?

Virtual Learning

Just as many of us have come into the coaching field in the last decade from related fields such as training or facilitation, I believe that there is opportunity for more integration of a coaching approach in the traditional virtual learning opportunities. Webinars are becoming more mainstream, almost like teleseminars were 10 years ago. Even in using a webinar platform, we can incorporate a more engaging coaching approach.

Questions to Consider

What virtual learning opportunities do you want to incorporate in your business?

What value will they add to your client's experience?

Making Technology Work for You and Your Clients

There is no doubt that technology will continue to provide us with new opportunities for how we connect with teams and groups and how we deliver our work. We have seen throughout the book how different coaches are using technologies such as Skype and the Web to bring groups together. In the face-to-face environment, think of the vast changes over the last few years with tablets, smartphones and iPads making their way into our everyday work, as well as into the learning environment. Continuing to ensure that technology is an *enabler* rather than a *barrier* will be key with our work.

Question to Consider

How can you utilize some of the newer technologies to connect group and team members, fostering better goal setting, action, awareness and accountability?

Support for Execution and "Silo Softening"

Coaching as a modality provides many benefits with its focus on both relationships and results. There is great potential for group coaching to be positioned for silo softening, by starting the conversation and building relationship across the silos that exist within organizations. Helping teams expand their view outward to stakeholders that they work with, and work through, can also support silo softening.

Coaching as a modality focuses on accountability. There is great need for more focus on execution and follow-through in our businesses today.

Question to Consider

What role can you play in supporting execution with the groups and teams you work with?

Longer-Term Impact of Doing More with Less

Doing more with less has been a common theme in many businesses since the economic downturn began in 2008. This has also impacted the learning and development industry. According to a 2011 study by the Conference Board of Canada, spending per employee for on-the-job training peaked in 1993, and has declined 40 percent since then. For every dollar American organizations spend on learning and development, Canadian counterparts spent an average of 64 cents.[6] What is the longer-term impact of these reductions?

The 2012 ASTD State of the Industry Report "estimates that U.S. organizations spent approximately $156.2 billion on employee learning in 2011," and "the average direct expenditure per employee decreased in 2011 to $1,182."[7]

In terms of focus areas, the top three learning areas in which organizations invested were managerial and supervisory; profession-specific or industry-specific; and processes, procedures, and business practices. These were stable from the year before.

With pressure on resources, there is opportunity for organizations to make the most of the money invested. The add-on of a series of group coaching conversations to current training initiatives may boost retention. The cost of incorporating two to four hours of a group coaching conversation, or building in a peer-coaching process, may be negligble in the long run in terms of the enhanced business impact obtained.

At the same time, should investment in development continue to decline in countries such as Canada, it is likely that dysfunctional team and individual issues will continue to emerge. Coaches may find themselves working in a more reactive, rather than proactive, manner. Working with dysfunctional teams on key topic areas such as team toxins, the Four Horsemen, navigating conflict and holding difficult conversations may be commonplace.

It is also important to underscore the message that coaching is a process of change, a process that does require time. Coaching in the context of teams takes even more time. The famous analogy is moving one person versus moving a ship. Over time the "two degree rudder change" can take us to a whole new continent, but in the short term we may not be aware of this subtle change.

---

[6] Neil Sandell, "Skills Shortage a Self-inflicted Wound" (Atkinson Series), *Toronto Star*, December 7, 2012, http://www.thestar.com/news/canada/article/1299478--atkinson-series-skills-shortage-a-self-inflicted-wound.

[7] Laurie Miller, "ASTD 2012 State of the Industry Report: Organizations Continue to Invest in Workplace Learning," *T+D Magazine*, November 8, 2012, http://www.astd.org/Publications/Magazines/TD/TD-Archive/2012/11/ASTD-2012-State-of-the-Industry-Report.

Question to Consider

Within your work, what do you see as the longer-term impact of the context of doing more with less?

Voices from the Field: What Do You See as Trends?

I was very interested in seeing what other coaches noticed as trends. Here is what they indicated.

Jacqueline Peters: Team coaching needs to be professionalized and as team coaches, we need to ensure that we are not just working based on what we or the team or the leader think might work, nor solely work on interpersonal dynamics because that's what we were asked to do. We need to educate ourselves on relevant team effectiveness research, choosing approaches that fit the research and the stage the team is at. We also need to link coaching outcomes and measurements to business performance, as defined not only by the team members, but also by external stakeholders of the team.

Catherine Carr: I agree with Jacqueline! I also can see requests for just peer coaching or, as occurs now, conflict coaching/mediation.

Kevin Stebbings: With research indicating that team building events offer very little in terms of return on investment (ROI), team coaching has a huge opportunity for organizations.[8] Team coaching builds upon previous helping roles and works well with the emerging generation of employees who want to have a sense of ownership and choice in how their organizations operate. As team building fades, team coaching has the potential to emerge as the powerful process of choice for organizations that desire to develop their personnel and profits.

With the advances in Internet technology making it so much easier to connect virtually, group coaching offers an excellent way for individuals to be part of global group conversations. I see individuals being able to access and then join a themed group so that they can have group coaching in the field of their particular interest. For example, a leader in India who wants to be part of a group that coaches on "Principle-Centered Leadership in Asia" will have an opportunity to join a themed group and draw from the wisdom of his peers. Or a mother in Europe who joins the group entitled "Starting a Business from Home" will be part of the global conversation that group coaching facilitates.

(Continued)

---

[8] Wageman et. al., "Senior Leadership Teams: What It Takes to Make Them Great."

Knowledge of the power of group coaching needs to come first. Then awareness of and access to themed groups needs to be expanded and made available.

Renee Brotman: More attention to group and team coaching. Both are more cost effective than individual coaching. Provide real-time feedback to real-world experiences. However, the best of both worlds would be recommended—group/team coaching and time for some one-on-one coaching. Sometimes the "most personal" behavioral issues are not addressed in a group. Confidentiality and trust may be the reason.

Ursula Lesic: Future trends within group and team coaching will be part of day-to-day corporate America with internal and external coaches being available to enhance performance.

Shana Montesol: Organizations can leverage the power of group coaching to increase the return on their training investments. I regularly facilitate a 2.5-day soft skills training at an international organization (on topics such as effective workplace communication, how to manage your boss, how to work cross-culturally). Part of the design of the program is a two-hour group coaching session that takes place three months after the 2.5-day workshop is completed. It's a great chance for the participants to cement their learning, revisit the course content and be coached in areas where they have gotten stuck. It's also an important additional data point in terms of evaluation. Trainings often end with a written evaluation form, but the true test of an effective learning experience is whether skills are applied outside the classroom. This group coaching session is a way to get a glimpse into that.

Michael Cullen: Regularly scheduled "drop-in" sessions that allow for topic themes to organically emerge for peer-to-peer exploration and discussion—supervised/facilitated by a certified coach.

Kim Ades:

- Journaling as a standard
- More coach-the-coach models in place
- More self-run groups using materials and content of lead coaches
- Organizations that build their cultures on coaching models

Ray Rigoglioso: I see group coaching as a way to foster community—a need I have noticed very keenly among members of both of my groups. Group coaching can create the kinds of conversations people long for, but for which there are few outlets or forums. I see group coaching as a powerful tool to build community.

Sharon Miller: Fully leveraging the team is an untapped source of competitive advantage. The current paradigm lets us invest in an individual high performer. A team focus is not built into current HR systems. It's absolutely a must and I think it will happen. It will require a paradigm shift.

Work is done and life is lived in and through relationships. Period. The end. Communication is the vehicle of relationships. It's how relationships happen. Communication may be verbal or be the other 93 percent (face, tone, energy, body language). Communication happens in team meetings. But we face the "death by meeting" syndrome. They can be a waste of time. What's important is how you leverage your resources, but not in a way that turns the vise tighter. Team coaching and relationship coaching is paramount in having the conversation—even bringing two people together who need to collaborate to get better business results can make an improvement. You are leaving capability and capacity at the table by not focusing on results.

Although this is a priority—everyone is working so hard—something has to give. What is giving right now is development. Patrick Lencioni's new book on culture is called *The Advantage*.[9] Dave Ulrich, in his book *The Why of Work*, explores how culture is the differentiator.[10] In today's world, businesses can access all the information they need, which people will copy so easily. So, how are you going to differentiate? How will you attract and retain talent?

Phil Sandahl: Trends include the growth of the global marketplace: more virtual teams, more multicultural teams. Diversity is another trend. There will be dramatic growth and reliance on virtual teams—more awareness and focus on team diversity and the value of that diversity. By 2020 there will be five generations of workers in the workplace. By 2020 an organizational lifespan will drop from 45 years to 10. Organizations will need to be very agile. Everyone will need to know how to collaborate—this will be the skill set for survival. The need for our work is growing.

WHAT'S NEXT?

In closing, *what's next for you? What do you want to create in your work and with the people you support?*

---

[9] Patrick Lencioni. *The Advantage: Why Organizational Health Trumps Everything Else In Business* (San Francisco: Jossey-Boss, 2012).

[10] Dave Ulrich and Wendy Ulrich, *The Why of Work: How Great Leaders Build Abundant Organizations That Win* (New York: McGraw-Hill, 2010).

I believe that we are at a time of great opportunity for more coaches, leaders and allied professionals to be incorporating team and group coaching approaches in the work they do. The sustained focus of the coaching process provides teams and groups with opportunities to pause, reflect, set new goals and take action. The longer-term orientation also provides a "stickier" solution, where changes may be sustained for the longer term. The sharing of alternative perspectives provides an opportunity for enhanced understanding and potentially more innovative solutions.

As I have stressed throughout this book, coaching many provides us with the opportunities to connect more people to the coaching process, through scalable solutions. The added befits of silo softening and communicating across differences are tangible benefits for today's world of ongoing change, enhanced collaboration, and doing more with less.

As in any coaching conversation, I have posed a lot of questions for you to consider throughout this book. It was my intention to support you in reinforcing what you may already know, stimulate some new thinking, as well as to provide you with multiple perspectives to give you a wider lens of insight. All of this has been with the intention of providing you with a wider variety of approaches and tools for the work that you do with your client groups and teams.

End-of-Chapter Questions

The impact of coaching is in the awareness stimulated and the action then taken. What is the mark you want to make? What are your next steps?

EXERCISES, TOOLS AND RESOURCES FOR TEAM AND GROUP COACHING

Questions form the backbone of any group coaching conversation.
—Jennifer J. Britton

Coaches and leaders can draw on a number of tools, exercises and other resources to stimulate the conversation within groups and teams. Remember that coaching is all about supporting the *planning, goal setting, awareness and action* of our teams and groups. As such, coaches and leaders may find themselves adapting more traditional training activities to sustain the conversation, deepen the insights for teams and groups, and support enhanced accountability.

This appendix explores exercises, tools and resources for team and group coaching. It includes:

- Working with resources, activities and exercises as a coach
- The backbone: powerful questions for team and group coaching conversations
- Working with visuals
- Assessments you may want to incorporate into your programming
- Adaptations for the virtual channel
- Voices from the Field: journaling in team and group coaching (JournalEngine)
- Group and team coaching activities, including a listing of exercises you may want to consider in:

- Establishing the coaching agreement
- Opening a session
- Goal setting
- Creating connection
- Boosting collaboration
- Deepening awareness around themes
- Leadership
- Commitment
- Facilitating action
- Closure

Throughout this appendix you will find the words *exercise, tool, process* and *activity* used interchangeably. A key component of successful coaching conversations is using the *language that appeals to the clients we work with*. My own personal experience base has had me working with teams and groups across multiple client groups, ranging from business owners to professionals in the safety industry, financial services professional women to stay-at-home moms. My experience across industries has ranged from coaches to individuals working in the transportation, safety, education, mining, and health care industries. A key success factor in working with these diverse groups has been in adapting the language of exercises or tools or resources, positioning them for the different groups I work with.

WORKING WITH EXERCISES, ACTIVITIES AND RESOURCES AS A COACH

As you review the exercises, activities and resources included in this section, it is important to recognize that group and team coaching is an extension of our core coaching processes. Many, if not most, of the individual coaching tools and resources we use can be adapted for the team and group coaching context. Masterful coaches will have a wide variety of tools and processes to choose from.

Second, as coaches it is important to place emphasis on the core coaching competencies of *planning and goal setting, action, awareness* and *accountability*. Just as the first ICF Global Coaching Client survey found in 2009, clients distinguish coaching from related professions (such as training) in these four areas. Keep in mind that teams and groups may be at different stages of the group program continuum during our work together. Key to mastery is choosing an activity with intent.

A common question from coaches is, "Aren't these activities that are also used in training and team building?" As coaches our focus with the groups and teams will likely be around goal setting, action, awareness and accountability. Placing emphasis on these four areas moves exercises into the realm of coaching. As you will note, many of these activities are familiar. Where we place the emphasis is key.

Goal Setting, Action, Awareness and Accountability Are Key Focus Areas of the Coaching Process

As coaches we want to work with our clients to set better goals. SMART-E goals are goals that are Specific, Measurable, Achievable, Realistic and Time-bound, as well as Exciting. If a goal is not exciting to the person being coached, internal motivation will drop. Goals should also connect with the metaview or the 30,000-foot view of "What is really important?" in their life and/or work. As coaches, helping clients keep a focus on the metaview through our activities is very important.

Second, as coaches we want to remember that the terrain of the coaching conversation takes place over the action and awareness realms. How are our activities, questions and exercises supporting our group and team members in *deepening awareness* around key issues of importance and their goals? How are the activities supporting the clients in *taking action* around these key issues? And how do our processes (through check-ins and check-outs), as well as action planning, support the *accountability* that will take them toward their goals? Remember that group and team coaching is a sustained conversation over time.

The appendix of *Effective Group Coaching* explored how many of our core coaching tools and activities could be adapted for the group coaching context. These included:

- The Wheel of Life (or Leadership, or Career, or High-Performing Teams)
- Values work: checklist, values clarification
- Perspective work
- Creating a powerful vision
- Metaphors

This appendix will serve to provide additional exercises, tools and resources as well as a reminder of some that were covered in *Effective Group Coaching*. You will also want to refer to the chart at the end of the appendix that outlines when different activities may be used.

CREATING POWERFUL ACTIVITIES

In creating powerful activities in the team and group coaching processes, coaches and facilitators will want to consider the following:

- A review of the experiential process
- Sequencing activities
- Debriefing activities

A Reminder of the Experiential Process

Experiential learning is grounded in a multi-step learning process. At the start, we—individuals, groups or teams—have an experience. Perhaps it is the experience of a new team forming due to an acquisition or merger, or a group coming together to explore how to be better parents or leaders. The experience in itself is not enough for learning to occur. For learning to occur, we need to provide an opportunity to reflect on what has happened.

As coaches during the experience and reflection stages we will be encouraging our teams or groups to look at the "What?" questions. These may include:

- What happened?
- What changes have occurred?
- What's working?
- What's not?
- What's needed to move from A to B?

Once we have had a chance to pause and reflect, it is useful to generalize—to think about how this can apply to other situations. This is known as the "So what?" phase of the experiential learning process. In this stage, coaches may be asking questions such as:

- So what's important about this gap you have identified?
- So what past lessons or approaches can you apply this time?
- So how does this show up in the workplace or on the team every day?

The learning cycle is completed when the team, group or individual moves into the application stage—the "Now what?" As David Kolb asserts, "the learner must possess decision making and problem solving skills in order to use the new ideas gained from the experience."[1]

The "Now what?" stage helps the group or team apply their learning and insights. Questions often used at this stage are:

- Now what experiences can you take forward?
- Now what are you going to do differently?
- Now what is important to keep an eye on?

You may also wish to refer to the digital chapter Team Coaching in Action (www.groupcoachingessentials.com) for the Tower Building team activity to see how the "What? So what? Now what?" questions can play out.

Sequencing Activities

Sequencing activities is a key consideration for successful team and group coaching engagements. In tandem with the focus areas of the group, sequencing considerations include:

---

[1] Wikipedia. "Experiential Learning," accessed October 11, 2012, http://en.wikipedia.org/wiki/Experiential_learning.

The level of trust and relationships among the group members: How well do members of the group know each other? Do relationships span outside of the coaching context? How much risk does this activity/conversation entail? What lead-up would benefit the group? How does the activity get contextualized?

Where the group is in terms of its own development: Is this a newly forming group or team that do not know each other, or is this a group that have developed strong bonds of trust and intimacy? What do they need from you as a coach?

Level of comfort: It is likely that there will be varied levels of comfort zones within the group or team. Encourage people to engage at a level that is supportive to them, and remind them that they are "at choice" to engage at whatever level works for them. *Remember that a stretch for one may not be a stretch for all.* Sensitivity of group and team members around these comfort zones is important.

Previous experience with the coaching process: Different groups will have different experiences with the coaching process. Build on what they have done already. In an organization, is there a coaching culture that already exists? Ensure that members are clear about what they can expect from the process—for example, coaching versus training.

Progression of topics: Looking at the priorities set by the group, what is the link back to past conversations and activities? How does this link to where the group is going? You may want to ask the group, "What do you see as the connection to the past topics we have explored?" and "How can this activity serve as a foundation for doing things differently?"

What does the group enjoy in terms of pace and engagement? Each group has its own unique rhythm and culture. Some groups love deep conversation as a large group, whereas others feel more comfortable connecting in smaller groups. Some groups enjoy a deep dive around a small number of core topics whereas others enjoy exploring a broad swath of topics. Adapt your approaches based on what you know of your group or team's preferences around how they like to engage, and at what pace.

Range of the group: Deepening self-awareness is key to the coaching process. Different group members may have a different range in terms of the depth at which they can explore issues. Consider the range of the group collectively and individually.

Amount of risk: How much risk does this activity entail? What's at stake if the activity or conversation does not work?

How much time do you have together? Never underestimate how much time it takes for conversation, reflection and action planning. I often talk about the 2:1 ratio, which means that we want to leave almost half the time for group discussion (pairs, triads, small group or large group) as the activity itself. For example, if you undertake a values checklist, it may take 10 minutes for group members to complete it. The real value may be in the conversation that follows, where group or team members may discuss these questions: How are people honoring these values? How are values being stepped over? What's the cost of this? What focus do they want to take?

What people can expect as a takeaway: A key place to start in selecting activities is considering what members want as an outcome of the session: exploration around an issue, clarity, goal setting, action or something else? Consider how different activities can be adapted for different purposes, or if in fact they suit one approach better than another. An example would be activities that support action planning versus exploration around an issue. This appendix highlights exercises that can be used with emphasis and focus. For example, the Wheel of Life can be used in designing the coaching agreement, as well as for planning and goal setting, and as an accountability structure.

Link back to everyday experience: Refer to the experiential model earlier in this appendix. Exercises and conversation should support team and group members to convert their learning to everyday experiences.

THE BACKBONE: POWERFUL QUESTIONS

Powerful questions are often the bulk of what a coach brings to the coaching conversation. What follows are some common questions coaches may want to incorporate. There are two sections:

- Questions for different stages of the group and team coaching process
- Team coaching questions

Questions for Different Stages of the Group and Team Coaching Process

Pre-program One-on-One Group Questions

- What led you to enroll?
- What would you like to get out of the program?
- What are your primary needs/questions/challenges regarding X (topic/theme/program)?
- What should I know about how you learn best?
- What topics would you like addressed in the program?

Pre-program One-on-One Team Questions

- Tell me about your role. (How long in role, in company?)
- What are key priorities for your work?
- How does your work relate to the work of others in the team?
- What do you see as key priorities for the team?
- What are you looking forward to from the team coaching process? (Mine for expectations.)
- What resources and support do you need to enhance your team and individual performance?
- What will success look like for the team?

During Introductions in the First Call, Have Participants Share with Each Other

- Who are you? Where are you from?
- What's brought you to this program?
- What do you want the group to know about you?
- What do you bring to the group that's unique?

Session Check-In Questions (One or More of)

- What have been your actions or insights since our last contact?
- What has been interesting for you since we last met?
- What has been important for you since we last met?
- What progress did you make with the commitments you mentioned last time?

After a Laser Coaching of a Group Member

- What did you find interesting or important about what you heard?
- What synergies exist?
- What ideas/topics did you connect around?
- What did you think of while you were listening?
- What action is this prompting for you?
- What insights is this prompting for you?

Check-Out at End of Session

- What worked well?
- What are you taking away?
- What should we do differently next time? *Or* It would be even better if...
- What was most interesting takeaway? *Or* What is your biggest takeaway?
- What are you going to commit to doing *no matter what*?
- What energy are you leaving the call with (temperature check)?

At the End of the Coaching Process

- What are you most proud of accomplishing during the time we worked together?
- What do you want to continue to keep an eye on (going forward)?
- What will sustain your results/focus?
- What might get in the way?
- What do you need to do now to move forward?
- What do you want to acknowledge others (in the group/team) for?
- What's your favorite memory/high point from our process?
- What do you want to say to other group members?

Final Group and/or One-on-One Call

- What have you learned about yourself? Your strengths?
- What are you proud of accomplishing?
- What outstanding questions do you have?
- What are your next steps?
- What accountability can you build into your everyday work/business, etc.?

Team Coaching Questions

- What will success look like for the work that we are doing together?
- What's the most pressing issue facing this team right now?
- What skills are not being used?

- What strengths does the team have?
- What strengths are not being used?
- Which strengths are being overused? What blind spots are being created? Exist?
- What does accountability mean for this team?
- What does the team need to be accountable for?
- What does commitment mean for this team?
- What's not being said? (What's the elephant in the room?)
- What's needing to be said?
- How are accountability and commitment important for this team?
- What is this team capable of?
- What does this team need to excel?
- Where does the team need to rest/recharge?
- What does the team need to stop doing? Do more of?
- What's going to stretch the team?
- What is taboo for this team?
- What's really important for this team?
- What's our level of trust?
- What single action, if you took it, would make a huge impact on the team, right now?
- What can this team do better than any other team?
- What will you commit to doing *no matter what*?
- What's the temperature/weather within the team right now (temperature check)?
- What is the "shiny object" that is distracting the team from what's really important?
- What do you need to do to sustain the momentum?
- What might get in the way of your success?
- What is going to enable you? Derail you?

Team Roles

- What roles are present in the team (e.g., devil's advocate, champion)?
- How do the roles support the team?
- Who fills these roles?
- What roles are missing?
- What roles no longer serve the team?
- What roles will support the team in achieving X?

KEY SUCCESS FACTORS WITH ACTIVITIES AND RESOURCES

Don't try to incorporate too much: A common pitfall in designing team and group coaching work is trying to fit too much into the schedule. A walk-through of the tools and activities you will want to use can serve as a good litmus test as to how much it will take. You will also want to consider what you know already of the natural pace of the group or team. Remember, the value is in the conversation. If we try to fit in too much, it may actually serve to put the group into overwhelm.

Create connection in multiple ways: As you can see in Table: GCiA.1 in the digital chapter Group Coaching in Action (www.groupcoachingessentials.com) Different Approaches to Working with Groups, there are multiple ways we can be creating connections within groups and teams. These include one-on-one conversations pre-program, learning partners, and hybrid touch points.

Role of language: As we have explored throughout the book, coaches are encouraged to use "language" that works for the client, watching for the overuse of "coach-ese."

Meet people where they are at, and the stage they are at: Recall the dynamics of groups and teams (refer to Table 8.1). When you are thinking about the flow of conversation, field work and activities, consider the stages that groups and teams are at. How will this activity support the group where they are at? You will also want to get a sense of where each individual member is at. The use of scaling questions ("On a scale of 1 to 10, with one being low and 10 being high, where are you?") is another way to take a quick pulse check.

Stance of the coach: Your stance and confidence as a coach also have tremendous impact on how exercises are received. What are you confident about? What are you unsure of? What space do you want to create in your session?

The 2:1 ratio: For coaches working in the team and group coaching arenas it is important to leave sufficient time for the debrief of any activities or tools being used. What is of greatest value is the conversation that ensues from any activity, assessment or resource that you are bringing in. The peer learning process, and hearing about others' perspectives, can be as enlightening as individual reflection.

In design work I often think about the 2:1 ratio. If it takes 20 minutes to undertake an activity, I like to ensure that there is at least half that time to debrief or have discussion. For coaches, questions form the backbone of any coaching conversation, be they individual, group or team coaching conversations. Questions create an opportunity for individuals to pause and reflect on their learning and the "What next?"

Questions to Consider When Selecting an Activity

What are the themes you are working on?

What stage of development is the group in (forming, performing, etc.)?

What adaptations may be required for this group or team? (Consider learning styles present, virtual or in person.)

What purpose does this tool or activity serve:

- To support planning and goal setting?
- To deepen awareness?
- To foster connection/collaboration?
- To support action?

How does this activity support the notion of "Do It Now"?

How does this connect with other activities you have used?

What follow-up is needed?

WORKING WITH VISUALS

Visuals are a very powerful tool in any learning, coaching or group process, one that is often overlooked, with emphasis being placed on the auditory channel.

Ian Jukes of the 21st Century Fluency project writes:

> Tests have further shown that people can remember the content of over 2,500 pictures with 90 percent accuracy several days after exposure, even though they see each picture for only 10 seconds. Recall rates after one year remain at about 63 percent.
>
> The same research, however, shows that when information is presented orally, after 72 hours people only remember about 10 percent. Add picture content to the material, however, and the retention skyrockets up to 65 percent. This is because the brain processes images 60,000 times faster than it does text.[2]

---

[2] http://www.njasa.net/Page/770

Over the past few years I have continued to expand the way I have brought visual images into the group and team coaching process. I describe a couple of ways in the Field Journal below.

There are a great number of visual resources we can choose from, including:

Visual Explorer: Center for Creative Leadership. CCL has come up with a number of different options for purchase: large (full size), postcard size and digital versions of this tool.

JICT Images Kit: Journey with Intuition and Creativity to Transformation. Available through CoachingToys.com. The 72-card deck is very portable, yet large enough for visibility with a group.

The Coaching Game: Points of You. An excellent visual deck to use with clients. The Coaching Game has evolved a number of processes to use the Points of View with individual and group clients. The company also offers a certification program for coaches. You can also create your own decks from your own photos, postcards or even old calendars.

Field Journal: Visual Decks

Many of you have heard me speak about how much I love the Visual Explorer tool from the Center for Creative Leadership. Consisting of more than 300 colorful images, this tool has been useful to me in team and group coaching work ranging from health care, to work with the police, to work with internal HR professionals, to multicultural community groupings. Whether you opt to use Visual Explorer, or another visual deck such as the JICT Images, or if you create your own with postcards or your own photos, here are some suggestions on how to incorporate images into your group and team coaching work:

In Person

Lay out the cards around the room. (Make sure everyone is safe to move.) Have people select the photo that resonates with them. Here are some of the questions I've used with different client groups and teams:

- What does personal productivity look like for you? (Audience: 120 people)

(Continued)

- What does it mean to be an internal HR professional? (Audience: 6–30 HR professionals.)
- What is the photo that represents your vision for this team/organization next year/in five years (team and organization focus)?

Give people several minutes (three to five minutes) to reflect on and take note of their photos. You may prompt them with some additional questions such as, "What's in focus? What's dominant? What's striking?" Have people write this down.

Next get people to work in small groups (pairs, triads or groups up to five). Depending on the time available, give each person three to five minutes to share their photo with others in the small group. Invite group members to point things out and share their observations.

Even if group members don't know each other, it is really interesting to see what other individuals point out. For teams and groups whose members do know each other, it can be extremely powerful to hear perspectives from their peers.

As a wrap-up, ask people to note in their workbook or manual what they found significant, and what they want to take forward from this activity.

In the Virtual Domain

You can send out a scanned copy (be aware of copyright) to participants by PDF, or if you are using a webinar platform you may be able to show several of the photos by screensharing. Follow a similar process:

1. Individually, select a photo and note what's important and significant about it.
2. Have each group member share the one they have selected and why. Open up dialogue for additional insights and perspectives.

Prompting questions may be:

- What's significant about this?
- What's the connection between this and where you are right now? Where you are going?

ASSESSMENTS

As we know from team coaching, assessments can be a very good tool in supporting both team and group coaching. Assessments provide a check point for individuals, groups and teams, which can be revisited at strategic times during the coaching process. For example, a pre-program team assessment can provide you with information about the strengths and blind spots as a team. This can create the foundation of some of the initial work you do with a team at an offsite, and can be used to create or co-create a roadmap of the themes you will be covering in your work together. Depending on the coaching length, you may wish to revisit the assessment at mid-point or at the end of the coaching process.

Role of the Coach in Using Assessments

Just as in selecting other activities, when using assessments we will want to place emphasis on goal setting or awareness building. In a team or group coaching conversation, the data can serve as the conversation starter from which new awareness is created, goals are shaped and new commitments are made. In the team coaching context, team assessments such as the DiSC or Team Diagnostic, which provide a snapshot of where the team is, can be supplemented by individual assessments such as MBTI or DiSC or StrengthsFinder to support individual team members in seeing the differences among themselves. Many team and group coaches have noted that they incorporate assessments on multiple levels.

Types of Assessments

There are a number of assessments that coaches may want to incorporate, including:

MBTI: The MBTI is a very popular assessment for coaches and HR professionals to utilize. Certification programs are held throughout the year around the world.

Personal Styles Inventory (PSI): Available through HRD Press, the PSI is an easy to use inventory that provides group or team members with basic information about their style. This can be very useful in starting to explore the impact of style in communication and decision making. No certification needed to use.

Leadership Circle Profile: The Leadership Circle Profile is "the only 360-degree assessment that measures leadership competencies and the inner assumptions that drive behavior. In an instant, managers discover what they are doing, why they are doing it, and key opportunities for development. Ultimately, this assessment cultivates awareness and insights that enhance effectiveness in leadership and impacts performance." Also available is the Leadership Culture Survey, which "identifies how your leadership culture is impacting productivity, turnover, and bottom line metrics."[3]

Strengths: VIA Strengths, StrengthsFinder 2.0 are two very good tools for working with strengths.

DiSC: The DiSC provides individual and team assessments.

EQi 2.0: The EQi 2.0 has become a very popular assessment for coaches who are interested in looking at emotional intelligence with their teams. Certification programs run globally throughout the year.

Team Diagnostic Assessment: The Team Diagnostic is an excellent assessment which maps out the 14 strengths of a team along productivity and positivity measures. Refer to the Voices from the Field section by Phil Sandahl in Team Coaching in Action at www.groupcoachingessentials .com.

Keys to using assessments effectively as a coach:

- **It's not about the data, it's about the conversation:** Key to bringing in an assessment is the conversation it provokes at the individual, team and/or group level.
- **What the team notices in the data that is provided:** Let the team comment on what they notice. Use questions to expand the review of the material
- **Certification required:** Many, if not all, of the assessments require some level of training and/or certification in order for you to use, or deploy, them. As a coach, consider where you may be asked to support teams or groups, and, if assessments have already been done, how can your work dovetail into this. You may be able to partner with someone internal who deploys the assessment, working with them as a co-facilitator.

---

[3] The Leadership Circle, accessed May 7, 2013, http://www.theleadershipcircle.com.

EXERCISES TO CREATE CONNECTION

"Business is conducted through relationships and trust is the foundation of effective relationships."
—Dennis Reina and Michelle Reina[4]

As we have seen throughout the book, the added value of any team and group coaching conversation is the peer sharing and learning that occurs. A reminder of things you can do as a coach to create connection among group members are the following:

- Pre-program one-on-ones and first session
- Communication channels between calls/touch points (email, Facebook, JournalEngine, etc.)
- Learning partners
- Hybrid group/individual approach
- Confidentiality

A fuller list of specific activities is included in the table that follows.

Using Geography or the Body in Coaching

One of the riskier, or edgier, areas for coaches is bringing "geography" to the coaching process, or getting group or team members to use their body in coaching. Intuitively there may be some real wisdom uncovered by giving people the opportunity to notice what is present and available as they move through activities.

Geography lends itself to exercises such as:

- The Wheel
- Perspectives
- Styles work (see case studies)
- Strengths work

[4]Dennis Reina and Michelle Reina, *Trust and Betrayal in the Workplace* (San Francisco: Berrett Koehler, 2006), 5.

Field Journal: Foundational Coaching Tool—Wheel of Life/Work/High-Performing Teams (Kinesthetic)

The Wheel of Life can be a very useful tool in supporting team and group coaching clients in:

- Planning and goal setting
- Deepening awareness around where you are at
- Action and accountability

In addition to using the wheel on paper, consider how you can integrate body-centered coaching or the skill of geography in having people physically "walk the wheel."

I bring the physical wheel into a lot of the work I do with teams, groups and pairs. There are always some great new insights in making it very kinesthetic. Take a look at the instructions that follow. How could you adapt this for your groups or teams? Maybe it is a Wheel of Business, Wheel of High-Performing Teams, or Wheel of Leadership.

The Wheel of Leadership (Floor)

Time required: 15-45 minutes.
Materials needed: Tape, labels of wedges (leadership competencies).
Instructions:
Let us say you decide to create a Wheel of Leadership for a new group of managers. Using colored masking tape, tape off a wheel on the floor and label each "wedge" with a different leadership competency. When I use this I will try to use the names of the leadership competencies that already exist within the organization. Some wheels may have six wedges, some eight or ten. Ensure that the circle is large enough for all members to walk around. Clear the area of any items that people may trip on.

Give group or each person members an opportunity to walk around the wheel once and think about what each one means to them. What do they notice in the different wedges? This is done in silence.

Next, ask each person to move to the wedge that represents their strength. Pause. Have group members notice where each person is at. Ask group or team members to share with others in their wedge what's important about that strength. How does it support their work and relationships? How does it get in the way? What blind spots does it create? Give groups some time to do this, and then have each group member share with the rest one or two things about their strength.

The next request may be, "Move to the part of the wheel where, if you placed emphasis or focus, it would make a tremendous difference in your work." Get people to notice where the group or team moves to. As in the first round, give people time to share with others in their wedge their thoughts on why this would make an impact on their work. Have them quickly share this with the larger team.

Next round: "What is the one area you would like to place attention on going forward?" Have group or team members notice. Allow each member time to share what that is, why it is important, and how they would like to be supported.

If the wheel on the floor is way outside of the comfort zone of group members, or if the room will not facilitate it, you can also get people to draw their own wheel on a piece of paper, and move to different breakout areas for discussion around the questions you pose (strength, greatest potential for impact, focus area going forward).

Other Questions to Incorporate into Your Coaching Using a Wheel with Clients (Individuals/Teams/Groups):

- What do you notice about your wheel?
- Where are you strongest?
- Where are you weakest?
- Where do you want to place attention?
- In which wedge do your strengths lie?
- How are you using these?
- Which wedge are you ignoring (or do you want to ignore)?
- What's important about this?
- On a scale of 0 to 10, what would you rate your level of balance/skill/ confidence/competence in this area right now?
- What would be an optimum rating on a scale of 0 to 10 in each of the wedges?
- What will it take to get there?
- What do you need to say yes to? No to?

With teams and groups, have members observe the synergies: What's similar? What's missing? Where is it overbalanced?

TEAM COACHING ACTIVITIES

Team coaching activities will often focus on deepening awareness for individual group members and team members collectively, as well as strengthening relationships and creating a common experience. A focus on goal setting and accountability are also key to the team coaching process. The adoption and development of a set of shared behavioral agreements, along with shared skills and models, can also be very useful. For example, in working with a team with new leadership, work around strengths and styles can be of benefit individually and collectively. With a team where turnover is prevalent, work around roles can be useful. In working with a team as a systems approach, even if people change, a systems approach will stress that the roles will stay the same.

Skill development may be another area of focus for teams. We need to remember that sometimes people are not doing things, such as providing constructive feedback, because they do not know how to do it. Teaching of these foundational skills—such as how to *give feedback, hold difficult conversations* and *navigate conflict*—can be very useful. It provides team members with a common framework they can all use.

In a team coaching process it is about the skill development as well as the application of the skills and checking in with the team to see how the skills are being used and refined by the team.

Some of the activities that are specific to a team coaching context include:

- Tower Building (Team Coaching in Action at www.groupcoaching essentials.com)
- Working with Strengths and Styles (Team Coaching in Action at www .groupcoachingessentials.com)
- Team Action Planning with Post-its (Team Coaching in Action at www .groupcoachingessentials.com)
- Team Story Board (Appendix)
- Wheel of Work (Appendix)

Check out the table at the end of the appendix for additional coaching activities that can be useful in the team coaching context at different stages.

VIRTUAL COACHING ACTIVITIES

Chapter 7 goes into great depth around setting up virtual coaching activities. Some of the best practices already covered to keep in mind when in bringing in virtual activities:

- Offline pre-work: What pre-work will benefit this conversation or set the members up for success?
- Breakouts: Not all conversation needs to take place in the large group. How can you incorporate virtual breakout groups? One service that facilitates virtual breakout groups easily is Maestro Conference.
- Provide clear instruction.
- Remember that the impact of coaching does not always happen during the calls. How can pre-work and post-work benefit the group?
- Always have a back-up!

THE IMPORTANCE OF CLOSURE: ENDING YOUR PROGRAMS

The latency and recency effects state that we will remember the start and end of things. What happens in the middle is sometimes a blur. We often place a large focus on the start of a group or team coaching process, but may not sustain the same focus at the end. Closure is key to a group or team coaching process, for several reasons:

- It allows space for reflection and sharing of successes.
- It provides a pause to capture key learning.
- It provides an opportunity to support the transfer back to the workplace.
- It provides an opportunity for celebration.
- It provides an opportunity to say thank-you.

Some key questions coaches will want to think about before this last session is:

- What kind of space do you want to leave for thank-yous and learning to be shared among the group/team?
- What benefit would there be in scheduling either an individual or group follow-up down the road to see what further action they have taken, and/ or insights they have acquired?
- What is the tone you would like to set in this final session?
- What pre-work will support group members before the final call (e.g., self-assessment, structured questions)?
- What connection is the group eager for, going forward?
- Is there a physical takeaway you would like to leave with group members, or have them create for themselves (e.g., a box, a vision board, an action plan, etc.)?

Voices from the Field: Journaling in Team and Group Coaching by Kim Ades, JournalEngine

Throughout the book we have talked about the sustained nature of the team and group coaching conversation. Many coaches incorporate journaling into their group and team coaching contexts. One platform that allows team or group members to journal in a secure environment is JournalEngine.

JournalEngine Software is an "insulated" online social network where people express their hopes, their dreams, their challenges and their frustrations, and receive support from their coach and other participants in the group as well as members in the community. Essentially JournalEngine does four things:

1. It provides a safe place for people to express their deepest thoughts and work with a personal coach in an intimate and accelerated way.
2. It delivers automated content.
3. It supplies a focused social network to a group of people who share the same interests, challenges or goals.
4. It provides a series of marketing tools that simplify the process of lead generation, lead conversion and client retention over the lifespan of client service.

Here's what coach and founder of JournalEngine Kim Ades has said about her experience in using JournalEngine in her group coaching processes.

> Journaling lays down the foundation for coaching between a coach and a client. In a group context, I ask my clients to journal so that I can help them create significant momentum and move them forward by leaps and bounds.
>
> Here's how I use JournalEngine: Clients typically go through a 10-week coaching course. They have a one-hour call with their coach each week and are expected to journal every single day for the duration of the coaching period. They are given a journaling assignment to address on a daily basis and as the coach, I am able to read their journals and comment on what has been written. The traction that takes place as a result of this process is astounding. Tremendous trust is built quickly, allowing me to address very deep and personal barriers to success instantly.

In a group setting, enabling group members to connect with one another and chat before the course even begins adds tremendous value to the experience. The idea is to provide homework assignments on a weekly basis that they can work on together within the group, allowing them to comment and interact with each others' journals. As a coach, the content extracted from these journals serves to fuel the coaching process and provide an exceptionally personal and meaningful group coaching experience.

Fast forward to 2012. Here's what we have seen from the journaling process:

- Results: much deeper and more personal
- Tap huge blocks faster
- Trust and intimacy established more quickly
- Coach plays a key role in setting the tone for the work

As a coach using JournalEngine, I read my client's journal entries and I am instantly informed about the mindset and experience of the client. I am always up to date and able to work with the data to identify challenges, limiting beliefs, patterns of behavior, and interpretations of events that may cause my client's progress to slow down. Addressing them right away provides powerful just-in-time coaching.

In groups I usually work with 12 people or fewer. What's important in working in the group context is that each participant experiences a personal shift through our work together. This means that each participant must be seen, acknowledged and coached directly through the journaling process.

Impact of Journaling on Coaching

Coaches are often ill-equipped to coach. They often show up on calls looking forward to being caught up in the lives and work of their clients in between touch points. Clients deserve a coach who is prepared to jump in and coach. Journaling provides timely and relevant data, allowing the coach to be prepared, to be on point and to address issues that are recurring and still hot on the client's agenda.

(Continued)

Coaches may have prep forms but these are not as rich, or as consistent. The coaching client may be filling one out quickly in a few minutes before the call, rushing to get it off to the coach. Many times these comments are brief, to the point, missing the emotion. With journaling there is never a loss of momentum in between calls, as clients capture their thoughts in the moment. There is a constant touch, which shows the evolving state of the clients. Emotional insights are apparent throughout the writing. The relationship is also built between the client and coach. This trust, intimacy and communication between client and coach is very important.

With journaling, clients can see the degree to which they have traveled. It is documented. The coach can also comment on the journal and provide tangible evidence of the impact of their coaching and how it caused growth moments.

Application to Group Coaching

In group coaching there is the added benefit of group cohesion and support at a much deeper level with groups. Establishing expectations about frequency of journaling and interaction early on in the coaching cycle is critical to the success of the coaching experience. Group members need to understand that everyone is responsible for journaling and reading other group members' journals (as they choose to share). There is great value from the extra support. In a group you can ask, "Where are you?" and the group members know that they matter.

The results I've seen in a group coaching context are dramatically higher when group members are asked to journal. They are doing the work every day, getting feedback every day and they are in conversation every day. This allows them to learn fundamental skills and principles without coaching, leading to greater sustainability.

Application to Teams

In team coaching there are different elements at play. It's important to be aware of conflict-of-interest issues and create a safe environment where coaching clients feel at ease about journaling honestly. What we have found is that leadership transparency is a vital part of opening up the lines of communication. The more the leader supports the process, the more willing the team to jump in and play. It is clear that teams who journal experience a significantly higher level of employee satisfaction.

Kim Ades

JournalEngine, www.journalengine.com

Resources for Inspiration, Ideas and Materials: Get Sparked

Marcy Nelson Garrison of CoachingToys.com uses the term "sparkers" for things that get creative juices going. Here are some resources you may want to check out for inspiration:

- CoachingToys.com.
- Fundoing.com from Dr. Chris Cavert. Also check out his wonderful blog posts on topics ranging from big questions to digital icebreakers.
- Wilderdom.com.
- BusinessBalls.com.
- David Megginson and David Clutterbuck, *Techniques for Coaching and Mentoring* (Burlington: Butterworth-Heinemann, 2005).
- Dale Schwarz and Anne Davidson, *Facilitative Coaching* (San Francisco: Pfeiffer, 2009).
- Sara L. Orem, Jacqueline Binkert and Ann L. Clancy, *Appreciative Coaching* (San Francisco: John Wiley & Sons, 2007).

Voices from the Field: What Are Your Favorite Exercises and Resources to Bring In?

One of my favorite questions for other coaches interviewed is, "What are your favorite tools, resources or exercises?" Here's what coaches responded.

Jacqueline Peters: I love doing Tower Building or Bridge Building activities to get people working together and experience planning and executing in the moment. We talk about what they observed/noticed, etc., and ask, "How was this experience just like work?"

(Continued)

Catherine Carr: Building peer coaching skills and practice sessions works well for teams to create excitement, momentum and change.

Kevin Stebbings: A favorite activity with teams is having each member of the team write three important team values on three index cards. The team sits in a circle, and the values index cards are then spread across the floor in the middle of the team circle. The coach asks the team about their observations and what they've noticed from the values cards before them. Each team member, one at time, is invited to choose five values from the cards and to line them up in order of importance. After each turn the coach asks the team about their observations of the five cards and the order in which they have been placed. The team is also invited to ask the team member about the reasons for choosing and ranking the values the way they have. The order of values for each team member is recorded on a flip chart. After each team member has had an opportunity to rank and discuss their team values, the flip chart sheet is placed in the middle of the circle. The coach then asks the team to share their observations about the rankings of team values as a whole. The coach facilitates discovery with questions such as, "What does this mean for us a team? Where are the opportunities here? Where are the challenges? What can we do together to move forward as a team?"

Renee Brotman: Favorite activities: role play, when appropriate; use of participant-written case studies, as well as coach-presented cases.

Shana Montesol: In the final meeting of the group coaching program, I take a few minutes to acknowledge each group member, often contrasting where they were when they started the program and the progress they have made to date. I then invite other group members to acknowledge this person. It's a moving and meaningful way to wrap up the program.

Sharon Miller: I draw on a lot of my training provided by the Center for Right Relationship and their the Organization and Relationship Systems training including Lands Work, Inner Role Work, Working with Team Toxins, Best Team Exercise and Perspective Wheels.

Michael Cullen: Group coaching: around the circle check-ins and check-outs at the start and end of the sessions.

Kim Ades: Group journaling. Group members each receive the same journaling assignments throughout the week and journal in a private and secure space for just the group. This generates group interaction, bonding, and dramatic movement for each individual in the group. The value of this level of depth and interaction is astounding.

Phil Sandahl: Something we learned from Appreciative Inquiry: Tell us about your best team experience. What made it memorable? What were the qualities of that team that stood out, that made it a best team?

Additional Exercises

Team Story Board Exercise

Purpose: To create a visual representation of key themes the group members have taken away from the workshop, and a vision of where they want to place focus. in the months ahead (you can determine the timeframe: 6, 12 or 18 months)

Materials: Large Bristol board or foam-backed board (2 by 3 feet), glue, scissors, words, markers, etc.

Instructions:

Ask one member of each group to collect a package of materials and one hard back board, markers, scrapbook materials, etc.

Say, "Over the course of our work together we have explored a number of themes and had rich dialogue around a number of topics. I want to give each group an opportunity to visually capture your key learning from our discussions. What you have in your package are materials to create your own storyboard of the key themes we have discussed, and a vision of where you want us to go (insert timeframe)."

Give teams 12 to 20 minutes to come up with their storyboard. At the half way mark get the group to pause and remind them to include both their vision as well as themes and learning.

Each group should be given two minutes to present these to the rest of the team.

Vision Road Map Exercise

Group size: 3–12.

Time required: 20–30 minutes (often dependent on group size).

Purpose: To help participants identify key milestones toward their future goals.

Materials needed: Markers, stickers, magazines, card stock or construction paper.

Preparation: Bring materials together.

Instructions:

This exercise is useful when looking at bringing vision work to life. Once participants have developed a clear vision for their work/life/career, etc., it may be useful to have them create an actual road map, a visual representation of those key goals.

Provide participants with materials (markers, stickers, magazines and card stock), to map out what they want. For example, you may have them draw a road and put the years, along with key goals reached or events undertaken.

In the couples retreats I ran for several years, couples were given the materials above and a large board to visually map their goals and vision. They placed key goals and timelines on the left, and also had a vision board on the right. This brought together two processes (vision board plus the timeline), which we sometimes keep separate.

Field Journal: Working with Values— Hospital Foundation

Team and group coaches are likely to find themselves doing a lot of work around values. For group coaches, the values may be on the individual level, as well as exploring those values in light of the relationships around them. For example, a couple or parents might look at their own individual values and then have discussion sharing these with each other. This could be followed up with the development of a shared values list for themselves as a couple or parenting unit.

At the team level, we may be facilitating discussion around values at the individual, team and organizational levels. For example, in working with a health care foundation team years ago, the team was faced with a new set of values being rolled into the organization. It was important for this team to also look at individual and team values. We started with an individual values checklist where members were given a list of 15 to 20 values and asked to consider if each was of high, medium or low importance to them. It was followed with a series of questions for team members to individually reflect on, such as:

- Which are the top three to five values?
- Which ones are they aligning with in their work? In their life?
- What changes of focus would they like to make to more fully honor/ align with their values?
- What would this look like?

After this, team members shared their top one or two values with the larger group. This was an important part of fostering connection among the team. It also gave team members an appreciation of what they valued (for example, detail or excellence).

The second part of the activity had the team break into different smaller groups, each taking a look at one of the organizational values that was being rolled in. The question for each group was, "What does the practice and integration of this value look like in our work?" Each sub-group looked at one of the organizational values, and defined it for the team. This built onto how the organization had defined it. Sub-groups posted their lists of activities and behaviors the team could use to embrace these values, presenting them to their colleagues. Other team members were asked to add onto these organizational values lists. This gave the team a list of practices and behaviors that would support the organization's values.

Finally, we brainstormed a list of values that the team wanted to hold for themselves as a team. This was prioritized down (using dots) to half a dozen. These values became part of a story board they later created (see Team Story Board Exercise, above).

As you will note in the chart of activities, coaches can also work with values by undertaking a Word String (refer to Chapter 11's co-facilitation Word String example) or Peak Experience Visualization.

Table A.1: A Selection of Activities for Team and Group Coaches

Activities for Establishing the Coaching Agreement	Instructions
Pre-program One-on-One Calls	Refer to Chapter 8 for pre-program call questions for teams and groups.
Hopes, Fears and Fantasies	As outlined in *Effective Group Coaching* (page 246), this activity supports initial dialogue within a group around key aspirations or hopes for a program, those things participants are looking forward to. At the same time participants are also encouraged to share their fears—things they are nervous or concerned about with the coaching. Fantasies are the most "zany" things that could occur during the program. This puts a light spin on the work, and also encourages group/team members to dream. The activity can be undertaken in 10 to 30 minutes in a larger group, or within smaller groups with sharing back to the larger group.

(Continued)

Table A.1: (*Continued*)

Activities for Establishing the Coaching Agreement	Instructions
Using Colored Dots: Dotmocracy Adaptation (What are your key focus areas?)	Using colored dots is a visual way to identify key priority areas for the group or team, once a brainstormed list of key coaching topics is identified.
Ways of Working/Agreement	Setting up "ways of working" or agreements is key to the coaching process. When working with teams you may have two levels of agreements: agreements for the team coaching process (such as confidentiality, start and end on time, focus) and a separate set of Behavioral Team Agreements. These Behavioral Team Agreements spell out what is appropriate/acceptable for each team member.
Pre-program Questionnaire	Pre-program questionnaires can provide a snapshot of interest areas and needs before the program starts. This is useful particularly if you cannot create contact with your group or team members. It may also be appropriate to have group members share some, or all, of their responses in the first call, circulating it afterwards.
Wheel of Life/Business/High-Performing Teams	The Wheel as a coaching tool is important as it creates a baseline view of where group members are at. Adaptations of the Wheel are endless: life, business, health, high-performing teams, etc. You may wish to get group or team members to look at this at the start of the program, mid-point and at the end of the coaching process.
Activities for Opening a Session	
Check-In	Select from some of the check-in questions listed in the Team and Group Coaching Process questions earlier in the appendix.
Personal Logos	Outlined in *Effective Group Coaching* (page 246) or the Field Journal in Chapter 3.
Hopes, Fears and Fantasies	As above.
Visual Deck	Have photos available and ask the group or team members to select the photo that represents: • What they are bringing to the process OR • What they are eager to create with others OR • Their focus for your work together
Theme-Based Activity	Make your own list of activities that would be useful in exploring the themes of your programs.

Activities for Goal Setting	
SMART-E Goals	Work with the team or group members around SMART-E goals: S - Specific M - Measurable A - Achievable R - Realistic T - Timebound E - Exciting This may be part of action planning on an individual, team or organizational level.
Priorities	Working around priorities is likely in most coaching processes. Throughout the book we have seen different ways to prioritize with setting the focus of coaching topics (Chapter 8), to Team Action Planning digital Team Coaching in Action chapter at www.groupcoaching essentials.com.
4D Model	This is a great model to share with teams, groups and individuals to support prioritization in time management. The 4D model encourages people to think through "Do It, Dump It, Defer It and Delegate It." This originally comes from the book called *The Power of Focus* by Jack Canfield, Mark Victor Hansen, and Les Hewitt.[5]
Values	Connecting teams and groups back to their values: How do these values show up in your goals. What is missing? What is not aligned?
Activities for Creating Connection	
Personal Logos	Give group or team members a minute to create a logo that represents what they bring to the group or team that is unique. This is a great icebreaker, or kick-off activity for teams that know each other and groups that don't. Have the grouping note what is similar or common among the group.

(Continued)

---

[5] Jack Canfield, Mark Victor Hansen and Les Hewitt, *The Power of Focus* (Deerfield Beach, FL: HCI Books, 2000).

Table A.1: (*Continued*)

Activities for Establishing the Coaching Agreement	Instructions
Hopes, Fears and Fantasies	Refer to *Effective Group Coaching*, page 248.
Email/Photo Introduction	Described in Chapter 8.
Table Image: Virtual Programs	Refer to Chapter 8 and the Virtual Table Image. This visual representation can be a great support for you as a facilitator and also helps group members feel more connected in the virtual domain.
Ways of Working/Agreements (Ground Rules)	At the start of every program, work with teams and groups to identify their agreements, "ways of working" or "ground rules."
Activities for Exploring Relationships	
Spider's Web	The Spider's Web is a great way to close off a team or group coaching process, bringing to light the relationships that have been built. It is also good for acknowledgment. I have used this for decades. Have ample thin rope to circle the group several times. Starting with one person, have them hand off the rope to another group member (still holding onto the one end). As they pass it off have them acknowledge another for what they have brought to the experience, one of their strengths or something about their relationship. The question should be the same for all group members. As the coach, "fade out" to the edges. At the end, have everyone notice the web that has been created and that exists whether they are together or apart.
Traffic Light List: Red, Green, Yellow	In our work context we have a series of relationships, some strong (green), some that need attention (yellow) and some that are in crisis (red). It can be useful for team or group members to identify their key internal and external stakeholders, color coding each connection (red, yellow, green). This is a very visual way to start exploring the topic of relationships that are strong, those that require attention and those that are okay. It can be followed by action planning.

Relationship Mapping	Have individuals identify all the external and internal stakeholders they work with. Get them to place these on a web (similar to MindMapping). The relationship mapping can be highlighted in the red, yellow and green to signify the status of these relationships.
Activities for Boosting Collaboration	
"Ways of Working"	See above.
SWOT	The SWOT tool comes originally from Strategic Planning processes, and gets us to look at our internal strengths and weaknesses, as well as external threats and opportunities. It is a great tool for co-facilitators to complete together to gain a common understanding of their strengths and weaknesses as a partnership, as well as the opportunities and threats in the context they operate within. Coaches may find the tool useful when coaching: • Group members undergoing transition (e.g., career transition) • Groups of new managers (e.g., look at their team or territory context) • Groups of new business owners Teams can explore the context they operate within, and identify their own strengths and weaknesses. May also be used at the organizational level. Refer to page 256 of *Effective Group Coaching*.
Strategic Issues Mapping	Strategic Issues Mapping is another strategic planning tool that can help a team expand awareness around the context in which the team operates. Refer to the digital Team Coaching in Action chapter at www.groupcoaching essentials.com for more description. Strategic Issues Mapping can help a team with their productivity results and with alignment issues.
Force Field Analysis	Kurt Lewin's Force Field Analysis tool is useful in the context of change. Have group or team members draw a line down the middle of a page. On one side the group or team should list the things that will support the change ("Driving Forces"), and on the other side list the things that will hold back the change ("Restraining

(Continued)

Table A.1: (*Continued*)

Activities for Establishing the Coaching Agreement	Instructions
	Forces"). The team will want to consider things such as culture, time, resources, policies, stakeholders, etc. Given that coaching is a process of change, this tool can be shared for the team to look at what is enabling or supporting their team into the change, and what perhaps is holding them back from making the changes they need to make.
Styles Work: Large Group Process	Table Top Exercise: refer to DiSC Styles Field Journal in Chapter 10.
Working with Strengths (Team)	Ideal for newly forming teams or teams with a new leader.
Best Team	Phil Sandahl mentioned the Best Team exercise as one of his favorites. Stemming from Appreciative Inquiry, in the best team exercise each individual is encouraged to think about the best team they belonged to and share this with the others. This creates a positive emotional field and also provides an opportunity for conversation and sharing to occur. Also helps to support connection among team members.
Best Team Visual Explorer	Using Visual Explorer or other visual deck, have individual team members select a photo which represents what a "best team" has looked like for them. Have them share with the rest of the team, and create a cumulative list of what the characteristics were of their membership of a best team.
Strengths Work (Individual/ Team)	Working with strengths is likely to be a rich area of exploration for teams and groups. Refer to VIA Strengths, and Team Coaching in Action at www.groupcoachingessentials.com text box.
Vision	Group and team coaches may work around creating a vision using questions or a visualization, or have teams create a team story board or vision board.
Values	As outlined in *Effective Group Coaching*, coaches can work with teams and groups using a Values Checklist, Peak Experience Visualization or Word String exercise.

Story Board (Team, Group, Couple)	Refer to description in this appendix. The Team Story Board can also be used in group coaching conversations for families, couples, business partners, etc.
Roles	Roles are a foundational topic many teams and groups may explore.
Activities for Deepening Awareness Around Issues	
Vision	As above.
Values (Organization, Team, Individual)	As above, with a reminder that values can be examined at these different levels: organization, team and individual.
Force Field Analysis	As above.
Ways of Working	As above.
Limiting Beliefs	Just as coaches work with Limiting Beliefs with individual clients, this may be a rich area for exploration with group and team clients.
Inner Critic Work (Modeling)	Our inner critics are always at play. Refer to *Taming Your Gremlin* by Rick Carson.[6]
SWOT	Strategic Planning Tool: as above.
Strategic Issues Mapping	Refer to Team Coaching in Action at www.groupcoaching essentials.com.
Benefits and Opportunities	As a tool for decision making, benefits and opportunities can be explored by teams. Similar to the SWOT matrix, benefits and opportunities can be mapped out.
Lines in the Ground	For in-person programs, having people move around a line or space to indicate interest or agreement can be a very visual way to get a "mapping" of where people are at. In Chapter 2 we looked at the Group Program Continuum. I have made this activity more kinesthetic in sessions by posting the three labels (Coaching, Training and Consulting) on the wall, and having group members line up where they see themselves naturally. We have then moved to where they see their clients wanting them. As with other activities, the value is in both the movement and the conversation that ensues. The line can be used in any sort of scaling question (1–10) or to explore gradients.

(Continued)

---

[6] Rick Carson, *Taming Your Gremlin: A Surprisingly Simple Method for Getting Out of Your Own Way* (New York: HarperCollins, 1983).

Table A.1: (*Continued*)

Activities for Establishing the Coaching Agreement	Instructions
Activities for Building/ Exploring Leadership Capacity	
Assessments	Refer to Team Coaching in Action at www.groupcoaching essentials.com and appendix on assessments.
Styles	Refer to Working with Styles, and also the DiSC Field Journal in Chapter 10. In addition to leadership styles, coaches may find themselves working around communication styles or conflict styles.
Strengths	Refer to Working with Strengths and Styles.
Vision	See vision exercises section below.
Values	See various exercises under values section below.
Activities for Facilitating Action	
Action Planning	Refer to Team Action Planning with Post-its in Team Coaching in Action at www.groupcoachingessentials.com.
Index Cards	A quick way to get teams and individual group members into brainstorming options is to use index cards. Have them write one idea per card around their focus or goal area. Index card use can be combined with other tools such as Marshall Goldsmith's Feedforward (see below).
Brainstorming	A foundational facilitation technique that may be used in everything from identifying the coaching focus, to setting goals, to creating an action plan. Some members may like to make a list, others will want to use Post-it Notes, and others, index cards.
MindMapping	MindMapping is an invaluable tool for everything from program design through to supporting clients in getting unblocked or exploring options. Originally created by Tony Buzan, MindMapping is now a technique that is widely incorporated at the individual, team and group levels. Coaches and clients can go low tech using pen and paper, as well as use paid or free MindMapping software such as MindMeister or MindJet. Those on the iPad have additional apps they can access including iThoughtsHD.

Force Field Analysis	As above.
Top 50	Top 20 or 50 lists can be a quick brainstorming technique to support the expansion of options. It might be a top 50 list of contacts, etc.
Marshall Goldsmith's Feedforward	The purpose of the Marshall Goldsmith Feedforward tool is to provide individuals, teams and organizations with suggestions for the future and to help them achieve a positive change in behavior. Feedback usually focuses on what has been done in the past; Feedforward provides possibilities for the future. Goldsmith has provided instructions on how to use Feedforward through many articles and a YouTube video he has posted online. At the end of the Feedforward activity, follow up with a couple of minutes for individuals to note the new ideas and add them to their action plans or MindMaps.
Team Action Planning: Post-its	Refer to Action Planning text box in Team Coaching in Action at www.groupcoachingessentials.com.
Commitments (individual or collective)	Ask each person, "What is the one thing you are going to commit to doing *no matter what* before our next point of contact?" Encourage communication and sharing in between the sessions or at the start of the next conversation.
Activities for Creating a Vision	
Team Story Board	As above.
My Vision for the Team (Visual Explorer)	One of the ways to use visuals, such as Visual Explorer, is to have each team member select a photo that represents their vision of where they see the team going.
Flipchart (Team Vision)	Another way to get the team to start creating a vision is to have them create on a flip chart some of the elements of where they want to be going and what they want to be doing.
Vision Questions	A set of vision questions can also be very useful in supporting group and team members in identifying what they want their vision to look like.
Index Cards	Similar to using Post-it Notes, index cards can be a great way to capture team ideas about what they see as the vision. You can have everyone share and post their ideas—it's interesting to point to similarities, etc. It can be a great conversation starter.

(Continued)

Table A.1: (*Continued*)

Activities for Establishing the Coaching Agreement	Instructions
Activities for Working with Values	
Peak Experience Visualization	The Peak Experience Visualization outlined in *Co-Active Coaching* (by Laura Whitworth, Karen Kimsey-House, Henry Kimsey-House and Philip Sandahl) is a great way to connect team or group members to what is really important to them.
Values Checklist	Refer to Field Journal: Working with Values in the appendix.
Team and Individual Values	Refer to Field Journal: Working with Values in the appendix.
Values Shield/Values Quilt	Using collage, a shield or quilt can be created to summarize all the values a person holds. This can be a powerful visual representation.
What is really important (Visual Explorer)	As with other iterations of using visuals, multiple cards can be laid out and members are asked to select the photo that represents what is most important to them.
Activities for Closure	
Appreciation	Creating time at the end of a program, or at specific milestones, for appreciation of each team or group member can be very powerful when trust and connection exist. This activity can be done verbally or in writing. If you decide to write it, have each group member write their name on a blank piece of paper and post it on the wall. Give group or team members time during the program to write their comments about others. Distribute the filled-out pages before the end of the program, giving people time to read them.
Spider's Web	As above.
Modeling	Refer to Team Coaching in Action at www.groupcoaching essentials.com.
3 questions	What worked well? What are you taking away? What should we do differently next time OR What would be even better if…?

About the Author

Jennifer J. Britton is the founder of Potentials Realized, a Canadian-based performance improvement company. An award-winning program designer, she works with groups, teams and organizations in the areas of leadership, teamwork and performance.

Drawing on more than two decades of experience as an experiential educator and former manager with the United Nations and other international organizations, Jennifer's global clients span government, corporate and non-profit sectors, from financial services to education and healthcare. Since early 2006, her Group Coaching Essentials™ program has supported hundreds of coaches in the creation and implementation of their own group coaching practice. Jennifer offers a range of group coaching programs and retreats for the general public in addition to the coaching and training services she offers to organizations.

Credentialed by the International Coaching Federation, Jennifer was originally trained and certified by the Coaches Training Institute. She has also completed advanced coaching training in the areas of ORSC and Shadow Coaching. A Certified Performance Technologist (CPT), Jennifer holds a Master of Environmental Studies (York University) and a Bachelor of Science in Psychology (McGill University).

Connect with Jennifer:

Email: info@potentialsrealized.com
Phone: (416) 996-8326
Web: www.groupcoachingessentials.com and www.potentialsrealized.com
Group Coaching Ins and Outs Blog: groupcoaching.blogspot.com
Twitter: @jennbritton
Facebook: facebook.com/effectivegroupcoaching
Pinterest: pinterest.com/jennjbritton
YouTube: youtube.com/effectivegroupcoach

Index

Want to connect?

Like us on Facebook
www.facebook.com/wileyglobalfinance

Follow us on Twitter
@wiley_finance

Join us on LinkedIn
Wiley Global Finance Group

Watch us on YouTube
Wiley on YouTube

Subscribe to our newsletter
Pfeiffer Training Newsletter

Go to our Website
Wrox.com

WILEY

If you enjoyed this book, you may also like these:

Effective Group Coaching,
by Jennifer J. Britton
ISBN: 9780470738542

Team Advantage:
TM LDR Guide,
by Darelyn "DJ" Mitsch,
Barry Mitsch
ISBN: 9780470463369

Appreciative Coaching,
by Sara L. Orem,
Jacqueline Binkert
and Ann L. Clancy
ISBN: 9780787984533